T0245612

A Seat at the Table

A Seat at the Table

THE LIFE AND TIMES OF
SHIRLEY CHISHOLM

DRS. GLENN L. STARKS AND F. ERIK BROOKS

Lawrence Hill Books
Chicago

Published by Lawrence Hill Books
An imprint of Chicago Review Press Incorporated
814 North Franklin Street
Chicago, Illinois 60610
ISBN 978-1-64160-926-5

Library of Congress Control Number: 2023950374

Typesetting: Nord Compo

Printed in the United States of America
5 4 3 2 1

*"If they don't give you a seat at the table,
bring a folding chair."*

—Shirley Chisholm

CONTENTS

INTRODUCTION

"You don't make progress by standing on the sidelines, whimpering and complaining. You make progress by implementing ideas."

S HIRLEY ANITA ST. HILL Chisholm rose from being the child of immigrants to running for the highest office in the land. As a Black woman, she achieved this not in spite of her background but because of it. Thanks to the influence of her parents and her own sheer tenacity, she was both the first Black woman elected to the US Congress and the first Black woman of a major political party to make a serious bid for presidency of the United States. She made history not only for her political runs but also for her accomplishments while in office. She broke down racial and gender barriers, opening the door for so many who have followed, including minorities and women of all colors who have been able to achieve political success because of the precedents she set. In November 2020, for example, Kamala D. Harris became the first woman and first woman of color elected as vice president of the United States.

Chisholm was aware that her legacy would have a lasting impact and once stated, "I want to be remembered as a woman . . . who dared to be a catalyst of change."[1] She was an unapologetic feminist and civil rights champion, unwavering in her support for the issues she believed in. She was direct and presented her policy positions plainly for all to see.

Chisholm attained such success during a time when both Black people and women in this country faced blatant racial and gender discrimination. The few female and Black officials then in office felt they could not challenge the White male establishment or they'd be drummed out of office. Chisholm herself faced discrimination not only from White people, and particularly White men, but also from Black men. Yet she was not afraid to directly challenge the political establishment, which she referred to as "the machine."

In doing so, she gave a political voice to so many marginalized segments of society—women, minorities, the young, members of the gay community, domestic and agricultural workers, and the poor—not only in her home district in Brooklyn, New York, but across the country. Her run for the 1972 Democratic presidential nomination may not have ended in victory, but it was successful in the way it forged a unified grassroots campaign in which the voices of the previously voiceless joined together to vote for someone who supported their diverse but collective interests. Chisholm's presidential run—and her broader drive for change—was fueled by her own experiences growing up as the daughter of Black working-class immigrants in a country hostile to all these demographics, and by the strong lessons her family taught her about being dedicated to high principles of integrity and self-respect. When asked why she would dare run for president, she boldly turned the question on its head: *Why not me?*

This book explores the life of this remarkable individual, discussing the events of her youth that shaped her life, her contributions to education, and the arc of her political career. It also explores her

personal life, including the challenges and opportunities that contributed to her becoming an icon of American and even global politics.
There are few historical figures who have made such an impact and
who continue to influence the political landscape decades after leaving
public office. As many historians have pointed out, without Shirley
Chisholm's grit and determination there may not have been a Hillary
Clinton, Barack Obama, or Kamala Harris.

1

CHISHOLM'S EARLY LIFE

"I wasn't even born with a brass spoon in my mouth."

SHIRLEY ANITA ST. HILL was born November 30, 1924, in Brooklyn, New York. Her parents, like thousands of others, had immigrated to the United States in the early 1900s from different parts of the Caribbean, which was then suffering from massive crop failures caused by hurricanes, floods, and drought. These Black immigrants were also escaping systemic oppression by the White European ruling class, which was exploiting their labor to overcome the competition for the Caribbean's major crop, sugar cane, from other countries such as Brazil. One estimate is that by 1924, over twelve thousand Caribbean immigrants came to the United States each year.[1]

New York City was the hub of immigration to the US, and it was common for immigrants to have family members or friends already living in the city. Tens of thousands of immigrants from Jamaica and Barbados entered through Ellis Island, settling in Manhattan and Brooklyn. From 1900 through 1925, over three hundred thousand immigrants

from Barbados immigrated, leading to 16 percent of the city's population comprising of citizens from the Caribbean by 1930. A distinguish-
ing characteristic of these immigrants was that they were highly literate
and skilled. They aspired for education and made up the majority of
Black teachers, doctors, dentists, and lawyers in the two boroughs.

Chisholm's father, Charles Christopher St. Hill, was born in Guy-
ana, then known by its pre-independence name of British Guiana,
in 1901. He was orphaned at age fourteen, lived in Barbados for a
while and then for a year in Antilla, Cuba, and arrived in New York
City on April 10, 1923, aboard the SS *Munamar*. Chisholm's mother,
Ruby Leona Seale St. Hill, was born in Christ Church, Barbados, in
1901 and arrived in New York two years earlier than her would-be
husband aboard the SS *Pocone* on March 8, 1921. Many immigrated
from Barbados during the building of the Panama Canal because it
offered good-paying jobs that allowed immigrants to send money back
to their home countries. Chisholm's grandfather was one of those
immigrants and sent money home so his daughter Ruby could come
to the United States.

Chisholm's parents met at one of Brooklyn's Bajan social clubs,
Bajan being an English creole spoken widely in Barbados. After following a strict traditional courtship, they were married. Chisholm was the
oldest of their four children, all daughters. Two of her sisters, Muriel and
Odessa, were born within three years of her. Odessa was born in 1926,
while Muriel was born in 1927. The youngest, Selma, was born five years
later in 1932. Chisholm was the most vocal child and would later recall
that her siblings and mother were sometimes afraid of "her mouth."
She explained, "Mother always said that even when I was three, I used
to get the six and seven year old kids on the block and punch them
and say, 'Listen to me.' I was a fat little thing then, believe it or not."[2]

Taking care of their children was financially challenging; it was especially trying for a Black family to find work during the Great Depression.
Charles was an unskilled laborer who worked as a baker's helper and for

a factory making burlap bags, but sometimes only a few days a week. Ruby worked as a seamstress out of her home after her daughters were born so close in years. The family couldn't afford day care or a nursery school. When the children were older, she was a domestic worker for White families. The parents never complained about working so hard; a strong work ethic was part of their Caribbean culture. The children were raised as they were, with discipline, learning to value hard work and to be proud of being Barbadian Americans. These were all lessons that would well serve Chisholm throughout her life.

As most parents do, the St. Hills wanted the best for their children, including an opportunity to pursue their education. So in early 1928, when Chisholm was around three years old, the parents sent her and her two sisters to Barbados aboard the MS *Vulcania*. Ruby accompanied the girls on the nine-day trip on the tumultuous Atlantic Ocean to live with their maternal grandmother, Emmeline "Emily" G. Chase Seale, who had visited her family in Brooklyn when Chisholm was an infant. Although a hard decision for the parents, this would allow them both to work and save money for a home and the girls' educations. The family had originally planned to travel aboard the *Vespress*, but Ruby changed her mind due to a feeling of foreboding that ended up saving their lives, given that the *Vespress* sank after setting sail.

Grandmother Emmeline was a tall woman. Standing over six feet with a stentorian voice, she was stern and deeply religious, but loving. Chisholm later recalled how her grandmother preached the virtues of pride, courage, and faith from morning to night. After Emmeline's first husband died, she married Kirby H. Seale, and Ruby was born in Barbados on August 31, 1901. They owned a farm in the Vauxhall village of Christ Church, Barbados. When the St. Hill children moved there, Barbados was still economically controlled by an oppressive White planter class, and the island's Black residents were beginning their revolt against British rule. The Black struggle for independence would have a lasting impact on Chisholm's own views on fighting for equality.

Chisholm's mother stayed with the girls for six months until they were settled into their new environment. The girls had plenty of company since their maternal aunt, Violet, had also sent her four children to live at the farm until she and her husband were doing better financially in the United States. Chisholm's uncle Lincoln (Ruby's younger brother) and aunt Myrtle (Ruby's older sister) also lived there and helped care for the children. Lincoln was a newspaper editor, which shaped the children's thinking about the professional possibilities available for Black people. Chisholm later described the family as "a strongly disciplined family unit."[3] The home had no running water or electricity, so the family depended on drawing water from a well and read by a kerosene lamp at night. However, the large farm provided space to play and the clear Caribbean water to swim in.

Under her grandmother's watchful eye, Chisholm attended the one-room Vauxhall Primary School that served as the village's Methodist church on Sundays. Because the island was still a British colony, the local school followed traditional British pedagogical norms such as wearing school uniforms and teaching reading, writing, and arithmetic. However, it was run by Black administrators, and the children were taught by Black teachers. Chisholm later recalled how noisy the schoolroom was, since it was divided into seven sections of teachers simultaneously instructing one hundred students in different grade levels, but it allowed for a great community of learning. Living and being educated in Barbados led to Chisholm having a slight clipped British West Indies accent for the rest of her life. She would always consider herself a Barbadian American and was proud of her heritage. As an adult, for over thirty years she took part in the annual West Indian American Day Carnival Association's parade in Brooklyn.

As an adult, Chisholm credited her parents sending her to live with her grandmother and being raised in such as strict household following the British style of teaching with contributing to the strong speaking and writing abilities that she would draw on for the rest of her life. Her sister Muriel later recalled, "When you started school in Barbados, you went right into reading, writing, and arithmetic. There was no such thing as kindergarten and playing around with paper. You came to learn how to read and write and 'do sums' as they said."[4]

Their grandparents were very religious and took the children to church every Sunday. Emmeline worked as a domestic for a British family, but her farm sustained almost all the basic needs of the family with a variety of vegetables and animals, including cows, sheep, goats, chickens, ducks, and turkeys. (During one Christmas, the children were upset one of the turkeys they considered a pet was the main course.) Chisholm attributed so much of her later success to the influence of her grandmother, alongside the examples of Mary McLeod Bethune and Eleanor Roosevelt.

Chisholm also pointed out, "Granny gave me strength, dignity and love. I learned from an early age that I was somebody. I didn't need the Black revolution to tell me that."[5] Both her mother and grandmother were Quaker women who instilled an appreciation for discipline in the young Chisholm. She later noted, "I'm very religious, but I don't wear my religion on my sleeve. Being brought up as a Quaker Brethren, your mind and body are very disciplined. Everything is anchored in God."[6]

Chisholm and her sisters returned to New York on May 19, 1934, aboard the SS *Nerissa*. Per the ship's manifest, their mother, Ruby, went back to Barbados to bring the girls home. The manifest shows they left Barbados on May 11 and reports that when they arrived back in New York, Ruby was thirty-two, Chisholm was nine, Odessa was seven, Muriel was five, and Selma was two. Ruby was listed as a "house wife," Chisholm and Odessa were listed as in "School," and the other girls each as a "Minor."

In the short time the girls had been gone, Brooklyn's demographic makeup was already starting to become more diverse. The borough's population was now almost 3 percent Black, and immigrants were almost 35 percent of the population. For the first time, Brooklyn was the largest borough in New York City, and would remain so through 2010. The children had lived in Barbados for six years and barely

SS *Nerissa* manifest. *Immigration Service, US Department of Labor, 1934, courtesy of Ancestry.com*

remembered life in Brooklyn. They returned to the heavily Jewish Brownsville neighborhood during the height of the Great Depression, so their parents continued to financially struggle. The children were sensitive to the cold after living in warm weather for so long. Besides the sometimes-brutal New York weather, they lived in a four-room flat and relied on a coal stove for heating water. When their mother went shopping, the girls would stay in bed to keep warm.

The family didn't receive support from government relief programs. President Franklin D. Roosevelt's New Deal policy was established to provide economic stimulus packages to farmers, the unemployed, and groups hardest hit and to reform the banking and lending industry. However, it did little to improve the economic conditions of Black people in Brooklyn and most other parts of the country. Programs under the New Deal such as those administered by the new National Recovery Administration and Work Progress Administration rarely included support for Black people or women.

The St. Hills couldn't afford toys for the children, and there weren't any places for them to play. Chisholm recalled how she and her sisters created their own ways of having fun, such as parroting the local Jewish rabbis as they prayed. Their mother was furious when she caught them.

The girls had to become accustomed to living in the crowded, diverse neighborhood versus the spacious farm. Their densely populated poor neighborhood, with buildings often falling apart, was home to over two hundred thousand Black, Italian, and Puerto Rican people, all living in a two-square-mile radius. Reflecting on her early life, Chisholm would explain that although some called their neighborhood a "ghetto," many of the residents were first-generation Jews from Europe who came from much worse conditions. The residents were proud of their heritage and active in protests and progressive politics. Many of the daughters' friends were Jewish, as the school they attended was predominantly White and Jewish.

Regardless of their socioeconomic status and their parents' work struggles, the children had a fortunate upbringing. Chisholm later explained that her mother ensured the girls learned poise and grace in addition to their formal education. Their parents used their scant resources to buy the children a piano, and Chisholm would take piano lessons for nine years, doing so well that her parents sacrificed and bought a new piano on credit, paying it off over time.

Her father, Charles, was proud, handsome, intelligent, and an avid reader. He had a keen interest in politics (subscribing to multiple newspapers), unions (he was a member of the Confectionery and Bakers International Union), racism, and British colonialism in the Caribbean. Charles would invite his friends over nightly for lively conversations, and he always kept alcohol on hand for his friends, though he did not drink. While the men debated in the kitchen, Chisholm would lie in bed and listen. Charles would also have conversations with her on race and politics. Later she would reflect that her father was a remarkable man who taught her and her sisters pride in themselves and their race. Charles adored President Franklin D. Roosevelt—who along with his wife, Eleanor, was sympathetic to the struggles of Black people—and believed passionately in the ideals of Marcus Garvey, a Jamaican-born political activist. This was not surprising, given that Garvey, known as the "Black Moses," advocated for Black pride and independence and famously proclaimed, "The Black skin is not a badge of shame, but rather a glorious symbol of national greatness."[7]

Chisholm's parents enrolled her at PS 24 in 1935, when she was eleven years old. She had always been a bright child, reading the Bible when she was just three years old, learning to write when she was four. However, in school she was a rambunctious student who often got into trouble. She would catapult spitballs using rubber bands. A third-grade teacher luckily realized this was because she was bored and not being academically challenged. An IQ test revealed she was academically gifted, so she was assigned a tutor in history and geography. With that increased attention to her intellectual needs, she fell in love with education and was inspired to make it a lifelong dedication.

The family moved to the Bedford-Stuyvesant neighborhood the next year, when Chisholm was around twelve years old, to another four-room apartment but with larger rooms and steam heat. Unlike Brownsville, which was mostly White and Jewish, Bed-Stuy was roughly half Black. However, it was in this neighborhood Chisholm first encountered racial and ethnic slurs directed at Black and Jewish people. Historically a middle-class White neighborhood, Bed-Stuy's demographics were rapidly changing, largely owing to the Great Migration of Black people to the area from the US South and the West Indies, all looking for better opportunities in life.

Chisholm witnessed the racial tensions that resulted from the demographic shift. In 1936 the Independent City-Owned Subway System extended its A line, connecting Harlem to Brooklyn. Many Black people embraced their newfound mobility to escape crowded Harlem for the relatively more spacious Bedford-Stuyvesant, resulting in White residents becoming increasingly angry at the growing Black population. Though the neighborhood had been racially segregated since the early 1920s, redlining was used to ensure a strict segregation of Black and White residents. Wilder explains that the result of the purposeful concentration of Black residents between the 1930s and early 1950s was a "vast Black ghetto stretched across Brooklyn and was becoming the largest concentration of its kind."[8] Chisholm experienced this racism firsthand when she was enrolled at the local PS 28 school, where she faced racial hostility, fear, and resentment from some of her peers and teachers. She later moved on to middle school at PS 178.

Even with all the demographic changes and tensions, the St. Hills prioritized the girls' education. Each Saturday, Ruby took the girls to the library, where each would check out the maximum three books. At Christmas their gifts would be books. Ruby would often do the girls' chores so they could focus on their homework. The parents continued to work multiple jobs, including Ruby as a maid, so Chisholm as the eldest took care of her siblings when her parents were not home. This included meeting them at PS 28 each day to take them home for lunch and then return them to school before Chisholm returned to PS 178. She walked them home again at the end of the school day.

In fall 1939 Chisholm began attending the Girls' High School in the Bed-Stuy. Charles got a better job as a janitor for the school, so the family lived for free in a six-room apartment. While the neighborhood was predominantly Black, the school was diverse, with half the student body being Black. The school, located at 457 Nostrand Avenue between Macon and Halsey Streets, was built in 1885 as Brooklyn's first high school and is considered a masterpiece of Victorian Gothic style. Until it opened, public-funded education ended with grammar school. It was opened to girls first, and a separate school for boys was constructed a few years later. The students, for their time, were progressive thinkers. For example, in 1942 they led a protest because the girls were not allowed to wear pants.

The school was both integrated and highly regarded for its education of girls. According to an 1895 article in the *New York Times*, "It is the ambition of every Brooklyn girl after graduating from the public schools to enter the Girls' High School, where she may enjoy the advantages of advanced education, and be prepared for college or for more immediate concerns of life." Courses included various foreign languages, zoology, the sciences, advanced mathematics, economics, ancient to modern history, and "literary masterpieces, both American and English."[9] Parents from all over Brooklyn sent their daughters there. Chisholm did well and became vice president of the girls' honor society, Junior Arista, at a time when few Black students were elected to student offices. She also became proficient in French. While she was sometimes teased for her West Indian accent, she ignored it.

Chisholm was a great student but still had a rebellious nature. She sometimes played jazz on the family piano and allowed a few boys to kiss her after walking her home from school, even though the girls were forbidden from dating. She also loved to dance, which was something her mother hated. While her father tried to convince his wife to allow their daughters to explore some parts of being American teenagers, Ruby was adamant about maintaining a strict Caribbean upbringing, replying, "Charles, we've got to be strict on them if we want them to grow up to be something."[10]

Chisholm graduated in 1942 with high marks, a testament to her parents' attention to the children's study habits and barring them from dating. After graduating high school, she was accepted to both Vassar in Poughkeepsie, New York, and Oberlin in Ohio, and she received several scholarship offers. However, her parents couldn't afford the room and board, so she chose Brooklyn College, where New York students attended tuition-free and she could stay at home in the city, where the family then lived at 707 Kingsborough Walk.

Later in life she commented how Brooklyn College was the right choice: "If I had gone to Vassar, the rest of my life might have been different. Would I have become one of the pseudo-White upper-middle-class Black women professionals, or a doctor's wife with furs, limousines, clubs and airs? I can't believe that would have happened, but one never knows."[11] She described her mother being glad her daughter was going to college instead of pursuing a passing interest in becoming an actress, a profession her mother hated: "My mother always thanked God that I had brains and got to college on scholarship. Had I not been able to go to college I would have gone to the devil in the theater, she thought."[12]

Brooklyn College had just been established in 1930 by the Board of Higher Education of the City of New York and quickly gained a reputation for being academically challenging. Its administration was reluctant to admit women because they believed women to be mentally inferior to men and saw female college seekers as only interested in finding a husband. Thus, women who were admitted had to have a high school grade point average higher than what was required of male applicants. When Chisholm entered the school as a freshman, she was one of only sixty Black students out of the total student population of ten thousand. The college president and all members of the upper administration were White. The same was true of the student council, the college yearbook staff, and the newspaper staff. But Chisholm was undeterred; she had a responsibility to her family to do well.

Although she knew she wanted to teach, and it was the only professional field open to Black women, she majored in sociology, with a minor in Spanish. Her background in Spanish would later serve her well politically, given the diverse population of Brooklyn. Her sociology department was all White and all male. However, Brooklyn College brought her into contact with students from different backgrounds, and she was able to join clubs that exposed her to Black history. The campus was alive with World War II protests, in addition to academic and political clubs constantly holding events. This was a social and academic awakening for her, contrasting with how sheltered she had been by her protective parents.

Her college experience also revealed to her how racism was woven into the fabric of American culture. Guest lecturers invited by one her clubs, the Political Science Society, would make statements about Black people being limited or refer matter-of-factly to Black people's supposedly innate vocation as laborers requiring the White population's help. Chisholm noted how some Black people were expectedly subservient to White people, even if that White person was less intelligent or talented. She would always be upset about racism and how trivial skin color actually was. As she later put it, "My God, what do we want? What does any human being want? Take away an accident of pigmentation of a thin layer of our outer skin and there is no difference between me and anyone else. All we want is for that trivial difference to make no difference."[13]

These experiences of prejudice did not deter Chisholm from being active on campus. She was a member of the Pan American Student League, the Harriet Tubman Society, and the Social Service Club. The Harriet Tubman Society held discussions on Black leaders such as W. E. B. Du Bois, Mary McLeod Bethune, and Frederick Douglass. Invited speakers included Adam Clayton Powell Jr., the first African American elected to Congress, and musician and political activist Paul Robeson. Club members circulated petitions demanding integration of the military, more Black faculty members, a Negro History course on campus, and an end to poll taxes for voting. As a member of the club, Chisholm for the first time heard other people openly discussing and supporting an end to White oppression and embracing Black pride and Black racial consciousness.

Chisholm took an interest in debate, sociology, and political science, but remarked to a White political science professor who asked her why she didn't aspire to be a politician that she couldn't because she was a woman and Black. Still, this professor, Louis A. Warsoff, who was blind, became the first White person she grew to trust— she referred to him as "Proffy"—thanks to his encouragement of her potential. Warsoff recognized her quick mind and debate skills, and the two often actively engaged in political discussions.

Once, having won a debate in a New York City contest, she met another person who would influence her life: Eleanor Roosevelt. Chisholm would later share a touching memory in which Roosevelt told her, "Shirley St. Hill, you're very smart. You're intelligent. You must fight. You must get up and don't let anybody stand in your way—even a woman can do it."[14]

Chisholm loved the debate club and supporting women running for student offices, and she and some fellow Black female students formed a group called IPOTHIA, which stood for "In Pursuit of the Highest in All." The sorority-like club grew in number, since Black people were not welcome in the other social groups, which were mainly led by White men, and the few women members were the wives of male leaders. IPOTHIA would be the first Black women's student group at the college, with almost thirty members at one point.

Chisholm continued to be keenly aware of the bias she faced being a Black woman and so joined a number of off-campus organizations that strove for racial as well as gender equality. These included the Brooklyn League of Women Voters, the Brooklyn chapter of the National Association for the Advancement of Colored People (NAACP), the Brooklyn Urban League, the Brooklyn branch of the National Association of College Women, and the Democratic Party club in Bedford-Stuyvesant. She joined an illustrious legacy of prominent members of the League of Women Voters, including Jeannette Pickering Rankin, the first woman to hold federal office in the United States after elected to Congress in 1916, Eleanor Roosevelt, and Claudia "Lady Bird" Johnson. With the Urban League, she volunteered and taught children arts and crafts, and put on plays. She also volunteered with the Brooklyn Home for the Aged.

Chisholm would be as active as the other members of a group she joined but sometimes switched organizations if they didn't accomplish anything. Besides the NAACP, political organizations in Brooklyn were dominated by White members. This drove her to try to persuade organization leaders to address issues important to the Black community. She worked with other local leaders to increase Black voting and getting Black leaders elected. It was during her sophomore year that she became seriously interested in politics after hearing a speech from New York political leader Stanley Steingut. Chisholm was upset this White politician declared that Black people could only make achievements with the help of White people.

When Chisholm was a senior, her hairdresser introduced her to Wesley McDonald "Mac" Holder, who would later become her political mentor. He was an influential politician in Brooklyn after World War II, known as "the sly old mongoose" and "dean of Black Brooklyn politics." Like Chisholm, Holder's roots were in the Caribbean and he came to New York City from the same country as Chisholm's father, British Guiana, where Holder was born June 24, 1897 in Friendship Heights Village on August 31, 1920. His wife, Thelma Herod, immigrated from Panama in 1918. After graduating from New York City College, where he studied mathematics, Holder joined the Marcus Garvey movement, organized Black members, and pushed Garvey's philosophy that Black people should start their own country in Africa.

His oratory skills furnished him with unique ways of getting out of trouble. In Miami, Florida, and Arkansas he was jailed for speaking publicly against the Ku Klux Klan. When he asked for a lawyer in Arkansas, he was told the nearest was in Oklahoma. He defended himself and was only fined five dollars. When Holder returned to New York, he began his political career managing candidate Samuel Leibowitz for Brooklyn district attorney. Leibowitz was noted for his defense of the Scottsboro defendants, young Black men falsely accused of rape, in the 1930s.

As Chisholm described him, "Mac Holder comes once in a life-time. Hours and time mean nothing to him when he becomes involved in a political campaign. He has been responsible for watching my back through the years while I have been in Washington, and my success is attributable to him."[15] Others Holder helped shared Chisholm's sentiments. For example, Holder helped Democrat Roger L. Green win his New York State Assembly seat representing the Fifty-Seventh District in 1980. Describing Holder, Green stated, "I call him the sly mongoose. He has an uncanny knowledge of the Black body politic in Brooklyn. So many people call on him because it's like returning to the source of knowledge to receive advice and counsel."[16]

At the same time as Chisholm began realizing her interest in the political world, her parents realized their dream of buying their own home in 1945, proving to their daughters that hard work leads to reaching their goals. They purchased a three-story brownstone at 1094 Prospect Place between Kingston and Albany Avenues for $10,000. This was a momentous achievement for a Black family working any jobs they could while living through the Great Depression and raising four children. It was also a dream come true—as Chisholm once stated, Barbadians who moved to Brooklyn had two goals: a college education for their children and owning a brownstone. Their home was part of a set of row houses, and later one of Chisholm's sisters rented a room at 1081 Prospect Place, just across the street from her parents' home.

Chisholm graduated cum laude in 1946 with a Bachelor of Arts degree in Sociology and a minor in Spanish. Her sister Muriel graduated from Brooklyn College a year later, magna cum laude with a degree in physics. All the girls received college scholarships, a further testament to their upbringing. After graduating, Chisholm began looking for teaching jobs but was turned down repeatedly. She knew racism played a part, as she had all the required state teaching qualifications. In one interview at a school in an affluent neighborhood in the Bronx, the school administrator used the excuse that she wasn't qualified for the job. But Chisholm astutely discerned the real reason the administrator was not hiring her was because he finally discovered she was Black. Her petite frame and young appearance didn't help her career prospects; though she was twenty-one years old, she could've passed for sixteen. Some administrators feared older students just wouldn't take her seriously.

Chisholm eventually became a teacher's assistant at a nursery school, Mount Calvary Child Care Center, in Harlem in 1946. Like other school administrators, director Eula Hodges was reluctant to hire her. She even told Chisholm she looked like a child and asked if she could handle a classroom. Chisholm pleaded for a chance on a probationary term and said, "Give me a chance to show you. Give me a chance to find out whether I can do the job. . . . Don't judge me by my size!"[17] Her persistence persuaded Hodges to hire her on a probationary basis, but her exemplary skills as an educator soon landed her a permanent position. She continued her formal education while working days at the nursery school by going to graduate school at night. She earned a master's degree in curriculum and teaching specializing in early childhood education from the Teachers College at Columbia University on June 7, 1951.

While still in undergraduate school, Chisholm became romantically involved with an older man originally from Jamaica. She met him on the subway riding to her job at a Manhattan jewelry factory during Easter break in 1946. Their relationship lasted for five years. Her parents were concerned she was growing up too fast, and her mother warned her to eat meals alone and not fraternize with other workers. Her parents, especially her mother, never approved of the man. The two got engaged after dating for over a year, but Chisholm found out he was already married and had a family in Jamaica. She also learned he was part of an immigration fraud scheme bringing people into the country using false birth certificates and blackmailing them once they arrived. He was arrested and deported by the Immigration and Naturalization

Service. Chisholm was so upset she stopped eating and even considered suicide. Upon a doctor's recommendation her family sent her to a farm in New Jersey owned by family friends. She eventually returned home with a disdain for men and focused only on her career.

Her hatred of men changed while attending Columbia. While running from class to one of her many meetings, she met Conrad Quintin Chisholm. He was also an immigrant, and came to New York City from Montego Bay, Jamaica, in 1946. He was born October 7, 1916, as the fifth of John and Zillah Chisholm's twelve children. Chisholm was in love with the swindler when she'd first met Conrad years earlier, so initially she brushed him off. But while she was attending Columbia, Conrad began pursuing her, even though she would not immediately reciprocate his affection. As Chisholm later recalled, "Young men had always dropped me. If we were dancing, I'd talk about some world problem or other. I had a reputation as being too intellectual. But Conrad was fascinated by this young slip of a girl with this commanding voice."[18]

After Conrad's persistent attention and after gaining her mother's approval, Chisholm finally agreed to marry him. The two married on October 8, 1949, in a large West Indian–style wedding. She later joked, "I used to kid him that Jamaican men always want the best so he just had to marry a Barbadian girl."[19] The two lived with the St. Hills through the 1950s until they moved to 1066 Prospect Place in 1962. Conrad had first worked in the garment industry and then as a short-order chef before becoming a private investigator after his graduation from the New York School of Investigation. He specialized in compensation claims against the railroads and then worked as a city government senior investigator for the bureau of medical services in the New York City Department of Social Services. He was also a skilled ballroom dancer. The Chisholms made it a ritual of vacationing to the islands each year. They never had children, though she suffered two miscarriages, which she never talked about publicly; Chisholm preferred to keep her private life private.

Chisholm advanced quickly in her education career. After leaving Mount Calvary, she served from 1953 until 1954 as director of the Private Friend in Need Nursery in Brownsville, Brooklyn, and then as director of the Hamilton-Madison House Child Care Center in Lower Manhattan from 1954 until 1959. In this latter position, she oversaw a staff of twenty-four teachers and maintenance personnel, and 130 children ranging from ages three to seven years old. Almost half were Puerto Rican, and she dedicated herself to helping them all learn English to succeed. It was easy for her to assist them because she spoke Spanish fluently. All these positions gave her a firsthand look at poverty and inequality, and she was committed to educational improvements for children at the earliest age possible.

By the 1950s, Bedford-Stuyvesant was undergoing dramatic demographic changes. In 1950 there were 155,000 Black residents in this section of Brooklyn, or about 55 percent of the population, up from just 30,000 in 1930. This led to shady lending companies and individuals trying to take advantage of the Black population, whom they saw as vulnerable to being financially swindled. While local Black people were targets of credit and housing scams, the White residents were being enticed by real estate brokers to move out of the neighborhood. Jack Newfield explained, "White real estate brokers offer[ed] my Negro friends fifty cents an hour to slip circulars under the doors of White-owned houses, saying there was a buyer available." One White family reportedly just walked out of their home and never returned, leaving all their furniture and possessions behind. Added Newfield, "Real estate speculators easily obtained loans from banks, but the stable, hard-working Negro family next door to my house could not get a bank loan to rehabilitate their dirty, peeling frame house."[20]

These types of activities coupled with increased crime and corruption in local politics paved the way for political activism in Brooklyn and other urban areas across the country in the 1960s.

2

GETTING INTO AND OUT OF POLITICS

"It began to crystallize in me that I had something that could be used for people who had no input into things."

THE 1950s AND 1960s saw movements emerge among those who felt disenfranchised, including Black people for civil rights, women for equal rights, workers for better pay and union representation, the poor for better housing and jobs, and young people against government, religious, and social conservatism. The docile youth of the 1950s became forceful activists in the 1960s. While the 1950s was the Golden Age of Capitalism, the 1960s saw an economic reversal as the World War II economic boom waned. The Black community was hardest hit by this downturn. The sprawling urban cities of the 1950s became centers of crime and violence, fueling demands for urban reform. Public trust in the government was low, and Black people in particular saw politics as an illegitimate way to make changes. All of this served as a backdrop to Chisholm's entry into politics.

The civil rights movement was forcing the country to acknowledge the vestiges of slavery and discriminatory disparities and led to a swell of support for progressive liberal politicians who advocated social change and equality. While many in the movement embraced nonviolence and peaceful resistance, some organizations, such as the Nation of Islam and the Black Panthers, took a more radical approach, demanding equality through violence if needed. At the time, the population of Brooklyn had grown to 2.6 million and was now 14.14 percent Black, while over 19 percent of the borough's population was foreign born. The Bedford-Stuyvesant neighborhood's population was 80 percent Black.

Against this backdrop, locally and nationally, Chisholm's political life began through joining Brooklyn's local political clubs. In 1953 she joined the Seventeenth Assembly District Democratic Club, which supported party candidates running for office and vetted voter concerns. Although the district was majority Black, the Democratic Party candidates it supported were usually White, and the club was run by White Irish Americans. Chisholm was assigned the task of decorating the cigar box used to hold raffle tickets. Even in this minor role she was outspoken, gaining support from women but anger from men in complaining the women weren't given a budget—what she called "seed money"—forcing them to use their own money, or equal respect, although their raffle funded the campaigns of the men. The club leadership relented and gave them funds, but Chisholm was accused of "egging on" the other women by telling them to be vocal about their concerns. She also questioned the club leadership for not supporting Black neighborhoods, such as by having trash picked up a few days a week there while the schedule was daily in White neighborhoods. Most of the Black and female members had never before challenged club leadership.

She and the club members were politically successful in getting the first Black judge elected in Brooklyn to a municipal court bench

post. This was a struggle; what was referred to as the White political machine did not support qualified Black nominees, yet all forty-
nine civil judges in Brooklyn courts were White, even though most
of the cases heard involved Black people. The district's population
was majority Black, and Chisholm later recalled sarcastically that the
White machine wouldn't support a Black candidate even if the district
was 99 percent Black.

Lewis S. Flagg Jr. was the candidate Black leaders wanted to run
for a vacant municipal court position. He was a respected attorney,
activist, and Black civic leader. He had unsuccessfully run for the New
York Assembly in 1932 and 1933 as an independent candidate. In each
race, a Democrat won the seat. This was while he maintained his law
practice. He was also considered for a nomination to the US district
attorney's office in 1933, one of two Black lawyers being considered
for the first time for a position in that office. When Flagg announced
his interest in the vacant judicial position after the death of the prior
judge, the Democratic Party chose a White nominee who did not
reside in the Bedford-Stuyvesant neighborhood. Wesley McDonald
"Mac" Holder, whom Chisholm had met in college, organized the
Committee for the Election of Lewis Flagg Jr. Chisholm joined with
community leaders who were upset a Black politician had not been
elected since the early 1950s. Holder, Chisholm, and the others were
seen as rebels within the Seventeenth Assembly District.

At this time, Bertram L. Baker was the only Black person representing the district in the New York State Assembly. After immigrating
from the Caribbean island of Nevis (the birthplace of Alexander Ham-
ilton, as Baker was proud to point out) in 1915 at the age of seventeen
and becoming a US citizen in 1924, he joined the Democratic Party,
although most Black people were members of the Republican Party,
as it was still seen as "the Party of Lincoln." However, politicians such
as Baker, Holder, and Chisholm with Caribbean backgrounds were
more prone to become Democrats and were also not accustomed to

or accepting of segregation. Baker tried to recruit other Black people
to the party. "I went around here on Jefferson Avenue canvassing
to get signatures on the Democratic petitions and a Black woman
came to the door," recalled Baker at age eighty-seven. "She looked
at me astonished. She said, 'Young man, I'm ashamed of you. I was
a Republican born, I was Republican bred and I'll be a Republican
when I'm dead.' Bam. And she slammed the door in my face."[1] This
statement was symptomatic of the relationship between Black Americans and the Democratic Party at the time. Not only was the first
Republican president, Abraham Lincoln, credited with ending slavery,
but also Democratic segregationists implemented Jim Crow policies
throughout the South, where the majority of the Black population
lived. However, Black people began voting primarily Democratic
starting with President Franklin D. Roosevelt, and even more so for
President John F. Kennedy.

Chisholm joined Baker and other Black members when they
formed the United Democratic Association, with Baker as its leader.
Still, he acted as the "confidential inspector" for John Cashmore, the
Irish American Brooklyn borough president. Democratic bosses knew
their club couldn't remain all White with a growing Black population,
so they maneuvered Baker into an elected position. They made a deal
with John Walsh, also an Irish American politician, to accept a nomination for reelection to the state assembly but then withdraw after the
primary in exchange for a judgeship. When he did so, the Democratic
club nominated Baker as his replacement, under New York State law
and party rules allowing the party leaders to select a new candidate
if the primary winner withdrew. In November 1948 Baker won the
general election, becoming the first Black person elected to a political
office in Brooklyn. Representing Bedford-Stuyvesant in the assembly,
he cosponsored one of the nation's first laws against housing discrimination and became the majority whip, the highest state position held
by a Black person at that time.

At the same time, Holder taught Chisholm lessons she would always remember. As she recalled, "Mac taught me how to listen and observe men in the political arena. He taught me the techniques of getting out the vote and how to get on a ballot."[2] She also learned not to use the strategies of Baker in making backroom deals with the political machine. For Flagg's primary campaign, she was one of the leaders in visiting residents, holding meetings, sending notices, and raising money. She urged voters to challenge the White establishment, despite some Black voters in the community being afraid of causing trouble and not supporting the club for pushing for a Black candidate. Still, Flagg garnered two thousand names on his nominating petition during the first round of the Democratic primary, although only 750 were needed. The Democratic machine tried to invalidate his run by claiming that most of the names on the petition were forged, from voters not registered with the Democratic party, and included non-residents of the district. The case was brought before the board of elections, and the complaint was withdrawn.

On the Sunday before the 1953 primary, 1,500 supporters campaigned house-to-house. After Flagg won the primary by a slim margin of 147 votes (4,507 versus 4,360), his opponent, Benjamin Schor, contested Flagg's victory. Schor circulated false rumors that 1,179 ballots were missing and insisted on a recount. In response, Flagg accused Schor of trying to "thwart the will of the people and deny the mandate of the voters."[3]

After a four-day court hearing, on October 2, 1953, New York supreme court judge Benjamin Brenner ordered a recount of blank and void ballots and a recanvass in eight districts. Knowing he would lose, Schor switched to the Liberal Party ticket. Flagg's reaction was resolute: "Only too long have the people been told that we do not have the power and the strength to make demands upon the political party bosses—that we should be satisfied with the crumbs which fall from the table. Victory in November can and will be achieved if the electorate will go to the polls and vote for me."[4] Flagg won thanks not only to Black votes but also to support from Jewish residents and the United Electrical, Radio and Machine Workers of America and the United Auto Workers.

Chisholm aligned with Holder when he converted the Democratic committee that elected Flagg to the Bedford-Stuyvesant Political League (BSPL) in 1953. They described themselves as "rebels" with a platform of electing Black leaders, political reform, voter registration, and proper representation of the Black community. They had shown the local Democratic Party they couldn't just expect the Black vote while their needs were being ignored. The BSPL operated under the banner of LET'S MAKE HISTORY AGAIN after getting Flagg elected. They pushed for more Black elected officials for the state legislature and US Congress, and Holder ran for local political office. Though neither Holder nor any of the candidates the BSPL supported were able to win, they galvanized citizens to fight for housing equality and economic opportunities.

In 1958 Chisholm had a falling out with Holder when she became so active in the club that members persuaded her to run for BSPL president. This was partly because Holder helped Black candidates while still negotiating with White Democratic bosses whereas Chisholm steadfastly opposed being politically beholden to the bosses at the expense of voters. She also didn't approve of any politicians making backroom deals, where they secretly negotiated for their own personal benefit rather than openly for the full benefit of voters. Holder was furious, accusing her of disloyalty and turning her back on the person who taught her everything she knew. He used all his political tactics against her challenge, including packing the election meeting with loyalists and circulating flyers denouncing Chisholm. She lost the election, and the two remained at odds for nearly ten years following. The BSPL suffered early during this rift and folded a few years after Chisholm's loss.

However, Chisholm continued to attend Seventeenth Assembly District meetings, which were led by Vincent P. Carney. She later reflected, "I'll never forget the club house. Blacks and Whites sat separately, the Blacks on one side of the room and the Whites on the other. Carney and his henchmen sat up on a raised dais puffing on stogies and wearing big diamond rings. And I can still see the people sitting on those benches for as long as three hours waiting for a tap on the shoulder to go walk up to the platform, as if they were going to see God Almighty. It just got to me."[5] She felt it was ridiculous that residents were controlled by political leaders rather than the other way around. The Seventeenth Assembly District exemplified how politics was run more like an organized criminal enterprise based on special favors and personal patronage rather than a democratic process.

In 1955 Carney promoted Chisholm to the club's executive board. She knew this wasn't really a reward for her hard work but rather a ploy to shut her up, which didn't work. She was eventually thrown off the board and would later recall how they thought that would make her too embarrassed to return, but "the very next week I came to the clubhouse and sat out on the floor with the slobs. When they saw me out there, I saw them nudging each other. . . . I walked up and shook their hands and they got rattled. I kept on asking questions, kept on needling. It began to crystallize in me that I had something that could be used for people who had no input into things."[6] Chisholm would tell the women what happened during board meetings, enraging the men, but it did lead to women being placed into leadership roles.

Eventually she tired of feeling rejected by the club and left their politics in 1958, learning a powerful lesson that too many politicians were driven by personal power: "Political organizations are formed to keep the powerful in power. Their first rule is 'Don't rock the boat.' If someone makes trouble you change them, do it. If you can't get him, bring him in. Give him some of the action; let him have a taste of power. Power is all anyone wants, and if he has a promise of it as a reward for being good, he'll be good. Anyone who does not play by those rules is incomprehensible to most politicians."[7]

While Chisholm may have become disillusioned about politics, she was excelling in her education career and getting accolades for her work. In 1957 she was named alumna of the year by Brooklyn College and also received an award for outstanding work in child welfare from the Women's Council of Brooklyn. Due to her expertise, in 1959 she became an educational consultant to the day care division of New York City's Bureau of Child Welfare. In this position she supervised ten day care centers, 116 employees, including seventy-eight teachers and thirty-eight other staff members, and ran a budget of $400,000. This position required extensive planning, meeting with parents, and building community coalitions. She didn't give up on her community and remained involved with activities such as establishing youth programs, serving on the board of directors of the Albany Houses public housing project, and fighting for community improvements in sanitation and other services. For these efforts, Key Women of America acknowledged her in 1963 as their Key Woman of the Year and in 1965 as a Woman of Achievement.

3

GETTING BACK INTO POLITICS AND THE NEW YORK STATE LEGISLATURE

"If you need to have a discussion, have a discussion. But it makes no difference to me. I intend to fight."

C HISHOLM DIDN'T STAY AWAY from politics very long as Black activism in Bedford-Stuyvesant increased. She and other residents wanted real change, and she was never one to sit on the sidelines. Residents were tired of increased violence and racial unrest in Brooklyn. In 1961 gang wars erupted, resulting in several teen deaths in Bedford-Stuyvesant, Williamsburg, and Crown Heights. Riots between citizens and the New York City Police Department ensued because of the police force's oppressive and racially biased policies and practices. For example, riots in 1964 were caused by an unarmed fifteen-year-old teenager, James Powell, being fatally shot by a White police officer, reportedly for loitering. Many White residents moved to the suburbs, but police officers assigned to the predominantly Black Bedford-Stuyvesant and Harlem were almost all White.

Chisholm and residents were tired of housing discrimination, high unemployment, and a failure of White local government leaders to implement civil rights laws or address issues such as police brutality. There was also community tension between different ethnic groups. The majority Black residents wanted more control of the Ocean Hill–Brownsville school district's hiring choices and school curriculum, particularly in hiring Black teachers. This pitted Black residents against the majority White and Jewish teachers and their teachers' union, which resisted school integration and the hiring of more minority teachers. Community protests, including blocking union teachers from entering local schools, spilled into other neighborhoods, and all schools in New York City were shut down for thirty-six days. This gained national attention because it symbolized how slowly integration was taking place in schools across the country, with White people trying to control public schools since the *Brown v. Board of Education* decision. Wil Mara explained the mass exodus of White residents didn't change the political structure of all White political leaders and thus "left Blacks and other minorities with almost no employment opportunities, living in decaying neighborhoods served by indifferent local governments."[1]

In this charged environment, Chisholm reentered politics in 1960 when she joined the Unity Democratic Club (UDC), formed in 1955 by lawyer Thomas Russell Jones and others who supported the election of Flagg. Other members included James H. Shaw Jr. (later a member of the New York State Senate and then a judge) and Enoch Williams (later a city councilman). However, the club was controlled by Black Democratic boss Thomas R. Fortune, another case of a single person trying to control the democratic process and stifle the voice of voters by making backroom deals and leveraging personal power.

Before being named the UDC, it was called the Thomas R. Fortune Democratic Club.

Jones was described as a "golden-tongued orator" and created the UDC through his political contacts with Jewish radicals and local African Americans. The club was located at 1103 Bergen Street in a building owned by Marcus Garvey's Universal Negro Improvement Association, and its membership was integrated and included women and middle-class residents.

As with the BSPL, the leaders of the UDC were determined to combat the White Democratic machine. Chisholm later recalled the UDC's goal was to get rid of the White machine and establish Black self-representation in the Seventeenth Assembly District. The UDC's support of equality was reflected in its leadership. Along with Chisholm was the club's copresident, Ruth Goring, and Jocelyn Cooper, the wife of Black attorney Andrew W. Cooper, who is now famous for winning the case *Cooper v. Power* that created the Twelfth Congressional District in Brooklyn and ended gerrymandering in the borough.

The UDC merged in 1961 with the Unity-Nostrand Democratic Club (the two later split in 1962) to form the Committee for Full Registration and Adequate Representation. As its membership quickly grew to over eight hundred, Chisholm and others would take to the streets and knock on doors to get residents active for those running for office and to get voters registered. Andrew Cooper used Chisholm's home for meetings and recruitment. The UDC even joined the Brooklyn branch of the Congress of Racial Equality (CORE) to protest racial discrimination. Other reform Democratic clubs started supporting the UDC's stance against the machine.

Jones initially ran to represent New York's Seventeenth Assembly District in 1960 with an agenda of improving education, sanitation, housing, transportation, health care, and wages. He lost the Democratic primary by only 187 votes to incumbent Samuel I. Berman, who had been serving in the assembly since 1954 and who won the general election. Nevertheless,

Chisholm continued to support the works of Jones and other club leaders as they sought political office and fought to end discriminatory practices against Black people in the borough. She later recalled how she "walked these streets until I almost went crazy,"[2] knocking on doors and trying to educate local residents on the importance of activism.

The UDC then focused on getting Jones elected to the assembly during the next election in 1962, and Ruth Goring as a district leader. The UDC's greatest enemy was the toll years of discrimination and political exclusion had taken on the enthusiasm of Black residents to get involved in the political process. As Goring explained, "We felt that the district's Negroes were not represented politically. I was just sitting by and watching a community go to pot. People would go to the community leaders and not be seen. There were no responses to letters."[3] Jones garnered the counsel of Pat Carter and Carter's wife, Constance, to help with mailings and other election activities.

Jones defeated Berman and his old-line Jewish organization during the Democratic primary, as well as the two African American female contenders. He won the general election with 69.59 percent of the vote against Republican Priscilla Maddox and Liberal Miriam I. Eversley. Goring was successful against Carrie Lark, who was Black but sponsored by the Democratic machine. Jones's and Goring's elections were thought to be an end to the White male–dominated political machine in Brooklyn, and Chisholm thought the control of the White political machine was finally over in the Bedford-Stuyvesant district. However, White leaders would continue making alliances with Black political leaders in an attempt to hold on to their power. In 1964 Goring became assistant to the Brooklyn borough president. In that same year, Jones accepted a civil court judgeship on the New York City Civil Court after only spending two years in the state assembly.

After three years of aggressive support work, Chisholm was elected to UDC's executive committee and began to aggressively recruit other women. On October 14, 1963, she wrote a letter to Jones advising him to add Elizabeth Bond and Wima Pegg because she felt they were "loyal, ardent [and] matured persons. Such women are very necessary for additional strength as well as being dynamic, counteractive forces against the less mature elements on our executive committee who have 'too many axes to grind.'" She also gave him cautious advice, stating, "Tom, always be sure to check the club's constitution before you move in order not to have to retreat on your decisions" and "Just a few thoughts. You will act as you see fit."[4]

The local Democratic Party, while not recognizing it as a key decision maker, continued to provide limited support to the UDC, such as allowing members to attend local meetings and give comments on policies. The party also didn't push for Black candidates to represent the majority minority area or put forth policies to improve the community. That drove Chisholm to notify the UDC of her intention to run for the state assembly seat vacated by Jones in 1964. She had worked hard for the Democratic Party and refused to be denied because she was a woman. "They were shocked," she remembered. "It was the first time a Black woman had sought elective office in Brooklyn. But I knew I could do it. I felt strong enough. There were people in that club-house who were saying, 'Why not give Chisholm a chance? She's got it. She can lead.' So I told the club's executive committee, 'If you need to have a discussion, have a discussion. But it makes no difference to me. I intend to fight.'"[5]

Chisholm later talked about the opposition she faced even though the majority of club members wanted her to run. At a special meeting called at Jones's home, he waffled on running for reelection and Chisholm recalled, "I was moved to tears when I realized that all of this was a ploy to prevent me, as a woman, from being elected to the Assembly. I'll never know if it was my crying or the stirring, impassioned speech I made that night, but it ended up with me as the organization's candidate."[6]

Chisholm also had the support of her parents and her husband. Conrad told her, "It's what you want, Shirley, go out and get it."[7] His support of his wife was exemplified in his response to a reporter who once questioned his relationship with his powerful wife: "I am not threatened by her in any way. I grew up secure. I'm West Indian. Early in our marriage I saw Shirley's ability to get things done. I decided that she'd get the billing. I push her in any way I can."[8] He later commented on how much Chisholm's political career meant: "She came on the scene when America needed a voice of Shirley Chisholm. They needed someone who would stand up there and [be] strong and support certain causes. And help certain sections of the community that needed a voice."[9] Chisholm would often joke that people would suspect she was married to a weakling. Conrad was just the opposite, a strong-willed man who supported his wife's ambitions.

After Chisholm won the eventual support of the UDC, she still faced opposition from men in the community. While campaigning, some would heckle her, one man asking if she had fixed her husband's breakfast before going out to campaign and straightened up her house. But she didn't let the hecklers faze her; her qualifications were more important than her gender. She also benefited from the precedent set by other politically active women in Brooklyn, including Ada B. Jackson, Maude B. Richardson, and Pauli Murray.

Jackson, the daughter of a former slave, ran in 1944 and 1946 to represent New York's Seventeenth Assembly District, in 1947 for Brooklyn City Council, and in 1949 for the US Congress. Richardson, a former vice president of the Brooklyn NAACP, ran for Brooklyn City Council in 1945 and for the Seventeenth Assembly District in 1946 and again in 1948, and Murray, a lawyer and feminist activist, ran for Brooklyn City Council in 1949 under the Liberal Party. Under the campaign slogan "Good government is good housekeeping," her campaign was based on improvements in such areas as transportation, public facilities, and housing.

Chisholm's campaigning paused briefly in 1963 when her father, Charles, died of circulatory system failure after returning from working in the garden and complaining of a bad headache. When she was told the news while working at the Bureau of Child Welfare's division of day care, she screamed and collapsed in grief. His death opened a rift between Chisholm and her family that would remain largely unresolved from that point on. Charles had left the house to his wife, Ruby, and their other daughters. However, he left Chisholm a trust fund from his savings, which compounded lingering feelings that she was his favorite child because he gave her more attention than the other girls—such as talking to her about politics.

Despite her grief, Chisholm had learned from her father to keep fighting so soon resumed campaigning, even though she lacked funding as the result of the Democratic Party seldom supporting Black candidates and her lack of support from Black men. But she knew women were the core of the Democratic Party and mobilized them, leveraging her power as the Brooklyn branch president of Key Women of America. The organization was founded in 1954 by Bertha Nelms Harris and focused on improving the lives of children, families, and their communities. Members gave their full support to Chisholm's campaign.

Chisholm's call to action was exemplified in a speech given years later before the Conference on Women's Employment, organized by the House Committee on Education and Labor. She said, "Women in this country must become revolutionaries. We must refuse to accept the old, the traditional roles and stereotypes. . . . We must replace the old, negative thoughts about our femininity with positive thoughts and positive action affirming it, and more."[10]

She defeated rival Harold Brady during the June 1964 Democratic primary with 4,290 votes to 1,729. In the general election she received 18,151 votes compared to 1,893 for Republican Charles E. Lewis and 913 for Liberal Party candidate Simeon Golar. This caused a split between Chisholm and Jones. He wanted to change his political image as a judge by distancing himself from his liberal roots, and he used Chisholm as an example of what was wrong with a leftist view while he embraced a more principled view of political reform. This also caused a rift among members in the UDC. However, Chisholm was undeterred, as she was solidly a part of the liberal Democratic wave sweeping the country that was electing other prominent Democrats, including President John F. Kennedy in 1961 and Lyndon B. Johnson in 1964.

Chisholm became just the second African American female to serve in the New York State Assembly. The first African American was Edward A. Johnson in 1917, representing the Nineteenth Assembly District. The Republican attorney advocated for a civil rights act and the establishment of a state employment bureau. He lost reelection when his district was redistricted, and unsuccessfully ran for Congress in 1928. The first African American woman was Bessie A. Buchanan, serving from 1955 until 1962. She supported civil rights, ending discrimination in private housing, and the assignment of police officers to specific duties, and she wrote a song she unsuccessfully tried to have adopted as New York's state anthem. She later served under New York governor Nelson A. Rockefeller as a delegate to the White House Conference on Aging and then as commissioner for the New York State Division of Human Rights.

When Chisholm entered the assembly the first day, the legislators were hopeful she was just another puppet of Stanley Steingut, the "boss" of the Democratic Party in Brooklyn and leader of the Madison Club. Chisholm knew they had found out she was Black, but she would later speculate, "I think they were expecting a sedate buxom Black woman that the bosses had gotten together to get elected just to look good. When I walked in, one of them whispered, 'O, my God, she's so young-looking!' Another said, 'She looks easy.' But after my maiden speech they knew how wrong they were."[11]

Two important strategies Chisholm learned while in the assembly were compromise and making alliances, while still holding fast to her liberal progressive agenda to force legislators to address such issues as equality and education reform. She worked with other Black leaders from New York, including David Norman Dinkins, who later became the first Black mayor of New York City in 1990; Charles Rangel, who was elected to the House of Representatives in 1971; and Basil Alexander Paterson, who became deputy mayor under Ed Koch in 1978 and then New York's first Black secretary of state. (Paterson's son, David, became governor of New York in 2008.) Dinkins, Rangel, Paterson, and Percy Ellis Sutton (later Manhattan borough president and one-term New York State assemblyman) were known as the "Gang of Four" and the "Harlem Clubhouse" because of their political control in Harlem.

Chisholm served in the assembly from 1965 to 1968, sitting in the 175th, 176th, and 177th sessions. Because her district was continually redistricted, she had to run for reelection in 1965 (she won by 82.19 percent against Republican Frederick F. Shaw Jr.) and again in 1966 (she won by 80.42 percent against Republican Jesse Vann). Each time, she had to compete in both a primary and general election, gaining a reputation for being outspoken, which was controversial in the assembly given there were only six Black members in total—and she was the only Black woman. She was sometimes sidelined even in Democratic Party discussions, such as the two-month-long battle among Democrats in choosing the Speaker of the House. However, she was a leader on key assembly committees thanks to support from the statewide Council of Elected Negro Democrats, which fought for greater Black representation on committees.

On assigned committees, Chisholm was labeled a "troublemaker" by some and "maverick" by others, since she didn't abide by the "rules of politics" if it meant compromising her convictions. As a result, it was also a lonely time for her. Albany, New York, at the time was a majority White city, and it was not proper for women to go to restaurants and bars at night. Her male colleagues never invited her out for social events because she was a woman, and thus she spent her nights in the DeWitt Clinton Hotel, located across the street from the capitol building, reading over legislation. She later recalled, "I think there was a little fear of 'How do we handle her socially?' Men don't like independent women. Not many knew I was a regular gal. I think they were afraid to take the chance. I ate most of the time in my room. I had the TV and I read and I did my legislative homework. I went to bed early."[12] On the weekends, however, she did return to Brooklyn to visit Conrad, her family, and her constituents.

Chisholm had a cold relationship with Steingut. He only had his Democratic leadership position because he inherited it from his father, showing the corruption in the party. She remembered his visit to her college when he emphasized Black people could not make achievements without the help of White people. For years, he had cut backroom deals, preselected who ran for office, and cashed in on favors to control party votes. Chisholm would not support legislation just to appease him. In 1965, she did not support Steingut for Speaker but instead backed Anthony John Travia, who had been the Democratic minority leader.

Former UDC leader Thomas Russell Jones was close to Steingut, so Chisholm's opposition was surprising to Steingut. She explained, however, that Travia had served the party and deserved the chance to be Speaker: "They told me 'You don't do things like this, Chisholm,' and I point out that Travia was Democratic majority leader for seven years and gave yeoman service and now that his party was in power, they were kicking him aside. To me, this was creating a dangerous precedent and I said, 'Remember gentlemen, someday you may be in Anthony Travia's boots.'"[13] Travia defeated Steingut with 55.86 percent of the votes.

The bad blood between Steingut and Chisholm would continue even after she left the assembly when in 1968 she preferred Moses "Moe" M. Weinstein over Steingut for assembly minority leadership.

Weinstein had been acting Speaker of the House after Travia was appointed by President Johnson to the US district court for the Eastern District of New York but lost when the Republicans took over the assembly after the November 1968 election. This contentious relationship with Steingut because she wouldn't blindly agree with his crooked political decisions would later be an issue when Chisholm decided to run for Congress.

Yet Chisholm's actions were consistent with her commitment not to be owned by the Democratic machine, to include those who touted themselves as leaders of the reform movement in Brooklyn. As she once stated, "Don't talk to me about those reform Coalition for a Democratic Alternative people. They always try to claim me for their own because my views on legislation are progressive. Reformers? I have another name for them. We in the Black community have to be very careful whom we associate with. My husband is a former private investigator. I have dossiers on people."[14] She has always claimed she had dossiers, even in her early days in the UDC, but never revealed them.

Chisholm was an active legislator and dubbed by the Associated Press as one of the most militant and effective Black members of the General Assembly. Most legislation she supported was based on her personal experiences during her years working in education, remembering her mother's time as a domestic worker and struggling when she lost her job, the long hours both her parents worked, and her experiences with racial and sexist discrimination. She fought for publicly supported day care centers, all-day kindergartens, a slum insurance pool, a minimum state wage of two dollars, and an end to discrimination in mortgage financing and insurance. She earned the moniker "Fighting Shirley," though some of her colleagues used other names such as a "Pepperpot" due to her feistiness and the "Rock of Gibraltar" because she was stubborn and unyielding. Others called her "the female Adam Clayton Powell," whom Chisholm admired for his tenacity.

In the assembly she introduced fifty bills, of which eight passed. Her bills extended unemployment benefits to personal and domestic workers, whom President Roosevelt had excluded from his New Deal as a compromise with southern Democrats since most of their domestic workers were Black. This was the first law of its kind in New York and required anyone with a domestic worker to pay $500 or more a year to contribute to their unemployment insurance. She argued against the state's required literacy test in English, arguing that just because a person "functions better in his native language is no sign a person is illiterate."[15] She implemented the Search for Education, Elevation, and Knowledge (SEEK) program, providing scholarships and remedial education for disadvantaged students to attend the City University of New York (CUNY) or the State University of New York (SUNY). She worked with Julius C. C. Edelstein, a lobbyist for CUNY, on the program details, and with Dinkins, Paterson, and Sutton to finalize the request for funding and legislative proposal.

Legislation was passed to ensure female faculty members in higher education would not lose their accrued time toward obtaining tenure if they took maternity leave. She spearheaded a bill extending unemployment and social security benefits to agricultural workers. Her colleagues later recalled Chisholm's tenacity. According to Albert H. Blumenthal, former deputy minority leader, she was "a very tough lady, likable, but a loner. Unlike other women in the Legislature, she was never afraid to jump into a debate. Chisholm was never hysterical, she never flailed. She knew what she wanted to say and said it well. She wasn't quick to make up her mind, but when she did, you couldn't blast her out of it."[16]

The challenges Chisholm faced in trying to forge change were exemplified in a 1965 report by Daniel Patrick Moynihan, the assistant secretary of labor under President Johnson. *The Negro Family: The Case for National Action* was prepared to persuade the president that civil rights legislation alone would not lead to racial equality, and opened by discussing the plight of Black people at the time:

> In this new period the expectations of the Negro Americans will go beyond civil rights. Being Americans, they will now expect that in the near future equal opportunities for them as a group will produce roughly equal results, as compared with other groups. This is not going to happen. Nor will it happen for generations to come unless a new and special effort is made.
>
> There are two reasons. First, the racist virus in the American blood stream still afflicts us: Negroes will encounter serious personal prejudice for at least another generation. Second, three centuries of sometimes unimaginable mistreatment have taken their toll on the Negro people. The harsh fact is that as a group, at the present time, in terms of ability to win out in the competitions of American life, they are not equal to most of those groups with which they will be competing.[17]

Chisholm, however, opposed the chapter "The Tangle of Pathology," which described nearly a quarter of urban Black marriages being dissolved (through separation or divorce), a quarter of "negro" births as illegitimate, a quarter of Black families being headed by women, and the breakdown of the "negro" family leading to an increase in welfare dependency. Also disparaging was the discussed matriarchal role of Black women. One passage read, "The matriarchal pattern of so many Negro families reinforces itself over the generations. This process begins with education. Although the gap appears to be closing at the moment, for a long while, Negro females were better educated than Negro males, and this remains true today for the Negro population as a whole."[18] The report reinforced the stereotype of Black women taking education, jobs, and the role of head of household away from Black men. The male-centric report blamed Black people for their challenges—i.e., it blamed the victim without acknowledging the role of government or societal catalysts. Supporters hailed the report as prophetic. Chisholm saw it and similar propositions from sociologists as racist and sexist. The stereotype of the Black matriarch would be used against Chisholm when she later ran for president.

In 1967 Chisholm served as vice president of the New York City chapter of the National Organization for Women (NOW), an organization she helped cofound with twenty-seven other women the year prior. While heading the NOW-NYC campaign, she pushed legislation to guarantee women's equal rights and to legalize abortion access. This was groundbreaking, as abortion was a topic legislatures before her would not tackle. But for Chisholm this issue was not only a matter of women's rights; it was a civil right. It took three years, but the proposed legislature passed into law. It was a monumental feat, given the legislature comprised 207 men and only 4 women.

Other initiatives she supported but unfortunately did not pass were a minimum-wage law, cutting funding to schools run by churches, unemployment insurance for hospital workers, ending discrimination in the banking industry, and mandating state police officers to complete training in civil rights and race relations. Some lessons from the assembly bothered her. There was the chauvinistic attitudes of her male counterparts. She remarked, "This whole question of women, it gets to you. You can use women to do all sorts of tasks, but to put a woman in power, well that's another thing."[19] However, that never deterred her. As she once said, "If they don't give you a seat at the table, bring a folding chair."[20] Another thorn in her side was the tendency for legislators to vote to appease financial contributors and special interests, even for legislation they didn't support personally. This was something Chisholm would never do, because she was "unbought and unbossed"—to borrow the title of her autobiography. She had the support of Black people, women, and the rest her constituency, and they knew she supported them in return.

4

RUNNING FOR CONGRESS

"Ladies and Gentlemen . . . this is fighting Shirley Chisholm coming through."

CHISHOLM WOULD LATER EMPHASIZE she faced greater discrimination as a woman than for being Black when she ran in campaigns. Although such legislation as the Civil Rights Act of 1964 and Voting Rights Act of 1965 had been passed, there were still many in government and general society seeking to deny Black people their constitutionally guaranteed rights. When she first became politically active, she recalled warnings that "the White man is going to get you," and some Black people maintained this view through the 1960s. She recognized the impact continued racism and sexism had on the country: "In the end anti-Black, anti-female, and all forms of discrimination are equivalent to the same thing: anti-humanism."[1]

In August 1968 the Democratic National Committee elected Chisholm as the committeewoman from New York State. She finished her third term in the state assembly and decided to run to represent the Twelfth Congressional District, knowing she could make change in the US Congress. This new district resulted from a court-ordered redistricting of the Fourteenth District that would add all or parts of other neighborhoods to Bedford-Stuyvesant. While Bedford-Stuyvesant included Black, White, and Latino people—specifically Puerto Ricans—and was 80 percent Democrat, the addition of the other neighborhoods added Puerto Ricans from Williamsburg, Italians from Bushwick, and Jews from Crown Heights. Although the new district was 70 percent Black, White residents made up almost half of registered voters. Legislators boasted that the new district was established to give Black voters a greater voice, but many felt it cemented the idea that Black people couldn't win elections since White residents voted in greater numbers.

The new district resulted from attorney Andrew W. Cooper filing a lawsuit in US district court to halt any further Brooklyn elections until the districts were drawn to properly allow equal representation. Cooper described past redistricting efforts as being "in so tortuous, artificial and labyrinthine a manner" that Black people were stripped of their voting power.[2] As Chisholm later recalled, "You have minimized whatever potential power we had. You have come into Bedford-Stuyvesant, you've taken a ruler and a pencil and you have chopped us up in about four or five different ways so as to be sure that each of these little areas are attached to a White congressman."[3] The district court ruled the reappointment plan of 1961 was unconstitutional, and the US Supreme Court upheld the decision in December 1967.

As a result of the newly created district, Stanley Steingut wanted an African American representing the district, compelling Edna F. Kelly, the White incumbent, to seek reelection in another district. Kelly's anger with the Democratic bosses was evident in a letter she wrote to a constituent on July 19, 1968, in which she complained, "The recent reapportionment of New York's Congressional Districts by the New York State Legislature and the results of the June

18th Primary Election should leave no doubt as to how I feel about some of the 'leaders' of the Democratic Party in our State and the tactics they utilize and to which I have never subscribed."[4] The new map carved up parts of her old district into the Twelfth Congressional District and the remaining to the district Emanuel Celler represented. Kelly tried to run against Celler, who had been in Congress since 1923, but lost to him in the primary, carrying only 32 percent of the vote. Kelly and Celler both complained about the Twelfth District, with Celler charging it was just created for the "negro." Steingut wanted an African American elected because of the large Black population, but he wanted one the Democratic machine could control. He instructed the White Democratic clubs not to nominate any White candidates. Others saw this new district as a representation of the new urban America.

Before the redistricting plan was done, the Committee for a Negro Congressman from Brooklyn (CNCB) met in December 1967 to vet potential Black Democratic candidates. They held interviews with five potentials and selected Chisholm because she was an independent political thinker who challenged the White political machine. Chisholm recalled, "It was about three days before Christmas. About a quarter to twelve that night . . . I got a call. . . . I'll never forget this, I don't know where they got all the phones from, but it was a Jewish man on the wire, a Puerto Rican man, and a Black man. All wanted to break the news to me. This was my Christmas present, 1967."[5] The CNCB released a statement almost a week later on December 28: "The Bedford-Stuyvesant community is resolved to see to it that the White machine bosses no longer call the tune for Black people."[6]

Black leaders notified the Democratic Party they would not be ignored in influencing who represented the Twelfth District. If their wishes weren't respected, the party would lose Black voters at the local, state, and federal levels. The Council of Elected Negro Democrats warned, "If you fail to deal with us, you'll have to deal with our successors who'll make the Stokely Carmichaels and Rap Browns seem like conservatives."⁷ Carmichael (born Stokely Standiford Churchill Carmichael) and H. Rap Brown (later called Jamil Abdullah Al-Amin but born Hubert Gerold Brown) had both served as leaders of the radical Blank Panthers.

Chisholm was a detailed political strategist and later explained, "Before I make a move, I analyze everything."⁸ She analyzed the voting rolls of the new district and saw it had ten thousand to thirteen thousand more registered women than men. She knew she still would be hampered by male Democratic leaders who wouldn't support her, and they knew she wouldn't give them unwavering support if she disagreed with them. In the midst of analyzing how she would gain support, she got a call from Wesley Holder, her mentor. He offered his total support, explaining now in his seventies he wanted to live long enough to help elect both a Black judge and Black member of Congress. Chisholm also had support from Julius Caesar Claude Edelstein as her financial adviser and Thomas Fortune as her campaign manager.

Surprisingly, Thomas Jones, who Fortune had replaced as UDC leader after serving as club treasurer, also displayed an interest in running for Congress. A sign reading JONES FOR CONGRESS appeared in a storefront in early 1968, although Jones denied having encouraged it. As Fortune recalled, "He came around to the club, but there wasn't much support for him. You know, a judge is supposed to be above politics, and Jones hadn't been to the club in the last few years."⁹ Jones was the community's contact for Senator Robert Kennedy, even though Chisholm should have been. As she explained, "Kennedy didn't understand the district. I was the top vote-getter, but Kennedy never sought me out. I think there was some people who kept him from me."¹⁰ However, Jones never ran, reportedly after Kennedy told him he was more valuable running the Bedford-Stuyvesant Restoration Corporation, which was Kennedy's personal community development project. It was no surprise neither consulted Chisholm on the project, given the bad blood between her and Jones.

The project was as a failure, but Kennedy wanted to improve what he saw as a ghetto: "Even if we fail, we have learned something. But more important than that, something has to be done. People like myself just can't go around making nice speeches all the time. . . . We have to do some damn work, too."[11] Many credit Kennedy's actions to his not wanting Brooklyn to face the same riots as occurred in the Watts neighborhood of Los Angeles, California, in August 1965. However, his efforts did little to improve Brooklyn or the Bedford-Stuyvesant neighborhood.

The federal court approved the state assembly's new redistricting map on March 20, 1968, and the Democratic primary was set for that June. Chisholm competed against two other Black candidates: Dollie Lowther Robinson, who had served as special assistant to the director of the Women's Bureau of the Department of Labor under the Kennedy administration, and state senator William Colridge "Willie" Thompson Sr., who had served as a senator since 1965 and was the first Black state senator from Brooklyn. He had assured Chisholm he wasn't going to run but then filed a nomination petition near the deadline. She and others who supported her felt he was pushed as a "spoiler candidate" by Robert Kennedy and Steingut. She alleged that "Willie felt the White boys were going to get out the vote for him."[12]

Thompson, whose parents were also native Caribbean from Saint Kitts, was the most well financed and supported by the Kings County Democratic machine, and thus was secretly supported by Steingut, who wanted to give a public impression he was not involved in influencing an election in a Black community. Thompson was Brooklyn's first non-White state senator but was seen as controlled by White politicians, although he was a former protégé of Bertram Baker, who represented Brooklyn in the New York Assembly starting in 1948 and was a powerful Black Democratic leader. Thompson also served in World War II as part of the famed "Buffalo Soldiers" and received a purple heart. As Chisholm explained, "Everyone knew that silently they were backing the senator. . . . Thompson was the kind of person that they felt they could work with. . . . But you see they didn't want to come out openly for Senator Thompson because it would be thwarting the will of the people."[13]

Dollie Robinson was supported by Bertram Baker, and local Reverend Gardner C. Taylor endorsed her before his four-thousand-member congregation of Concord Baptist Church. Baker opposed Thompson because of his support from Kennedy, whereas Baker supported Lyndon Johnson and Hubert Humphrey during the 1960 Democratic presidential primaries. Thompson opposed Baker for previously supporting a Republican in a local race.

Baker disliked Chisholm for being an up-and-coming reform candidate who didn't answer to Democratic bosses like him, and his political power was slipping away. He didn't see her as the great reformer of Brooklyn, as she worked with Thomas Fortune, who was also a Democratic boss in Brooklyn. According to his grandson, Ron Howell, Baker went through Chisholm's 1972 book *Unbought and Unbossed* and highlighted by line things he felt were true or untrue because he had such political disdain for her becoming politically powerful in what he saw as his territory. According to Howell, "The disputes were for the most part not personal, but it was clear that Bertram saw her as an uppity and bitter woman and that she saw him as a relic of a political past that was going the way of the old Tammany Hall."[14] (Tammany Hall was a New York City political machine controlling Democratic Party politics from the 1890s until the 1960s when John V. Lindsay became mayor.)

None of the other seven assemblymen of area districts would weigh in for any candidate. Chisholm's strategy was to present herself as a candidate of the people while arguing her opponents were owned by the establishment. She saw Steingut's lack of support as him opposing her and stated, "Unless you have the political leadership in back of you in each of these areas, it's hell on wheels," and "The whole thing that bothered so many of these professional politicians is that I cannot be disciplined."[15]

Although the district was majority Black and Puerto Rican, Chisholm still sought White votes. As she saw it, "The White people of this community know me well enough to know I'm fair. I truly believe I am my brother's keeper."[16] She even had the support of local rabbis, some campaigning for her by going through neighborhoods and proclaiming her "our Shirley." She had support across the neighborhood. Her first campaign contribution of $9.62 came from a group of local residents on assistance who were at a bingo party and offered to have fundraising events every Friday night to help her. The money was delivered to Chisholm personally by a Black mother on welfare, carrying the money in a dirty envelope. Chisholm cried after she received the money, and it confirmed she made the right choice to run. By the end of her campaign her total budget had been just $20,000.

Chisholm's campaign team worked up to nineteen hours many days, and she and her supporters took to the streets. They canvassed voters and built confidence through face-to-face interaction. Her campaign slogan was FIGHTING SHIRLEY CHISHOLM: UNBOUGHT AND UNBOSSED, which she printed on flyers, posters, and bumper stickers to be distributed by her supporters. They would drive through neighborhoods with Chisholm's picture and campaign slogan on cars, handing out thousands of flyers they carried in shopping bags. As a symbol of women evolving from housewives to a political force to be reckoned with, the shopping bags featured her campaign slogan on them too. Black, Puerto Rican, and Jewish women would help her raise money through bake sales, barbecues, and raffles. Her husband, Conrad, later commented, "The women are fierce about Chisholm. She can pick up the phone and call 200 women and they'll be there

Shirley Chisholm reviewing data as she runs for the US Congress. *Photo by Roger Higgins, courtesy of New York World-Telegram and the Sun Newspaper Photograph Collection, Library of Congress Prints and Photographs Division*

in an hour. And she gives them nothing more than a thank you and a buffet supper."[17] When Chisholm called her women supporters for help, she announced, "We gotta go to war."

There was concern about Black voter turnout for the Democratic primary, so Chisholm knew she had to really push for the non-Black vote. She later recalled, "All I was doing was marching, night after night after night in the ten [assembly] areas. Jewish people's homes, Black people's homes, Puerto Rican people's homes, churches, every place I could go. Anybody who wanted me, I was running. . . . In the Black neighborhood I ate chitlins, in the Jewish neighborhood bagels and lox, in the Puerto Rican neighborhood arroz con pollo."[18] Fortune explained, "It was not easy convincing the Black people that they should register and vote. Too many of them felt that whoever they helped to put into office would only work for themselves once they got in. Also they were encouraged in this attitude by the authorities who were prepared to give them a little something for nothing in the hope that they would do nothing."[19]

Chisholm commented that her rival Thompson was sure he would win because he thought he could rally White voters to the polls. He even went on vacation to Cape Cod instead of campaigning. She fought for the White vote, mostly concentrated in the Bushwick neighborhood, by going after the women's support. She told Conrad, "I'm leaving you for three days, honey. Come and visit me. . . . Check on me every night, see what I'm doing, but I have to live for three days in Bushwick. . . . I have to organize."[20]

During the June 18 primary, voter turnout was low. Only twelve thousand voted in Bed-Stuy, while forty-three thousand voted in the district where Celler and Kelly competed. Still, Chisholm defeated Thompson by 788 votes over his 4,907 (Robinson received 1,848). She carried every neighborhood except Bushwick, which Thompson only eked out by five votes. Despite his defeat, Thompson found political success by later becoming the first Black administrative judge of the Kings County Supreme Court. He told a friend he wasn't upset by the loss because it led to him becoming a judge, and the courts were at the forefront of the civil rights fight.

For the general election, Chisholm ran against James L. Farmer, the famous civil rights leader. Although a Liberal Party member, Farmer ran on the Republican ticket because Republicans picked him as a Black man who could defeat Chisholm with majority Black voters. Local Republicans who opposed him were pressured to endorse him by national Republican political figures, and he was endorsed by Puerto Rican Bronx Borough president Herman Badillo and New York governor Nelson Rockefeller. Having Farmer as an opponent proposed quite the challenge. He was well known from his work during the civil rights movement, particularly as head of the Congress of Racial

Equality (CORE) and helping to organize the 1963 March on Washington for Jobs and Freedom. This was also not Farmer's first run for political office. In 1966 he sought the Liberal Party nomination to run for New York governor against Franklin D. Roosevelt Jr., thus making Farmer a veteran of the process. Roosevelt gained 82.28 percent of the Liberal Party vote but lost to Rockefeller in the gubernatorial election.

Chisholm and Holder were outraged when they heard Farmer was running, particularly since Farmer didn't live in Brooklyn, and they knew the Republican Party only chose him as a puppet so they could control the district. Farmer lived in Manhattan but had an apartment in Brooklyn on Herkimer Street near Nostrand Avenue for a local mailing address. He was also seen as an unwanted outsider by residents of the borough. The local CORE office was at odds with the national CORE office, so local Black activists did not support Farmer. Farmer charged the Democratic Party of ignoring Black voters, saying that Democrats "took [Black people] for granted and thought they had us in their pockets. . . . We must be in a position to use our power as a swing vote."[21]

Farmer also charged Chisholm with being part of the Democratic establishment, which was hypocritical considering the support he was receiving from the White Republican machine. He also had celebrity endorsements from the likes of Sidney Poitier, Mahalia Jackson, Lionel Hampton, Nina Simone, and Brock Peters. He was supported by the national CORE office, which was the first time in the organization's history backing a political candidate.

During the race, Chisholm became ill with a massive but benign fibroid tumor, confining her to the hospital for nearly three weeks to recover after its removal. She was in bed in a nearby hotel during the 1968 Democratic Party convention in Chicago held August 26–29. The convention was the worst in the party's history due to hundreds of thousands of anti-Vietnam and counterculture protestors who swarmed the streets demanding a change in government policies.

The leading two groups were the Youth International Party (called Yippies) and the National Mobilization Committee to End the War in Vietnam (Mobe). The protestors nominated a pig named Pigasus (also called Pigasus the Immortal and Pigasus J. Pig) as a Democratic candidate and paraded it through the crowds. They demanded Pigasus have Secret Service protection and a foreign policy brief until it was seized by the police and taken to a local humane society. A curfew was put in place by Chicago mayor Richard J. Daley as the police presence was drastically increased. The day before the convention started, police rushed protestors in Lincoln Park with tear gas and riot gear, resulting in bloodshed as protestors were beaten with clubs even after being subdued.

The convention itself was also chaotic. Inside the International Amphitheatre, disagreements over Vietnam grew so contentious that convention organizers moved a debate on the subject after midnight, hoping viewers would be asleep. Party leaders argued over the protests as well. Mayor Daley was shown on television cursing Connecticut senator Abraham Alexander Ribicoff for his speech denouncing excessive police tactics. Outside, protests continued each night, and on August 28 up to fifteen thousand gathered with a legal permit to protest. However, they were attacked by police, state National Guardsmen, and federal troops, all totaling over twenty-three thousand officers, in front of Chicago's Conrad Hilton Hotel. The smoke from the teargas was so heavy it entered the lobbies of nearby hotels. By the end of the convention over six hundred arrests had been made, and over a hundred people were injured.

Although Chisholm could not attend the convention, she was voted to replace Edna Kelly as national committeewoman for the New York State Delegation. Farmer seized the opportunity to make such statements as "Where's Mrs. Chisholm? We haven't seen or heard from her."[22] Angered by this, she called her doctor and said, "Look, the stitches aren't in my mouth. I'm going out."[23] And that she did—with a bullhorn and her sound truck, even after her doctor told her not to call him if anything happened to her.

From that point on, Farmer turned the race into a gender war. He made such comments as "women have been in the driver's seat" in Black communities for too long, and the district needed "a man's voice in Washington" versus the voice of a "little schoolteacher."[24] His tactics didn't sit well with women, particularly some Black women leaders who had been given a backseat role during the civil rights movement by such leaders as Farmer. Farmer's demeaning of Chisholm led Dorothy Height and others to start letter-writing campaigns protesting Farmer's attack on Black women. Some were upset he was making such statements while married to a White woman. He married Lula Peterson Farmer in 1949 after his first marriage to Winnie Christie in 1945 only lasted a year.

Chisholm gained support from prominent national feminist leaders such as New York attorney, writer, and women's rights activist Pauli Murray, who argued the type of gender inequality supported by Farmer was sustained through policies she labeled as "Jane Crow." These views were intertwined with the societal expectation that women were demure, nonaggressive, and accommodating to men.

Chisholm ran for office when the women's movement was trying to merge the parallel pushes for gender equality led by White women with female racial equality led by Black and Hispanic women's groups across the country. However, she didn't begin her campaign to organize women or run on a feminist platform. Beyond women, she also had the endorsement of the local Black paper, the *Amsterdam News*, and the American Federation of Labor and Congress of Industrial Organizations (AFL-CIO) of New York.

During the campaign, Chisholm labeled Farmer an outsider and puppet of the Republican Party and big donors, whereas she took no money from special interest groups. She reached out to voters by visiting neighborhoods and holding rallies. Her most notable campaign strategy was riding through the district in a sound truck announcing,

"Ladies and Gentlemen . . . this is fighting Shirley Chisholm coming through."[25] Describing her campaign style, Chisholm explained, "I have a way of talking that does something to people. I have a theory about campaigning. You have to let them feel you."[26] She had minored in Spanish in college and spoke fluently to Hispanic residents, which was a major leg up since Puerto Ricans made up 20 percent of the neighborhood. She had to be persuasive to Hispanic voters, as they often voted for a Hispanic name on the ballot regardless of that candidate's political agenda.

Major television and newspaper media, however, did not give Chisholm equal coverage, sometimes discussing Farmer running for office without mentioning her name. Coverage of the race was often also sexist. One article in the New York Times had the headline FARMER AND WOMAN IN LIVELY BEDFORD-STUYVESANT RACE. A weekend special aired by NBC, "The Campaign and the Candidates," almost exclusively featured Farmer. They justified airing Farmer would attract viewers; he was "noteworthy." Chisholm called television and radio stations to complain, only to be told Farmer had a national reputation. One even snarkily told her, "Who are you? A little school-teacher who happened to go to the Assembly."[27] When she did get media attention, it was often negative. Another article in the New York Times mentioned she "looked slight at 96 pounds" and another called her a "tiny yet torrid lawmaker."[28] This sentiment was not shared by all reporters. Local NBC reporter Gabe Pressman believed Chisholm would win and spent a half day covering her campaign.

Despite this, Chisholm and Farmer did agree on some issues, such as equal access to education, housing, and employment. Neither supported the Vietnam War, and both were in favor of community control in the fight over public school desegregation in the Ocean Hill–Brownsville section of Brooklyn. Still, Farmer would always come back to his record on civil rights and being a man as reason for being the better candidate. He touted his gender as superior, campaigning on the streets with a group of eight Black men banging bongo drums, a symbol of the male-dominated Black Power movement.

Chisholm touted the advantages of being a woman, as did Holder, along with her being a popular resident Democrat. She ran on her record in the assembly and her fighting spirit. She told one audience, "They call me Fighting Shirley Chisholm. My mother tells me I was born fighting. I was kicking so hard in the womb she knew I was aching to get out and fight."[29]

Chisholm defeated Farmer by a margin of more than two to one (34,885 votes compared to 13,777), with almost 67 percent of votes. There was also a Conservative Party candidate, Ralph J. Carrano, who received 3,771 votes. The *New York Times* would not give Chisholm direct coverage in terms of interviews or positive press in comparison to her opponent during the campaign, but the day after the election they announced her as the winner. In her victory remarks she stated, "My dear friends, tonight is a very important night, not so much for me, but for you, the people of this community. After many years of struggle and sacrifices on the part of several of you here this evening, we have at long last been able to elect today a voice that shall be your voice in the halls of the United States Congress."[30] She also promised, "As a United States Representative in Washington, I intend to represent all people—the Blacks, the Whites, the men, the women, and especially the youth. There are many new ideas abroad in this country, and I intend to speak for those ideas. And my voice will be heard."[31]

Christopher C. DeMuth, a speechwriter for the Nixon White House, had just graduated from Harvard College in 1968 when he worked on Farmer's campaign. He discussed Farmer's loss to Chisholm during an interview in 2008: "We were caught up in the changes in the civil rights movement, the old guard civil rights leaders were being pushed aside by a younger and much more racially self-assured group, and one of them, an assemblywoman named Shirley Chisholm, clobbered us. We just—we got creamed in the general election."[32]

Chisholm's platform and Farmer's support from the White political machine ultimately led to his loss. Farmer congratulated Chisholm on her victory and pledged his support. He told his supporters he would run again in the next election but never did. She and Farmer later became friends, and in his autobiography he playfully noted the distinction of being the first Black man in US history to have been defeated by a woman in a congressional race. He wrote:

> The Democrats held their primary and its winner was not Mickey Mouse, but extremely able state assemblywoman Shirley Chisholm. A poll I had conducted showed that as far as name recognition was concerned it was no contest. I should win hands down. What the poll did not say was the extent to which we could translate name recognition and preference into actual votes, considering the tradition of voting a straight Democratic ticket, regardless of candidates. Chisholm was a formidable opponent and an excellent campaigner.[33]

Chisholm's historic victory didn't initially garner media attention outside New York because the media was focused primarily on the presidential election, and Nixon's narrow defeat of Hubert Humphrey by less than 1 percent of the popular vote. The race was so close that results were not announced until the day after Election Day. Chisholm was initially upset that only the local Black paper, the *Amsterdam News*, covered her campaign. She was, however, featured on the cover of *Jet* magazine on November 21, 1968, with the cover title "First Black Woman In U.S. Congress." Within several months, however, word of her victory gained national attention, and she was featured on the cover of magazines and in nationally televised documentaries. She was on the cover of *Ebony* in February 1969 with the title "New Faces in Congress: Mrs. Shirley Chisholm Is First Black Woman on Capitol

Hill." Chisholm was celebrated as the first Black congresswoman, often referred to as a schoolteacher who won the election. Speaking on her achievement, she later reflected:

> There are 435 members of the House of Representatives and 417 are White male. Ten of the others are women and nine are Black. I belong to both of these minorities, which makes it add up right. That makes me a celebrity, a kind of show attraction. I was the first American citizen to be elected to Congress in spite of the double drawbacks of being female and having skin darkened by melanin. When you put it that way, it sounds like a foolish reason for fame. In a just and free society, it would be foolish. That I am a national figure because I was the first person in 192 years to be at once a congressman, Black and a woman proves, I think, that our society is not yet either just or free.[34]

5

CONGRESSWOMAN SHIRLEY CHISHOLM

"One thing the people in Washington and New York are afraid of in Shirley Chisholm is her mouth."

Oath of Office
of
Representative in the Congress of the United States
Ninety-first Congress

January 21, 1969

I,   Shirley A. Chisholm   , *do solemnly swear (or affirm) that I will support and defend the Constitution of the United States against all enemies, foreign and domestic; that I will bear true faith and allegiance to the same; that I take this obligation freely, without any mental reservation or purpose of evasion; and that I will well and faithfully discharge the duties of the office on which I am about to enter. So help me God.*

Representative in Congress

(State and District)

Oath of Office. *Records of the US House of Representatives, courtesy of National Archives*

CHISHOLM WAS THE only female freshman member of Congress when she entered the House of Representatives in 1969. There were only nine women already in the House and just one in the Senate. Congresswoman Pat Schroeder, first female representative from Colorado, would later recall the lack of women when she entered as a freshman in 1973: "We had no women anywhere: no women pages, no women at the doorkeeper's office, in the parliamentarian's office, no women Capitol Police. You couldn't go into the gym, where a lot of deals were cut—couldn't even go out on the balcony, which is off the Speaker's office. . . . The attitude of a lot of women when I got there was, 'Aren't we lucky they let us in here?'"[1]

Still, the number of women was starting to increase, along with their caliber of experience and other credentials. Historically, women had been elected as widows of congressmen in a symbolic measure to recognize the achievements of their deceased husbands. Starting in the mid-1950s, women such as Chisholm were being elected on their own merits. This was explored in a government document entitled "A Changing of the Guard" that discussed race and gender not being the only changes to Congress:

> In the decades between 1955 and 1976, a new type of well-educated, professional candidate emerged. Women's pre-congressional experiences merged reform backgrounds with specialized training, lengthy resumes and, increasingly, elective experience. Before 1955, just seven women in Congress held law degrees (the first was Kathryn O'Loughlin McCarthy of Kansas, elected in 1932). From 1955 through 1976, 10 of the women elected to Congress were lawyers, and several were graduates of the nation's premier law schools. Of the 39 women who were elected or appointed to Congress during this period, 34 (87 percent) had post-secondary education.

Significantly, 14 of these women had served in state legislatures, making the third generation of women in Congress the first in which women elected with legislative experience outnumbered women who were elected as widows.[2]

Chisholm joined Congress along with two other Black politicians, Louis Stokes of Ohio and William "Bill" Clay Sr. of Missouri, both their respective states' first Black representative. This increased the number of Black members of Congress to ten, up from six in the prior session and the highest in history until then. The ten included Chisholm, Stokes, Clay, Edward William Brooke III (the only Black Republican in the Senate, representing Massachusetts), William L. Dawson (House member from Illinois), Augustus Freeman "Gus" Hawkins (House member from California), Robert N. C. Nix Sr. (House member from Pennsylvania), John Conyers Jr. (House member from Michigan), Charles C. Diggs Jr. (House member from Michigan), and Adam Clayton Powell Jr. (House member from New York).

During her first term, Chisholm hired an all-female staff of six to exemplify her support for women's equality. Some wanted her to hire an all-Black staff, but she wanted a staff to represent the role of women behind the scenes of Congress who were often overworked and underpaid, so she hired four Black and two White staff members. Three had served as aides to former congressman Joseph Resnick of Ellenville, New York, who left office in January 1969. Her staff included Shirley Downs as her legislative assistant; Carolyn Jones, a secretary; Karen McRorey, who handled constituent services; and Patricia W. Lattimore—along with rotating college interns. The staff would marvel at how hard Chisholm worked. As Downs explained, "She's like a vacuum cleaner. I mark stuff for her to read and the next day she comes in and says, 'Let's get together at 2 o'clock and discuss it.' She reads anything and everything. The other day she waltzed out of here with 'The Valachi Papers.'"[3] (The Valachi Papers was an account of mafia activity in the United States revealed to a congressional committee in 1963 and later turned into a book.)

Chisholm's staff affectionately called her "Mrs. C" or "Chizzie," and they were fondly known as the "Chis-ettes." None of her immediate staff were from Brooklyn, as she needed members who knew their way around Capitol Hill. She later hired Travis Kane, the sole man in the office, as her administrative assistant. Her staff assumed the role her husband Conrad had filled in making sure she was on time and accompanying her to and from meetings. They were so dedicated that they even helped her select her wardrobe. As Chisholm explained, "I have a young staff that selects my clothes for me; they don't want me to look old-fashioned. Although I'm older than all of my staff members, they have a hard time keeping up with me."[4]

With the help of her political mentor, Wesley Holder, she also maintained a Brooklyn office at 1149 Eastern Parkway with both a female and male staff. Chisholm made frequent visits to her district to meet with residents, attended high school graduations and church socials, and even met with constituents over tea. She would walk down the street and be immediately recognized; she also personally knew many of the residents because she had lived there almost all her life. As she explained, "That's why they trust me. I know their problems. Many of my friends moved out of this neighborhood once they thought they had made it, but we decided to stay because the roots where you were reared, where you were educated, the associations you have made, the fights you have led, are not easy to give up."[5]

Muriel Morisey later served as Chisholm's constituent caseworker, press secretary, and senior legislative assistant. She described to a House historian the atmosphere of Chisholm's congressional office and what it was like to serve on her staff:

> There wasn't any issue of, "I wonder if a strong Black woman has a place here." And her D.C. staff was dominated by

women. Her press secretary was a woman. The senior legislative assistant was a woman. The chief of staff . . . was a woman. There was a young White man on the staff who was a terrific guy and beloved by everybody, but he was the [only] White man on the staff. . . .

I think we were aware that we were unusual—but we were working for Shirley Chisholm. We were the Chisholm staff, and that carried so much meaning because of who she was—and also that she empowered her staff enormously. So we moved through our work, and even our social lives, carrying the mantle of being one of Chisholm's staffers. And people knew that meant we really were very powerful by virtue of the confidence that she had, the way she relied on us, the trust she exhibited. So for me, it's hard to separate any of the experience from the fact that working for Shirley Chisholm, having a position of trust with her senior staff— that was a really big deal. That's what I remember. Most of the staffs had few women. I knew it, but I think at the time I was always feeling most people on the Hill don't enjoy the confidence and the trust and the capacity to make a difference that her staff did.[6]

One of her former legislative aides, Laura W. Murphy, recalled the reaction to Chisholm as she walked through the halls of the male-dominated Congress: "Congress would only give secretarial or clerk positions to people like me. People would stare at [Chisholm] when she walked down the hall, because invariably a large entourage of professional staff women followed wherever she went."[7] She was also an inspiration to the Black maintenance men and others, such as secretaries, who worked in congressional buildings.

A benefit of her congressional job was she and Conrad could now afford to buy a home. When they found a nice house in Brooklyn, the real estate agent curtly told them it was no longer for sale. This was typical of the racism Black people faced in the area. The agent eventually found out who Chisholm was and contacted them a week later to ask why she didn't reveal she was a member of Congress. Chisholm used "the strongest language" in her response, and she and Conrad purchased a home from a different agent.

Chisholm and Conrad had moved often before they bought their own home. From 1962 through 1963 they lived at 1066 Prospect Place. They lived at Betsy Ross Apartments at 751 St. Mark's Avenue until 1967. They lived at 1165 Sterling Place from 1967 until late 1968 when she was elected to Congress, and later that year in December owned their home at 1028 St. John's Place between Brooklyn and Kingston Avenues. Their home featured a wall with photos of Chisholm, a grand piano, and a full library; they would live there until January 1973. They also later purchased a former Jewish social club building on 1147 Eastern Parkway and converted it into an events space.

Chisholm additionally rented an apartment in Washington, DC, for her use while Congress was in session, though it was burglarized during her first weeks in DC while she was spending a weekend in New York. The burglars ransacked her apartment and stole all the new outfits she had bought to wear to Congress, amounting to $300 in clothing and furs. After that misfortune, she moved to a new apartment and unlisted her address and phone number. She only made one public statement about the incident, venting disappointment at her privacy being violated: "I don't want anybody to know where I live. I don't want anybody visiting my home."[8] She always felt the break-in was an "inside job" but would rarely talk about it because it bothered her so much.

She spent each week in Washington and each weekend in Brooklyn, reserving Saturday nights for spending time with Conrad. While she was still the woman of the house, she of course didn't have time for household chores. Her constituents also graciously helped her out with that. As she explained, "Black women in my community at home have volunteered to do the house-work for me, so that's all taken care of."[9] Conrad once commented on being there for his wife when she came home, explaining, "With the tension she has to go through, she has to have a shoulder to cry on when she comes home. I give her that moral support she so deeply needs, even though she was born with an abundance of self-confidence."[10]

Chisholm's first committee assignment was to the House Committee on Agriculture and its Subcommittee on Rural Development and Forestry. Although the committee did address issues such as food stamps and migrant labor, she had no desire to serve on it because she knew she could not make a difference there. She responded tongue in cheek to this assignment: "Apparently all they know in Washington about Brooklyn was a tree grew there. I can think of no other reason for assigning me to the House Agriculture Committee."[11] When she told her constituents about the assignment, they agreed there were no hogs grown or cotton fields in Brooklyn.

She was already opposed to the House system of appointments according to seniority that kept a very few White men in control, which she called the "senility system."[12] Along with this, she saw the need for campaign finance reform and felt there were scores of young, qualified people whose greatest obstacle to running for office was a lack of funding.

Chisholm was upset she wasn't placed on the Committee on Education and Labor, considering her background in education. She demanded to be reassigned and appealed directly to House Speaker John W. McCormack on the House floor. This was a very rare move, as freshman members of Congress were expected to focus on learning their new job and not challenge norms, and particularly not challenge senior members. After McCormack told her this is the way things operated and to be a "good soldier," it dawned on her that this attitude explained the dysfunction in Washington. Chisholm aired her concerns on the House floor to have an amendment made for her to switch committees. This was after the Speaker would not recognize her as she continued trying to get his attention, so she walked down to the floor to speak.

Her appeal went around the normal process of going through Chairman Wilbur D. Mills of Arkansas, then chairman of the House Committee on Ways and Means, who oversaw all Democratic committee appointments. Chisholm, of course, faced opposition to protesting the assignment, and she later recalled how this experience was typical of how she was treated as a woman:

> Every time I rose, two or three men jumped up. . . . Men were smiling and nudging each other as I stood there trying to get the floor. After six or seven attempts, I walked down an aisle to the "well," the open space between the front row of seats and the Speaker's dais, and stood there. I was half afraid and half enjoying the situation.
>
> "For what purpose is the gentlewoman from New York standing in the well?" Chairman Wilbur Mills asked.
>
> [Chisholm replied] "I have been trying to get recognized for half an hour but evidently you were unable to see me, so I came down to see you. I would like to tell the caucus why I vehemently reject my committee assignment."[13]

Mills unsuccessfully challenged her during her speech, asking if she would withdraw her amendment. Chisholm responded that she could not accept an assignment that was so far removed from the needs of her constituents. She also spoke of the just nine other Black representatives in the House and how all of them should be placed "where they can work effectively to help this nation meet its critical problems of racism, deprivation, and urban decay."[14]

Although not completely satisfied, Chisholm was reassigned to the Committee on Veterans Affairs, and she graciously acknowledged that "there are a lot more veterans in my district than trees."[15] Newly on the committee, her plan was to "make people more aware of their eligibility for the hospital and other veterans' benefits."[16] After her floor speech, some of her colleagues, including her friend Brockman "Brock" Adams from Washington, warned that she had maybe committed political suicide by going around Mills. Although Adams was one of the first members of Congress who befriended her, she didn't listen to him. Chisholm's view was that her job was to represent her Brooklyn constituents. Her actions set a precedent, as her challenge was the first ever made by a freshman member of Congress.

Chisholm's actions naturally drew ire from some of her White male colleagues, surprised at the audacity of a new member, particularly a Black woman, challenging an assignment and the chain reaction this could cause. Representative William Huston Natcher, a Democrat from Kansas, wrote the following in his private journal on January 29, 1969:

> Just before we had the vote on the Resolution Shirley Chisholm, the colored Representative from Brooklyn, New York, attempted to offer an amendment providing that she would be removed from the Committee on Agriculture where she is number 15, as a brand new Member, and placed on some other committee more commensurate with and more in line with the interests of her constituency in Brooklyn. She weighs about 98 pounds and is real dark, is a former school teacher and member of the New York legislature, and quite a rabble-rouser. In discussing her amendment, which was first ruled out of order and later held germane, after the resolution penalizing Rarick was acted upon, she stated that her first choice was presented to the Committee on Committees, which is the Ways and Means Committee, was the Committee on Education and Labor. This Committee, she said,

was more in line with the problems confronting her people in Brooklyn. This is the Committee that Carl D. Perkins, of Kentucky, is the Chairman of and the same Committee that Adam Clayton Powell formerly chaired. . . . Mrs. Chisholm was jubilant and made a dash for the swinging door which leads out to the Press section of the Capitol and, although I could not see her, I had a right clear picture of her standing in the corridor, waving her arms, and in her loud, shrill voice releasing the information that she had won her argument to get off the Committee on Agriculture where, she maintained, she was placed so that she could be controlled. I presume that a tree still grows in Brooklyn but as far as Shirley Chisholm is concerned, there will be no tobacco cut there this summer. This was quite a first for the Committee on Ways and Means and places a small dent in the shining armor of the Committee on Committees.[17]

Chisholm fighting for a better community assignment exemplified that she wanted to truly represent her district, and because it was so diverse she did not have patience for racism, whether from White or Black people. An issue in Brooklyn was the perception of racism between Black and Jewish residents, and the assertion by some political leaders was that this racism was driving Black activism more than a demand for change against the old Democratic machines. Chisholm would not subscribe to this idea being the primary reason Black voters were politically active, and she voiced the hypocrisy of White liberal political activists calling Black people racist while not implementing the many liberal causes they professed to support.

Speaking on these issues, Chisholm lamented:

I wish to God the mass media would stop playing it up. Don't they understand that what is going on is an anti-establishment feeling? Of course it is the Jewish land-lord and the Jewish shopkeeper in the ghetto that the Black man sees and reacts against, but it is not anti-Semitism that is at work. What worries me more is this new restraint I see on the part of White liberals who profess not to understand why Blacks are rising up in such hostile fashion. They were fine when they were relieving their pangs of guilt with their contributions and their participation in the panels and the forum groups, but now that it has come down to the stark reality, when it becomes a matter of putting into practice what you've discussed in your forums and panels, you've got a lot of hang-ups.[18]

Showing her support for her district and her heritage, on September 21, 1969, Chisholm and Adam Clayton Powell Jr. were the grand marshals of the first African American Day Parade held in Harlem. The parade was founded in 1968 by the Afro-American Day and United Federation of Black Community Organizations. It has been held annually on every third Sunday in September since 1969 to celebrate the culture, heritage, and unity of African Americans. Its annual attendance reaches into the hundreds of thousands, and almost one million in some years. Other grand marshals since 1969 have included David Dinkins, Spike Lee, Ossie Davis, Ruby Dee, Queen Mother Moore, Al Sharpton, Jesse Jackson, and Denzel Washington.

Also in 1969, Chisholm was made an honorary member of Delta Sigma Theta sorority. During the induction ceremony, she gave the audience a warning about leaders in Congress and her intended role as a freshman congresswoman:

You have no idea what those people in Washington with their hands on the power have been plotting and planning for us. Let me tell you. Do not be complacent. The Man says he knows we ain't never gonna come together. Oh, everyone is being so kind to me. They have such good advice. They tell me, "Shirley, you're just a freshman and you have to keep quiet as a freshman." I listen sweetly to them and then I say, "Gentlemen, thank you for your advice. I understand what you're saying. But when I get up there on the floor of Congress, I'm sure you'll understand that I am speaking with the pent-up emotions of the community!" One thing the people in Washington and New York are afraid of in Shirley Chisholm is her mouth.[19]

Chisholm didn't mince words when it came to her ambitions in Congress: "I have no intention of just sitting quietly and observing. I intend to speak out immediately in order to focus attention on the nation's problems."[20] She was not afraid to challenge norms and was unapologetic about her stance on issues she believed her constituents elected her to fight for. In a 1969 interview with the *New York Times* she stated, "If the day should ever come when the people can't save me, I'll know I'm finished. That's when I'll go back to being a professional educator."[21] She was uniquely compared to some of her congressional peers in focusing on the needs of those who elected her. She once commented it seemed she was speaking a foreign language when she used words such as "community" and "the people" to some other members.

However, her first few months were not easy, and she felt other members of Congress looked at her like someone who had come from the moon, as she described it. Many tried to ignore her, while others were openly sexist and racist. She later recounted just how challenging it was, detailing a Georgia delegate who refused to sit next to her in the Congressional cafeteria. She dealt with this by telling him, "You order your lunch, and if ANYBODY bothers you, you tell them to see Shirley Chisholm." Recollecting the experience in an interview, Chisholm remarked, "I thought this would embarrass him, but it did not. Here it is the funniest thing to me. It did not embarrass him. He went right over to the table and he sat . . . and he sat . . . and he sat down."[22]

This what not the only time her peers treated her badly because she was Black. An Arkansas congressman who sat in front of her every day would cough every time Chisholm would walk past him to take her seat. She thought perhaps he was ill, as he would violently cough and take out his handkerchief. She was later told by her friend Brock Adams that the man did this as she walked past him to spit in his handkerchief to symbolize spitting in her face. That night Chisholm purchased a man's handkerchief. The next day as she passed him, she waited for him to start coughing. When he did, she pulled the handkerchief she had purchased and spit into it. She told the congressman she had beat him to it, and he never coughed or spit into his handkerchief again. Reporters who watched the whole incident openly laughed in support of Chisholm until the House Speaker had to bang the gavel for order.

Another southern White colleague attempted to berate her by continuing to reference how much she was making as a Black American in Congress. Every day she came to the chamber to be seated, he would ask how she felt making $42,500 a year, the same as him, but pronounced it "forty-two five" in a long southern drawl. Chisholm was curt in telling him to "vanish" whenever he saw her coming so he wouldn't have to worry about how she felt about it, and that she was paving the way for more people like her to get to Congress so they could make "forty-two five." She also faced sexist questions from some on how her husband felt about her being in Congress.

She countered these and other racist and sexist congressmen with satire rather than anger. "I could curse them out,' Chisholm remarked, "but I didn't believe in that. Because I believe in being humorous and I believe in embarrassing them." Finley writes, "Her humor, edged with satire, at times allowed her to gain the upper hand over her detractors, many of whom were White men who were surprised that a Black woman

possessed the kind of intellectual acumen and mental toughness necessary to carry out a successful mainstream political career."[23] Chisholm
was known for her quick responses to outlandish questions or suggestions. She was once asked how she would respond to an invitation to
the then all-male Gridiron Club, which didn't fully admit women until
1975. Chisholm quipped, "Guess who's not coming to dinner."[24]

Chisholm focused on her work, and her congressional office was
always busy with constituents seeking her support. Because the District of Columbia did not have its own congressional delegate until
1971—the first being Walter E. Fauntroy after passage of the District of
Columbia Delegate Act—local residents and leaders came to Chisholm's
office. This was not unusual for African American and female members of Congress. They often served as "surrogate representatives" to
citizens from other districts or states who wanted to communicate
with a member of Congress who truly understood their concerns. As
explained by Representative Clay, these expectations of Black representatives included "personally returning all phone calls . . . attending all
PTA and block unit meetings; securing jobs; cosigning personal loans;
fixing traffic tickets; providing free legal service; acting as a marriage
counselor, child psychologist, and medical adviser."[25]

Chisholm's staff were busy with calls from Black constituents and
women from across the country because they knew she would listen. She was the only Black woman in Congress, and the only other
minority woman was a Japanese American, Patsy Takemoto Mink of
Hawaii. Mink was elected to Congress in 1965 as the first woman of
color and the first Asian American woman. Like Chisholm, she was
also against US involvement in the Vietnam War and supported education reform, women's equality, and improved social welfare programs.

In Congress Chisholm spoke out in support of civil rights,
women's rights, and the poor and against the Vietnam War. As her
husband once noted, "She was a mouthpiece for the underdog, the
poor, underprivileged people, the people who did not have much of a

chance."[26] In opposition to the Vietnam War, in her first floor speech on March 26, 1969, Chisholm railed against President Nixon's spending on the war versus social programs, contrary to the promises he made during his campaign. In her now-famous speech "People and Peace, Not Profits and War," she declared:

> For this reason, I intend to vote "No" on every money bill that comes to the floor of this House that provides any funds for the Department of Defense—any bill whatsoever—until the time comes when our values and priorities have been turned right side up again, until the monstrous waste and the shocking profits in the defense budget have been eliminated and our country starts to use its strength, its tremendous resources, for people and peace, not for profits and war.[27]

She was among many others who spoke against the Vietnam War that day. House Democrats gave speeches for four hours, including Chisholm, who also called for the support of "every mother, wife, and widow in this land who ever asked herself why the generals can play with billions while families crumble under the weight of sickness, hunger and unemployment."[28] Outside the Capitol, a crowd of women, estimated by police to be around 1,300 in number, dressed in black. All were members of Women Strike for Peace who opposed President Nixon's broken campaign promise to end the US's involvement in the war. The leader of the group, Amy G. Swerdlow from Long Island, New York, carried a letter for the president and gave it to a guard at the White House gate. It stated, "You have the power to end the immoral war now. We believe we cannot win in Vietnam. We believe we do not belong there."[29] An article in the New York Times described the scene as the "first sizeable demonstration since President Nixon's inauguration."[30]

Equally striking was Republican Representative Paul A. Findley of Illinois printing the names of the 31,379 US citizens who had died in the war so far in the daily Congressional Record under the headings DEATHS RESULTING FROM HOSTILE ACTION IN VIETNAM THROUGH DECEMBER 31, 1967; DEATHS RESULTING FROM HOSTILE ACTION IN VIETNAM THROUGH DECEMBER 31, 1968; and DEATHS RESULTING FROM HOSTILE ACTION IN VIETNAM DURING JANUARY 1969. Under each state and then MILITARY SERVICE, the list of names covered 121 pages, and Findley submitted it after he tried to convince President Nixon earlier that week to withdraw combat forces.[31] In 1973 Findley coauthored the War Powers Act to limit the power of a US president going to war without Congressional authority. This directly resulted from Nixon's bombing of Cambodia. It required the president to notify Congress within forty-eight hours whenever military forces were introduced to hostilities, and to provide continual updates for as long as forces are deployed. President Nixon vetoed the law, but Congress overrode his veto.

Melvin R. Laird, secretary of defense, spoke to the US Senate on the continuation of the war for at least two more years in 1969. Chisholm described this as "antiballistic missile insanity" and continued, "Two more years. Two more years of hunger for Americans, of death for our best young men, of children here at home suffering the lifelong handicap of not having a good education when they are young. . . . Two more years of too little being done to fight our greatest enemies—poverty, prejudice and neglect—here in our own country. . . . It must stop this year—now."[32]

Chisholm was deeply concerned about the welfare of the American people both at home and abroad, especially those in her local state of New York. While still in Congress, she remained active in local New York politics, although not without controversy. In both 1965 and 1969, she refused to support the Democratic candidates running for mayor in Brooklyn. In both cases, the Republican candidate she supported won, angering her local Democratic Party, though both Republican candidates were more concerned with the needs of local citizens. She went against the advice of some of her allies and was even threatened by some Democratic Party members that she would be removed from her seat as a national party committee member. This threat, however, never came to fruition.

Another instance of controversy swirling around Chisholm's involvement in local politics occurred in July of 1969 when she outraged Democrats by endorsing Liberal Party candidate John V. Lindsay for reelection as New York City mayor over Democrat Mario Angelo Procaccino. Lindsay was formerly a Republican but lost the primary because he was seen as too liberal. Conrad and her mentor Wesley Holder told her not to support Lindsay because of his party, but she felt he was most in touch with voters and would not cave to the political machines. The White Democratic machine and some Black leaders criticized her and warned that bucking party allegiances would damage her career. Chisholm countered that Democratic liberals who had designed policies such as the War on Poverty, including Procaccino, did not understand what the poor were going through.

Procaccino's campaign was dubbed one of the worst in history. He made out-of-touch statements while campaigning, such as telling Black voters his heart was as Black as theirs, and that his running mate would grow on them like a cancer. His "law and order" stance was seen as targeting Black and Hispanic people. In Chisholm's eyes, Lindsay was the clear better choice. As the mayoral race continued, other prominent Democrats joined her in support of Lindsay, including Percy Sutton and Adam Clayton Powell. Lindsay also gained the support of Black and Puerto Rican voters in Harlem, the South Bronx, Bedford-Stuyvesant, and Brownsville. On Election Day, Lindsay was announced as the winner, and the *Amsterdam News* later praised Chisholm for sticking to her convictions, dubbing her the "Black Joan of Arc."[33]

It's unclear whether Chisholm fully embraced the new moniker. However, her popularity was indeed growing, and she was invited to appear on the *The Dick Cavett Show* on August 8, 1969. She spoke

about her self-advocacy in being reassigned to a better-suited committee, the Committee on Veterans' Affairs, saying that she was serious
on the many communications she was receiving from veterans across
the country in having someone who really listened to their concerns.

Cavett asked her about her social life, and Chisholm explained
she was a regular woman and recently went to a cocktail party where
one of her congressional peers was shocked how well she danced after
asking her to "take a few steps." After dancing, he responded she
"didn't take a few steps, but moved." She spoke on being seen as an
intellectual and ghostwriter for many politicians but was really a "cud-
dly" person. During the interview, Cavett asked if she was sometimes
used as a "novelty" at events, given she was the first Black female in
Congress, and she responded she had run into being placed in a "glass
cage for exhibition purposes." However, she understood why she was
used by some and laughed it off graciously. Cavett ended the interview
by saying he wanted to play her when they did a movie of her life.[34]

That same year, NBC News aired a special on Chisholm illustrated
by Bill Ryan that gave rare insight into her personal life, which she
kept so guarded. The broadcast was excellent, revealing in Chisholm's
own words how she felt about being the first Black female member of
Congress, and about the derogatory labels others placed on her. "I'm
not concerned about labels," she said. "I am concerned about what
my behavior and my actions indicate to the masses of Black people
in this country, and also what my behavior indicates to the Whites in
this country. I see myself as a potential reconciler on the American
scene. Time will tell whether or not this will be so."

Shirley Downs, Chisholm's legislative assistant, spoke on Chisholm
being a warm person who was very hardworking and organized. She
laughed about the heavy briefcases Chisholm would take home at night
for homework and how her legislative style unhinged other members
of Congress. She also stated how Chisholm was clear on what in the
political system didn't work, that she wanted people to stand up for

what they believed in and were against, and that she had a rapport with other people because of that. Lewis Fisher, press and appointment secretary, commented how she had a quality not only lacking in public governance but in the country at large: honesty. He also commented on how Chisholm looked at issues on both a pragmatic and human level.

The NBC special covered her district and details of her life, such as her upbringing in Brooklyn and Barbados and her political achievements. It also aired a moving moment of Chisholm giving a speech during the graduation of students from the Bedford-Stuyvesant unwed mothers program for girls who dropped out of school but then reenrolled through this program. She told a story of being a child during the Great Depression and having to wear a dress her parents purchased from their monthly public assistance. She recalled being a proud girl who didn't want to return to school because she was teased by the other students who laughed at how the dress awkwardly hung on her slender frame. She told the story to let the audience of girls know that she did not hold herself above them, that she too knew hardship, and that in spite of their past or what they were feeling, they should look to the future.

From their home in Brooklyn, Conrad described Chisholm as "100 pounds of nuclear energy," and she described him as "200 pounds of patience," speaking on how he was committed to her success. He acknowledged his sacrifices but how it was worth it for what Chisholm was doing for all people in America. She was personable in discussing her love of dancing, reading in the very large library in their house, playing the piano, and writing poetry. She read a poem she had written entitled "Land of Our Birth"

> Land of our birth . . .
> Tell us in words, simple and plain
> The reason for all of our torturing pain.
> Are we not part of this nation strong
> For what have we done that is so wrong?

Land of our birth . . .
Tell us by deeds, sincere and true,
The reason we are not really part of the crew.
Did we not sacrifice and hoped not in vain
To be assured that there would be equal gain?

Land of our birth . . .
Tell us in song—hearty and loud
Amidst the singing, jostling crowd—
That we are all citizens of your realm
And that you are captain at the helm.

Land of our birth . . .
The time has come for action fast
We can no longer live in the past
This mighty land . . . powerful and free
Must demonstrate the real democracy.

The NBC News feature showed how Chisholm made recording sessions in Congress as a weekly broadcast to her constituents in Brooklyn, speaking on topics close to her such as the importance of children getting a good education. She spoke on how she felt Congress moved too slowly, and how she wanted to change the seniority system placing the fate of the country into the hands of select men who were not in their position because of intellect or ability. She was blunt in stating that some of these men were senile, and 90 percent were from the South and thus were "old men that make up the southern oligarchy." Far from receiving backlash for her statements, she earned from her constituents a greater appreciation of the challenges she had in Congress making change.

Her appearances on television were indicative of her support in her district. Chisholm expectedly won reelection in 1970 against the

Republican and Conservative candidates with 82 percent of the vote, and she was supported by both the Democratic and Liberal Parties (the latter thanks in large part to her earlier support of Lindsay for mayor). While campaigning, Chisholm stated she would be willing to lose to do the right thing: "If my tenure in the Congress has to be short because I can't behave, I don't mind. If I could bring about change, I don't mind being politically expendable."[35]

She also understood her constituents, recognizing that policies that tackled unemployment, substandard housing, and issues negatively affecting cities such as Brooklyn would be her main focus in Congress. "My people are interested in here-and-now answers to emergency questions that constantly arise from day to day. They're not concerned about foreign policy—the Vietnam War—except in so far as the war takes away from financial assistance."[36]

In the early 1970s opposition to the Vietnam War was at its height. It wasn't just students protesting but also some veterans and politicians. For example, Vietnam Veterans Against the War was founded in 1967. During their protest march ending at the steps of the Capitol in April 1971, notable speakers included Chisholm, Bella Abzug, Senator Edmund Muskie of Maine, and Congressman Ogden Reid of New York. Chisholm spoke against the war as she had in Congress on the needless spending and loss of American lives for an unwinnable war. The shooting of antiwar demonstrators at Kent State University and Jackson State College (now Jackson State University) led to outrage and a nationwide student strike that closed secondary schools, colleges, and universities across the country.

And the Vietnam War was just the beginning of Chisholm's focus during her tenure in Congress.

6

SHIRLEY CHISHOLM'S LEGISLATIVE FOCUS

_____

"You don't make progress by standing on the sidelines, whimpering and complaining. You make progress by implementing ideas."

CHISHOLM WAS VERY DEDICATED to various issues while in Congress, to the point of being an activist for some. Among these were her being a founding member of the Congressional Black Caucus, combatting apartheid, and supporting passage of the Equal Rights Amendment. Her support of these issues exemplified her fight for equality not only in the United States but globally. For example, she was just as concerned about the condition of Black people in South Africa and refugees from Haiti as she was about her constituents in Brooklyn. What can also be seen from analyzing how she navigated these issues was her growth in being politically savvy while still approaching issues as an educator for change.

Congressional Black Caucus (CBC)

In 1969 Charles C. Diggs Jr., who had been in the House of Representatives since 1955, felt isolated from the few other Black members in Congress. He and Adam Clayton Powell Jr. rarely communicated because of a difference in views and political styles. Diggs gained the support of Chisholm, Louis Stokes, and William Clay when they were elected to form the Democratic Select Committee. They formed to establish a coalition of Black House members growing in numbers, and to address political issues important to Black voters such as redistricting and legislation tied to the civil rights movement.

The founding members were frustrated at opposition to policies supporting Black people such as civil rights legislation and social programs from predominantly White members, such as Speaker of the House John W. McCormack, who was seventy-eight years old and struggling to hold on to power while House members tried to get him to resign due to his lack of leadership. As Arthur Levy and Susan Stoudinger explain, "The Black Representatives were compelled to look to their own ranks for leadership and direction. These were provided by three Black freshmen—Chisholm, Clay, and Stokes— who, by virtue of their background and experience, were relatively more active and more closely attuned to the moods of the Black community. Functioning as an 'active minority,' these newly elected Blacks fostered common identity, organized common legislative and extra-legislative tactics, and stimulated cohesive voting behavior among the Black Representatives."[1] By a motion by Charles B. Rangel of New York on February 2, 1971, including a name change, the Congressional Black Caucus was formed. It was initially made up of thirteen members.

Founding Members of the Congressional Black Caucus (CBC)		
Name	Political Party	State Represented
Rep. Charles C. Diggs Jr.	Democrat	Michigan
Rep. Shirley Chisholm	Democrat	New York
Rep. William Lacy Clay Sr.	Democrat	Missouri
Rep. George W. Collins	Democrat	Illinois
Rep. John Conyers Jr.	Democrat	Michigan
Rep. Ronald V. Dellums	Democrat	California
Rep. Augustus F. Hawkins	Democrat	California
Rep. Ralph H. Metcalfe	Democrat	Illinois
Rep. Parren J. Mitchell	Democrat	Maryland
Rep. Robert N. C. Nix Sr.	Democrat	Pennsylvania
Rep. Charles B. Rangel	Democrat	New York
Rep. Louis Stokes	Democrat	Ohio
Delegate Walter E. Fauntroy	Democrat	District of Columbia

Shirley Chisholm and members of the Congressional Black Caucus.
Photo by Warren K. Leffler, courtesy of U.S. News & World Report Magazine Photograph Collection, Library of Congress Prints and Photographs Division

In their first action as a newly formed caucus, Louis Stokes (D-OH) gave a speech on October 2, 1972, detailing the mission of the CBC and the urgent reasons for its creation:

> In 1969, Shirley Chisholm, Bill Clay and I came to Washington—bringing the number of Black representatives to nine. 1877 had been the previous high-water mark for Black representation in the House—with eight Congressmen. It had taken us 92 years to come back. The nine of us came together—under the leadership of Congressman Charles Diggs—to form the Congressional Black Caucus. It had been apparent from the start that we would have to serve as congressmen-at-large for minority, poor and disadvantaged Americans—for citizens whose voices had never been heard in Washington before.[2]

The same month the CBC was founded, *Ebony* magazine's February 1971 issue featured all Black members of Congress on its cover, accompanied by an article titled "Black Lawmakers in Congress," with pictures on each of these thirteen members. It discussed key issues each stood for, such as Chisholm's support of unemployment insurance for domestic workers and her opposition to the congressional seniority system. The members did not see themselves as civil rights leaders, but as legislators with common goals. They committed to a nonpartisan CBC as a formal network for Black legislatures to coordinate on issues where their success was bolstered by collective action rather than individual efforts. As member William L. Clay (D-MO) explained, "Black people have no permanent friends, no permanent enemies . . . just permanent interests."[3] Chisholm also referred to the CBC as "unbought and unbossed."

As soon as the CBC was formed, they were labeled by President Nixon as political enemies and later covertly placed on his aptly named "Nixon's Enemies List," which was discovered during the Watergate investigation. It contained the names of public and private figures the Nixon administration felt would challenge his domestic or foreign policies. Those listed were then targeted by the administration for surveillance with the goal of publicly humiliating them with any personal negative information uncovered to discredit anything critical they said about the administration.

Since the CBC opposed most of Nixon's policies, particularly his lack of support of programs improving Black lives, Nixon refused to meet with them after they requested a conference in 1970. As a result, the caucus publicly boycotted his January 22, 1971, State of the Union address that following January, refusing to be "part of his audience." The CBC saw his refusal to meet as representative of the country's same refusal to address issues important to Black Americans. Because the CBC gained press coverage from their boycott with interviews and nationwide media attention on the major news networks, Nixon met with them that March.

Congressional Black Caucus meets with President Richard Nixon. *Courtesy of White House Photo Office Collection (Nixon Administration), National Archives*

The group presented him a thirty-two-page document including sixty-one "recommendations to eradicate racism, provide quality housing for African-American families, and promote the full engagement of African-Americans in government."[4] They outlined their agenda for job creation programs, increased spending to combat poverty, a boycott of products from South Africa to protest apartheid, and an end to the US involvement in Vietnam. Caucus member Charles C. Diggs (D-MI) represented the group during the meeting and explained to President Nixon, "Our concerns and obligations as members of Congress do not stop at the boundaries of our districts, our concerns are national and international in scope. We are petitioned daily by citizens living hundreds of miles from our districts who look on us as Congressmen-at-large for Black people and poor people in the United States."[5]

The Nixon White House responded to the recommendations with a 115-page report but never issued any policies supporting their requests. Instead, they highlighted actions they were already doing and tried to use those as examples of addressing the CBC's concerns. On June 3, 1971, Diggs presented the CBC's *A Report to the Nation* to the House, formally outlining its disappointment with the president's response. This extensive report was detailed in articulating what policy changes were required and the shortcomings of President Nixon's administration. They specifically called out failings of the administration to address economic security and development, community and urban development, justice and civil rights, and foreign policy. The Nixon administration ignored their report and recommendations in terms of policy changes but increased its focus on considering the CBC as enemies.

The CBC wanted to further express their views on Nixon's policies after his next State of the Union address. They filed complaints with major television networks on February 1, 1972, for airtime to rebut Nixon's 1972 State of the Union address. The networks opposed, so the CBC filed a reply to the networks' oppositions on April 20, 1972, with the Federal Communications Commission demanding that ABC, CBS, and NBC allow the caucus to respond. Their primary complaint was that "although the President chose to discuss a number of important and controversial issues, he remained notably silent on the serious national problem of institutional racism against Black and other minority Americans," and that the networks denied their request "due to network policies which exclude all documentaries and other programming which discusses controversial issues and which is not produced and controlled by the network."[6] The commission denied the CBC complaint in February 1973.

The lone dissent came from Commissioner Nicholas Johnson, who was known to dissent on matters of public interest, separation of powers in the government, and the need for the television networks to uphold First Amendment rights in broadcasting. In his extensive condemnation of the FCC for allowing politics to interfere with public information, he closed by stating, "The networks cannot claim that the Black Caucus is demanding time for a cacophony of differing voices which the networks, given temporal limitations, could not accommodate. The Black Caucus has made it simple for the networks. It has consolidated the myriad positions of the nation's Black citizens into a neat package. The appropriateness of the face-off is manifest and the networks, whatever discretionary latitude is accorded them in establishing standards, cannot claim that it can offer better format or spokesmen for the ideological exchange."[7]

Despite this loss, the CBC did not end their criticism of President Nixon. In February 1973 they issued a statement in the House they called the "True State of the Union" about the president's continuing failure to address the caucus's concerns. President Nixon never fully addressed any of them, and the caucus would maintain their agenda for the next administration.

Apartheid

Chisholm began aggressively speaking against apartheid and US investment in South Africa in 1970. The country's government and social system of racial segregation was based on White supremacy (a system called *baasskap*) that existed in South Africa from 1948 through the 1990s. Adopted by the South African National Party during the 1948 general election, the Population Registration Act of 1950 banned mixed marriages, created social and economic classes based on race— Black (Bantu), White, Colored (mixed race), and Asian (Indian and Pakistani)—and defined where these classes could live, work, operate businesses, own property, and use public facilities. Social, political, and economic racial discrimination was both institutionalized and legally enforced. Laws required non-White citizens to carry passes showing approval to be in a White area; Black citizens were not allowed to vote or form labor unions; and government policies ensured they were given inferior educations. Demonstrations against apartheid were met with swift and brutal retaliation by the all-White government.

Speaking to corporate executives at a press conference in May 1970, Chisholm commented that American companies like General Motors had failed to respond "to the needs of Black Americans" for too long; GM's support of racist policies in South Africa was a reflection of its dismissive attitude toward equal rights in America.[8] Corporate leaders were complacent in their policies and were bolstered in their complacency by US government's support of South Africa. The CBC started combating apartheid soon after they were formed. This is one of the reasons they would become known as the "Conscience of the Congress." They wrote a statement to President Nixon in 1971: "Even though we think first of those we were directly elected to serve, we cannot, in good conscience, think only of them—for what affects one Black community, one poor community, one urban community, affects all."[9] Caucus member Ronald V. Dellums (D-CA) introduced a bill proposing sanctions against South Africa in February 1971. These sanctions included a full trade embargo, stopping US loans to its government, and a complete divestment of all US companies doing business there. Though it had no chance of passing, he stated,

"Nonetheless, we had raised the issue before the elected representatives of the American people, and our resolution provided an organizing device for those on the outside to use to begin to build pressure on Congress for legislative action."[10]

The United States had a dark history of supporting apartheid. President Nixon and his secretary of state, Henry Alfred Kissinger, adopted a "tar baby" strategy focused on publicly condemning apartheid but privately intensifying relations with South Africa's government. The term is based on an 1881 story by Joel Chandler Harris called "The Wonderful Tar Baby Story" in which the character Bre'r Fox laid a trap for his enemy, Bre'r Rabbit, using a doll made of tar and turpentine. Each time the rabbit came in contact with the doll, he became more stuck. Kissinger reasoned that if Blacks in such African countries as South Africa gained independence, the Soviet Union would swoop in and take control. Thus, he reasoned it was best the White-dominant governments remain in power as allies to the United States.

In March 1976 President Ford was being pressured by conservative congressmen and American business investors in South Africa to end a twelve-year ban on loans to South Africa through the Export-Import Bank. Chisholm obtained signatures from forty members of the House in a letter urging Ford not to lift the ban. In the Senate, Republican Senator Jacob K. Javits of New York obtained seven signatures in sending a companion letter to Ford. Ford, like Nixon, felt South Africa could be an ally against the Soviet Union and favored working with its National Party. In contrast, President Carter favored voting rights for all South Africans. He worked with the United Nations to pass UN Security Council Resolution 418, which imposed a mandatory arms embargo against South Africa. However, his overall policies were deemed ineffective in the midst of the Cold War.

The CBC significantly invested time and resources to combat apartheid. Per Jennifer Manning and Colleen Shogan:

Members of the CBC introduced more than 15 bills seeking to end apartheid and racial discrimination practices in South Africa. As a result of the CBC's Black Leadership Conference in September 1976, the CBC helped establish TransAfrica officially on July 1, 1977, a foreign policy advocacy group designed to raise awareness about African and Caribbean issues. Formerly called the TransAfrica Forum, it was led by civil rights attorney Randall Robinson. Besides endorsing legislative sanctions, TransAfrica and the CBC also lobbied corporations and universities to divest from South Africa. Through hearings, rallies, and protests in their home districts and in Washington, D.C., CBC members increased attention on apartheid in South Africa.[11]

When Ronald Reagan took office, he opposed US sanctions and would not condemn apartheid. His administration tried to ignore the oppression and suffering of Black people in South Africa because of the country's anticommunist stance, strategic geographic location, and supply of natural resources the United States could use.

In 1981 a seven-member Congressional delegation visited Africa on what they called a twenty-one-day "fact finding mission" on the United States' political, economic, and development policies' impact on African countries. The delegation was led by Clement J. Zablocki, chairman of the US House Committee on Foreign Affairs. The other members were Chisholm, Richard Ottinger, Berkley Bedell, Gus Savage, David Bowen, and George William Crockett Jr. The trip lasted from August 4 through August 22, 1981, and during the trip they visited Nigeria, Kenya, Somalia, Angola, Zimbabwe, and South Africa. In their report to Congress, they were detailed in their observations from their four-day visit to South Africa on the "dehumanizing system of apartheid and its police state tactics of maintaining and enforcing this racially motivated system of domination [which] have concerned a great many American citizens."[12] These observations were based on their seeing the conditions, and meeting with Black and White political leaders, church officials, labor union members, student activists, banned individuals, American businessmen, journalists and academics (including Bishop Desmond Tutu, then secretary general of the South African Council of Churches and later a Nobel Peace Prize laureate).

While they were visiting, they saw firsthand the brutal treatment of Black people in the country. On August 11, they tried to visit a camp of Black squatters that formed after a raid on the Nyanga and Langa townships that destroyed all homes and shelters and blockaded all food and medical supplies. The raid left more than a thousand Black people homeless, including women and children. The squatter camp in Cape Town was where the women could be near their husbands while they looked for work. The congressional delegation was barred from the site as the camp was burned down by police. Chisholm spoke at a press conference after the event and broke into tears when saying how deeply concerned she was by "what had been done to Black mothers and children."[13]

The delegation was shocked to learn the South African government was in the process of establishing independent homelands for its Black people, which were really just ten settlements that would effectively transform South Africa into an all-White country. The US policy of "constructive engagement" under President Reagan was supporting this, along with the violent oppression of South African Black people. They also concluded this would play right into the hands of the Soviet Union, who could champion Black independence while globally touting the US as a supporter of continued White domination.

The White-controlled government was not receptive to the delegation. The congressional visitors were not allowed to see Nelson Mandela, who had been in jail since 1962, and their ninety-minute meeting with Foreign Minister Roelof Frederik Botha turned contentious as he refused to answer questions and later accused the delegation of arrogance and obvious intolerance. He went so far as to later speak of them on a South African radio broadcast in which he referred to the delegation as Democrats who were not representing the position of then US president Reagan.

Chisholm's activism against apartheid continued after she left Congress in January 1983. The Anti-Apartheid Group started a fund in 1983 that raised $30,000 with her support. In December 1984 she was part of a protest in Washington, DC, outside the South African embassy. Sixteen members of Congress were arrested for demonstrating in a restricted area. Chisholm and members of the Jewish Community Relations Council of Greater Washington and the National Black Women's Political Caucus were among the one hundred protestors. Similar protests were taking place in other cities, including Pittsburgh and Seattle.

In 1985 CBC member Representative William H. Gray introduced a bill to prohibit loans and new investments in South Africa, as well as to levy sanctions on US imports and exports with the country. In 1986 CBC member Representative George William Crockett Jr. introduced a resolution calling for South Africa to free Nelson Mandela and other political prisoners and recognize the African National Congress. Neither of these measures passed.

Finally, in 1986 the Comprehensive Anti-Apartheid Act passed in Congress, imposing preconditioned sanctions and calling for the release of Mandela and other political prisoners. President Reagan vetoed the bill, but his veto was overridden by Congress. In a surprising turn of events, Reagan's former vice president, George H. W. Bush, fully enforced the sanctions of the new law when he was elected president, leading to South Africa caving to economic pressure. Other countries in Europe and Japan joined the US in imposing sanctions. South Africa repealed its apartheid laws, and Nelson Mandela was released from prison on February 11, 1990, after serving twenty-seven years. He became the president of South Africa in 1994. All these results were direct impacts of the years of activism by Chisholm and the CBC and related efforts by other groups and individuals.

Women's Rights, Abortion, and the Equal Rights Amendment (ERA)

The fight to add an amendment to the US Constitution guaranteeing women equal rights began in Congress in 1923 by the National Woman's Party and was written by Alice Paul and Crystal Eastman. Reenergized by the feminist movement of the late 1960s, it was again debated in Congress, with Chisholm being one of the leading voices. Speaking on May 21, 1969, she discussed the stereotypes women face in seeking employment that affect what jobs they are hired for and decrease their ability for fair promotions and pay equal to their male counterparts in her now-famous address on the ERA to the House:

> The unspoken assumption is that women are different. They do not have executive ability, orderly minds, stability, leadership skills, and they are too emotional. It has been observed before, that society for a long time, discriminated against another minority, the Blacks, on the same basis—that they were different and inferior. The happy little homemaker and the contented "old darkey" on the plantation were both produced by prejudice.
>
> As a Black person, I am no stranger to race prejudice. But the truth is that in the political world, I have been far oftener discriminated against because I am a woman than because I am Black. Prejudice against Blacks is becoming unacceptable, although it will take years to eliminate it. But it is doomed because, slowly, White America is beginning to admit that it exists.
>
> Prejudice against women is still acceptable. There is very little understanding yet of the immorality involved in double pay scales and the classification of most of the better jobs as "for men only." More than half of the population

of the United States is female. But women occupy only 2 percent of the managerial positions. They have not even reached the level of tokenism, yet no women sit on the AFL-CIO council or Supreme Court. There have been only two women who have held Cabinet rank, and at present there are none. Only two women now hold ambassadorial rank in the diplomatic corps. In Congress, we are down to one Senator and 10 Representatives. Considering that there are about 3½ million more women in the United States than men, this situation is outrageous.[14]

In 1969 Chisholm was named honorary copresident of the National Association for the Repeal of Abortion Laws (NARAL), the year it was founded at the "First National Conference on Abortion Laws: Modification or Repeal?" in Chicago, Illinois. Its precursor was the Association to Repeal Abortion Laws (ARAL), which was an expansion of the so-called Army of Three: abortion rights activists Pat Maginnis and Rowena Gurner, and financial investor Lana Phelan. Chisholm declined to be other than honorary because her schedule was already so busy, but she wanted to show her support. She was appointed along with Dr. Lester Breslow (president of the American Public Health Association) as copresident, and Senator Maurine Neuberger of Oregon as Vice President. New York City councilwoman Carol Greitzer was selected as the active president and Lawrence Lader as chairman.

Chisholm gave a press conference in September 1969 discussing NARAL's mission to ensure women had access to quality medical care and abortion consultation. She introduced an abortion bill in December 1969. Arguing "compulsory pregnancy costs money," she gave her congressional colleagues details on illegitimate children receiving benefits from Aid to Families with Dependent Children (AFDC). She knew this would get the attention of male peers who criticized AFDC as too costly. Congress, however, failed to take action on abortion rights after the bill's introduction.

Undeterred, when the Committee on Education and Labor held a special subcommittee session on discrimination against women in July of that following year, Chisholm gave another stirring statement discussing the disparities women faced, using her own background as a testament to the discrimination:

> In my own experience, I have suffered from two handicaps— being born Black and being born female. . . . During my entire political life, my sex has been a far greater handicap than my skin pigmentation. From my earliest experience in ward political activity my chief obstacle was that I had to break through the role men assign women. . . .
>
> Every sector of the American population has a stake in eliminating anti-feminist discrimination. To quote a brilliant Black woman lawyer, Dr. Pauli Murray, "Discrimination because of one's sex is just as degrading, dehumanizing, immoral, unjust, indefensible, infuriating and capable of producing societal turmoil as discrimination because of one's race." In both cases, please note this, exclusion implies inferiority. The stereotypes are closely parallel. The happy little homemaker, the dumb blonde, the bubble-brained secretary, are the same kind of distorted pictures, drawn by prejudice, as those of the contented old darky and Black mammy and little pickaninnies down on the old plantation.[15]

Chisholm built nationwide coalitions in addition to alliances in Congress to get legislation such as the ERA passed. The following is part of her speech, considered to be among the top one hundred speeches of all time by many in our field, before the House August 10, 1970, after a bill was reintroduced to the House for discussion:

I would like to make one point. Social and psychological effects will be initially more important than legal or economic results. As Leo Kanowitz has pointed out: Rules of law that treat of the sexes per se inevitably produce far-reaching effects upon social, psychological and economic aspects of male-female relations beyond the limited confines of legislative chambers and courtrooms. As long as organized legal systems, at once the most respected and most feared of social institutions, continue to differentiate sharply, in treatment or in words, between men and women on the basis of irrelevant and artificially created distinctions, the likelihood of men and women coming to regard one another primarily as fellow human beings and only secondarily as representatives of another sex will continue to be remote. When men and women are prevented from recognizing one another's essential humanity by sexual prejudices, nourished by legal as well as social institutions, society as a whole remains less than it could otherwise become.[16]

White and Black women saw equality differently, however, as was exemplified in 1970 with Lois Mark Stalvey's *The Education of a WASP*. The book chronicles the discovery of racism by a White woman during the 1960s and discusses the accounts of a self-proclaimed White Anglo-Saxon Protestant who was forced to question her assumptions of race relations during the tumultuous time. The book's introduction was written by Chisholm, who commented on the author's rude awakening to how "the extent and depth of racism is rendering America vulnerable to the attacks of opponents here at home as well as those abroad" such that the country stands "no longer at the crossroads but instead on the brink of the precipice."[17]

Chisholm called the book a must-read for White America. In her words, "Unlike many Whites, Lois Stalvey does not stick her head in the sand like the proverbial ostrich but rather faces and penetrates through often painful and embarrassing incidents."[18] She ended by commending how Stalvey's insight and pain recognized racism: "It is this recognition within each of us that is necessary as the first step toward progress through understanding in the United States." Stalvey updated and reissued the book in 1989. She opened the new book in stating, "When this book was first published, I hoped that it would soon become only a history of what racism used to be. I feel profound regret that it has not."[19]

The women's rights movement was at its peak when the ERA was being fought for. On August 26, 1970, more than twenty thousand women marched in New York City demanding equality. This was organized by the National Organization for Women (NOW). Speakers at the event included Betty Friedan, Gloria Marie Steinem, Bella Abzug, and Eleanor Holmes Norton. There were also labor strikes by such groups as the Service Employees International Union, Local 1199B Charleston Hospital Workers, and United Farm Workers Union. Chisholm was a member of many organizations supporting women's equal rights, including NOW, the Women's Action Alliance, the National Council of Negro Women, the Coalition of 100 Black Women, and the National Black Feminist Organization. She gave televised and magazine interviews, spoke at rallies, and was the featured speaker at conferences held by the many organizations she belonged to. She was not the only national figure in this fight, as among her supporters were civil rights leaders such as Coretta Scott King and Rosa Parks.

In 1971 Congress was still debating the ERA, and many individuals and groups from around the country wanted to testify but were not given the opportunity to do so. In an effort to help those who wanted to testify before Congress, Chisholm wrote a letter to Congressman William Donlon "Don" Edwards, chairman of the subcommittee responsible for conducting hearings, on April 14, 1971, voicing her concerns and her own intention to testify:

Shirley Chisholm with Rosa Parks. *Courtesy of
Library of Congress Prints and Photographs Division*

Dear Don:

As you know, I am deeply concerned about the hearings
currently being held by your Subcommittee on the Equal
Rights Amendment Force on the Status of Women Report.

In the past we haven't even been able to have a hearing
on these issues and now group after group is coming in to
me and other women of Congress, and I am sure to you, to
express their concern over the fact that they have not been
able to testify and were only able to file testimony. I, myself,
wished to testify on the opening day of the hearings but so
many witnesses were scheduled and it was taking so long to get
through the witness list that I decided to just file my statement.

I know that it is tedious and often boring to sit and
listen to many, many statements on the same issue but it

is equally important to realize the sensitivity of this issue. Many of these people who are asking to testify, especially the younger women, have never had an opportunity to express their views before. And when the Committee indicates that they don't have time to hear them, the results are sometimes explosive . . . as for example the case of the group of women from George Washington.

The disruption on March 31 never would have occurred if those women had had the opportunity to testify. I know that you have subsequently made arrangements so the GW group can be heard. I hope you will also provide that opportunity to other groups, especially groups representing our young women.

For example, I know that the Intercollegiate Associate of Women Students was very concerned that they did not have an opportunity to testify in person.

Your record in the field of Civil Rights has been exemplary. I hope you can use your position on the Judiciary Committee to help to create more understanding of and sympathy for the civil rights of women.

Cordially,

Shirley Chisholm

Congresswoman[20]

The women from George Washington University Chisholm referred to in her letter were members of the university's Women's Liberation and testified before the House in support of passing the ERA. The ERA had been amended to add a requirement for the military draft to extend to women as a means of the bill being defeated. The Liberation members were asked by a member of the House, "How many women do you know who want to be drafted?" They responded, "Just as many as the number of men who want to be drafted."[21] Not only was the draft question sexist because Congress forbade women from being drafted, but it was also insulting to women's intelligence, given another bill was in the Senate making its way through Congress to end the draft. Neither the actions of this hearing or those of Chisholm swayed the majority White male members of Congress to support the ERA.

In July 1971 Chisholm was cofounder of the National Women's Political Caucus (NWPC) to be the political arm of the women's rights movement. She founded NWPC with other feminists, including Gloria Steinem, Bella Abzug, Betty Friedan, Dorothy Height, Jill Ruckelshaus, Ann Lewis, Elly Peterson, LaDonna Harris, Liz Carpenter, Fannie Lou Hamer, and Eleanor Holmes Norton.

Chisholm tried to merge her coalitions demanding women's rights with her fight for Black equality. She knew Black women were stuck between the Women's Movement led by White women and Black movements led by Black men, thus proverbially falling between the cracks. She encouraged Black women to join the NWPC to ensure their concerns were being represented. However, it seemed the majority White female membership was more concerned with women's rights to the point of supporting unqualified women candidates over the qualified Black men candidates. Chisholm told members during its first meeting, "Black women want to be part of the women's movement, but we are also part of another movement—the liberation of our own people."[22] Concerned with an agenda always set by White members, the Black members drafted an antiracial resolution against any discrimination, which was adopted by the NWPC. Member Vivian Mason warned, "[Black women] would not like to leave you but are prepared to leave you if you cannot say to us 'We will have no part of racism in any of its forms.'"[23]

Chisholm gave an interview in March 1974 in which she really tried to explain the differences between what Black versus White women wanted in terms of equality. She was asked, "Do you feel that there has been much of an attempt on the part of minority women to understand the position of White women?" to which she responded:

> The minority women say, "Look! I don't mind being in the kitchen. I don't mind having all the appliances. I don't mind sitting down and staying at home because I've never known what it is to sit down and stay at home because I've had to be out there for so long." So you know, when some of my White sisters complain about the fact, "Oh! My goodness, I can't be myself. I can't express myself. I don't want to find myself living in the house with all these appliances. I have to go out, and find myself," many minority women wish that they could find themselves in that position.

The ERA passed in the House in October of 1971 and in the Senate that following March in 1972. By 1973 it had been ratified in thirty of the needed thirty-eight states, but by then its national support had been derailed by the STOP ERA campaign led by Phyllis Stewart Schlafly, a conservative and vocal antifeminist. (STOP stood for "Stop Taking Our Privileges.")

Even though she had a law degree, Schlafly advocated that women should relish being in the traditional roles of mother and wife. Further, her rhetoric presented women as inferior to men. In her speeches she would often open by saying, "I'd like to thank my husband for letting me be here tonight."[24] The STOP campaign's primary argument against the ERA was it would take away rights women already had, such as the right to alimony and child support, and the feminist movement would destroy traditional families. While the ERA needed ratification by a three-fourths majority vote from the states by 1982, it gained thirty-five and failed to obtain the final three needed to be made law.

Chisholm continued her fight for women's rights by also tackling reproduction laws. She gave a speech at one of New York's first pro-choice rallies in Union Square on May 6, 1972, along with Bella Abzug, Mary Lindsay (wife of New York mayor John Lindsay), and others. This demonstration was in opposition to the repeal of New York State's abortion law. In her book *Unbought and Unbossed*, she dedicated an entire chapter to the issue, which she titled "Facing the Abortion Question." She felt this was a woman's right and legislation was needed to stop the deaths of women who were getting unsafe, illegal abortions, particularly women of color.

She encountered strong opposition to her stance on abortion, particularly from men, as even some civil rights leaders and Black elected officials opposed abortion as a form of racial genocide. Some members of Congress warned supporting it would be politically unwise for future votes from conservative and religious men and even some women. She countered arguments from men by pointing out that rich women could get an illegal abortion safely while poor women had to go to bad doctors she labeled "quacks": "Women are dying every day, did you know that? They're being butchered and maimed. No matter what men think, abortion is a fact of life. Women have always had them; they always have and they always will. Are they going to have good ones or bad ones? Will the good ones be reserved for the rich, while the poor women go to quacks?"[25]

Abortion was repeatedly attacked in Congress after the Supreme Court ruling in *Roe v. Wade*. Reversing the court's decision was a driving preoccupation of conservative lawmakers and became a litmus test for nominee to the high court and for the presidents who appointed them. Debates in Congress would continue to be heated. In a 1980 debate, Chisholm became so frustrated on the House floor that she told her peers if abortion was to be banned and men failed to pay child support, then mandatory vasectomies sounded fair. While some were stunned by her comments, it showed both her support of the issue and fearlessness in speaking her mind.

Racism, Black Power, and Representation

Chisholm saw anti-Black racism enacted by Black people as just as destructive as anti-Black racism enacted by White people. On October 25, 1969, her views were captured in an article entitled "Rep. Chisholm Blasts Black 'Elitists'" in the *Manhattan Tribune*. Based on her speeches at Howard University and Federal City College, the article quoted her explaining, "Many of our would-be leaders are now running about trying to start and maintain an elitists revolution in the name of social revolution. Let me tell you here and now that no elitist revolution has ever done a thing for the people—the masses who are truly at the bottom of the economic and political power structure."[26] She didn't name any persons or groups, but the article explained she was targeting Black leaders who called other Black people "Aunt Jemima" or "Uncle Tom." The *Manhattan Tribune* took its own informal poll of Black leaders to ask if they concurred with Chisholm's view on elitism and found they agreed.

Chisholm also spoke on racism in direct response to the Kerner Commission's report on civil unrest, issued in response to 150 civil disorders across the country between 1965 and 1968. President Johnson's commission was led by Illinois governor Otto Kerner Jr. and John Lindsay. The commission had two Black members, Senator Edward Brooke and Roy Wilkins of the NAACP. The final report confirmed what many civil rights leaders had been stating for decades—"Our nation is moving toward two societies, one Black, one White—separate and unequal"[27]—and called for expanded aid to Black communities to prevent further racial violence and polarization. Unless drastic and costly remedies were undertaken at once, the report warned of a destruction of basic democratic values. The report's introduction summed up the overall findings:

The summer of 1967 again brought racial disorders to American cities, and with them shock, fear and bewilderment to the nation. The worst came during a two-week period in July, first in Newark and then in Detroit. Each set off a chain reaction in neighboring communities. On July 28, 1967, the President of the United States established this Commission and directed us to answer three basic questions: What happened? Why did it happen? What can be done to prevent it from happening again? To respond to these questions, we have undertaken a broad range of studies and investigations. We have visited the riot cities; we have heard many witnesses; we have sought the counsel of experts across the country. This is our basic conclusion: Our nation is moving toward two societies, one Black, one White—separate and unequal. Reaction to last summer's disorders has quickened the movement and deepened the division. Discrimination and segregation have long permeated much of American life; they now threaten the future of every American. This deepening racial division is not inevitable. The movement apart can be reversed. Choice is still possible. Our principal task is to define that choice and to press for a national resolution. To pursue our present course will involve the continuing polarization of the American community and, ultimately, the destruction of basic democratic values. The alternative is not blind repression or capitulation to lawlessness.[28]

In response, Chisholm stated the report pointed out an issue that was already well known by Black people but not addressed, "that prejudice and hatred built the nation's slums, maintains them and profits by them—White America could not believe it."[29] She also called racism the "bugaboo of America"—the cause of racial riots—and this made the US vulnerable to attacks from both inside and outside US borders.

She further saw racism as driving fear and mistrust in the country, and this was driving students to demonstrate. Chisholm had spoken on forty college campuses in the preceding eleven months and recognized the commitment of students to social justice movements. Students felt the government was broken, it was past time for Black people and women to have equality, and racism was the root of all discontent. She was clear that commissions like the Kerner Commission, committees, studies, graphs, and analyses were not the answer to solving the nation's problems resulting from political hypocrisy. Racism in the 1960s and 1970s was ingrained in society. Southern states had implemented Jim Crow laws, and even in the North there were laws supporting discrimination in housing, employment, and segregated schools. As Chisholm acknowledged on August 10, 1970, in her ERA speech, "Laws will not eliminate prejudice from the hearts of human beings. But that is no reason to allow prejudice to continue to be enshrined in our laws—to perpetuate through inaction."[30]

It was this climate of mistrust and blatant racism that drove her to consider running for president of the United States. She had experienced racism and sexism and was attuned to the genuine needs of all Americans. However, she knew she needed to make some changes in her approach as a legislator. In Congress she began taking a more compromising approach, which would later turn out to be private posturing in preparation for a bid for the presidency. She voted for some defense spending bills not related to the Vietnam War and compromised on some war-related legislation in exchange for support of legislation she proposed. She angered some of her colleagues by not supporting fellow CBC member John Conyers (D-MI) as House majority leader, instead choosing to support southern congressman Thomas Hale Boggs Sr. of Louisiana, and conservative Joseph D. Waggonner Jr. of Louisiana for the House Committee on Rules. This choice paid off, as Boggs appointed her to the Committee on Education and Labor in 1971. Boggs had earlier given a statement on his perceptions of Chisholm:

I've been very much impressed with Ms. Chisholm. I find her
to be a, a woman of strong convictions, I find her to be very
articulate, I think she represents her district, and she does
it ably and aggressively. And as a matter of fact, she has the
distinction of being the only person to my knowledge who
defeated the Committee on Committees. I think it impressed
everybody in the House that here was a Negro member and a
Negro woman, the first ever elected in history, who was able
to take over the Speaker, the Majority Leader, the Majority
Whip and everybody, and beat 'em.[31]

Chisholm served on the Committee on Education and Labor from
1971 until 1977. Some of her achievements included the creation of the
Special Supplemental Nutrition Program for Women, Infants and Children (WIC) and the expansion of the food stamp program. She fought
for minimum annual incomes for families, federal funding assistance for
education, federal funding to extend day-care center hours, a national
school lunch bill, and other issues that were based on her personal and
professional backgrounds. When addressing issues, she was equally
critical of Democrats and Republicans for inaction or opposition.

Chisholm also rallied against legislation that was obviously race
driven. The House debated legislation on detaining those accused of
being insurgents and spies. This included those the FBI was targeting,
such as the Black Panthers, but not others such as White supremacist
groups. Some wanted to use Cold War military forces domestically
on such targets. The specific justification was under the authority
of the Internal Security Act of 1950, 64 Stat. 987, also known as the
Subversive Activities Control Act of 1950, which was passed during
the Cold War to address the perceived growth of communism in
the United States and allowed the federal government to detain any
person suspected of espionage or sabotage. She explained her opposition during a House speech in which she protested the section of

the Internal Security Act allowing confinement of suspected domestic spies or saboteurs:

> My colleagues, history records that Rome was responsible for its own demise. Let not history record that we were responsible for ours. It is no longer the Red menace we face, but our own fanaticism, racism, and prejudice. Although the emergency detention section has not been invoked since its enactment, its mere presence on the books is an offense, especially to Americans of color. As I said earlier in my testimony, it was not the Italians and Germans who were rounded up, but the Japanese Americans who were easily identifiable because of the color of their skin. Today, it is not the KKK or the [crime] syndicate whose doors are being kicked in, it is the Black Panthers. Skin, skin, skin color, gentlemen, that's the criteria. It makes us special targets.
>
> I am concerned, as I know you are, about the escalation of violence in America. If we are seriously concerned about seeking a de-escalation of violence, we must deal not with the symptoms, but with its causes. They are both material and psychological. The word "inside agitator" I know is the growl of a hungry man's stomach. There can be no law and order without justice and human compassion. We must bind the wounds and restore the faith of the young Black and brown people of this country in "the system" by changing "the system." One of the places we can start is with the repeal of the Emergency Detention Act [Title II of the Internal Security Act of 1950].[32]

In that same vein, concerns of citizens being detained grew after President Nixon announced, "This strong country has no reason to fear that the normal processes of law—together with those special emergency powers which the Constitution grants to the Chief Executive—will be inadequate to deal with any situation, no matter how grave, that may arise in the future."[33] His reference to "emergency powers" suggested deploying troops and using other federal means to arrest those involved in civil demonstrations and riots. This was not surprising in light of his "law and order" stance.

Chisholm had never been a supporter of blind adherence to so-called law and order, and ran against candidates in New York who used this same rhetoric to stir up White voters and stoke fear of Black crime. She felt Nixon was trying to use the same fearmongering tactics and saw it as racist political posturing in which Nixon refused to address related issues such as equal justice under the law.

Congress took action to address this issue by passing the Non-Detention Act of 1971. It stopped the military detention of any persons unless approved by Congress.

Chisholm also knew such laws as the Detention Act were meant to target Black militant groups because they fought for equality and against government actions that impeded on this equality. On April 21, 1969, she gave a speech at Howard University addressing the need for Black Power to be expressed as part of the political system to be effective. She knew real change would also occur through mobilization of grassroots movements for more elected officials that represented Black communities. Black people also needed to mobilize their economic strength, as stated in part of her speech:

> And the Black man's responsibility today is to establish his own values and his own goals. In doing so he will be affecting the larger American society of which he is a part. The Black man and the Black woman cannot, however, act alone. They must act within a community or family, job, and neighborhood. Let us not kid ourselves into thinking that the White man is suddenly going to make the choice readily available.

The new day will come with honest Black pride, and unified Black action and education, politics and economics. Why it has taken us so long to discover this simple approach is one of the mysteries of the twentieth century. The Jews, the Poles, and the Slovaks discovered this phenomenon years ago. Compassion and understanding may moralize the system periodically, but it will never make it honest, just, and decent for us. Only the application of economic and political power can achieve that goal. "Black is beautiful."[34]

Chisholm's support of minority communities was also evidenced by her actions outside Congress. 1970 was a census year, and it was known that Black people and other minorities were reluctant to take the census because they either did not understand its importance, distrusted government, or feared that they might become targets for deportation, as in the case of illegal immigrants. Additionally, they were often excluded by census takers and thus undercounted, particularly in poor urban areas. There was also a shortage of census takers. In response, Chisholm became an official census taker, also called an enumerator, in Brooklyn. It was uncommon to see an elected official, let alone a member of Congress, walking with a census bag through the streets of any city, but she wanted to exemplify the importance of Black, Hispanic, and poor people being represented in the census. By participating, they could be supported through government funding and equal representation in the state and federal legislatures.

The Black Power movement had national attention, and Chisholm spoke against the arrests of Black Panther activists Angela Davis and Joan Bird. Both were imprisoned unjustly by law enforcement because of their connections to the Black Panther Party. Chisholm joined a national campaign to raise the $100,000 bail for Bird in June 1970, an effort organized by the Women's Union. In a public announcement with attendees including Bird's parents, Chisholm stated:

The whole thing that really concerns me is this whole question of the excessive bail. But if you take the incarceration of this young woman in terms of what's happening in our society—when we should be incarcerating those who are bringing narcotics into this country—and the big organized gamblers and criminals who are being protected in different ways—I think we have to ask whether or not this truly is justice.[35]

She tried to get other Black leaders to support Davis, later recalling how she "had gone to my brothers in Congress and in leadership positions elsewhere and asked them to join me, and they told me they could not because it was not politically expedient for them."[36]

Chisholm supported even militant Black groups such as the Black Panthers because she knew their ultimate goal was equality. While she did not agree with violent tactics, she knew their cause was just.

As part of her support to the Black community, Chisholm also supported prisoners because many were Black perpetrators who were imprisoned even for small offenses. As the justice system became more and more crowded, in the early 1970s prison riots increasingly cropped up in protest against inhumane treatment. She supported prison reform and was part of a negotiating team when prisoners rioted in the Long Island City branch of the Queens House of Detention on October 1, 1970. The prison was 95 percent over capacity and described as not fit for animals by prisoners, their families, and advocates. When the uprising in Attica prison in September 1971 culminated in thirty-nine deaths—including prisoners, officers, and other employees—after Governor Rockefeller ordered in troops, Chisholm demanded legislation guaranteeing prisoners basic human rights. Heather Ann Thompson described the conditions of the Attica Prison: "The building was archaic, hardly modernized since it first opened during the Great Depression. And it was crowded with bodies—jam-packed with anxious and angry men, young and old, from cities and small towns all across the state of New York."[37] She outlined how the majority of prisoners were young, urban, undereducated, and Black or Puerto Rican.

Inmates asked for Chisholm because they trusted her to lead negotiations when they took hostages and threatened to kill them in the DC jail on October 11, 1972. The inmates insisted they were not part of a riot but rather a revolution and were being treated like animals. The negotiations included Chisholm, DC delegate Walter Fauntroy, DC School Board president Marion Barry (later mayor of DC), and television and radio talk show host Ralph Waldo "Petey" Greene Jr. Chisholm took over negotiations when the situation grew more tense as the conflict continued and prisoners became agitated, and told reporters:

> I was there to see if I could break the situation because we had nine men's lives at stake and that was the overriding thing in my mind constantly. These men, desperate as they are, are not going to release hostages willy-nilly. You have to negotiate and bargain and plead. They say they are willing to die. You see, these men don't care about life anymore but in the process of being willing to die they may take others with them.[38]

Chisholm calmed the situation through her negotiation skills, and the prisoners were granted their request to speak to a federal judge. Their emergency hearing with US district judge William J. Bryant lasted past midnight, during which time the inmates outlined the poor quality of the jail built in the 1930s, the overcrowding, and teenage offenders being housed with hardened adult criminals. They complained this led to teenagers becoming true criminals, stemming from President Nixon's District of Columbia Court Reform and Criminal Procedure Act of 1970 (also known as the DC Crime

Bill) aimed at "law and order" by having sixteen-year-old offenders tried as adults for certain felonies. Judge Bryant ordered the immediate separation of juveniles and adults and lawyers assigned to the prisoners, and he gave inmates a note promising there would be no reprisals against them. The hostages were all released. Later, nine of the inmates were convicted on various charges for the incident. The old building housing the jail was torn down and a new jail built in 1976.

Just as Chisholm was a hero to many, such as the prisoners she negotiated for, she led efforts supporting women who had paved the way for her. On June 17, 1971, she spoke on the effort to raise funds for a memorial to honor Mary McLeod Bethune:

> When completed, the Mary McLeod Bethune Memorial will provide for the Washington, D.C., Black community a living symbol of this Black woman's contribution by providing facilities for outdoor cultural and recreational programs for low-income families. There is little doubt that in death, as in life, Mary McLeod Bethune will serve her people and her country nobly. She once told a group that she was leaving them "love, hope and the challenge to develop confidence in one another." The proposed memorial will forever enshrine these words and serve as a testimonial to her own selfless dedication to achieve a just society.[39]

The memorial was ultimately unveiled on July 10, 1974, in Lincoln Park in Washington, DC. It was the first monument in a DC public park honoring an African American or a woman. The ceremony was attended by eighteen thousand people, including Chisholm, Barbara Jordan, and Yvonne Brathwaite Burke. The statue, designed by Robert Berks, represents Bethune handing her legacy to two children, with an inscription at the bottom:

I leave you love. I leave you hope. I leave you the challenge of developing confidence in one another. I leave you a thirst for education. I leave you a respect for the use of power. I leave you faith. I leave you racial dignity. I leave you also a desire to live harmoniously with your fellow man. I leave you finally a responsibility to our young people.

With issues such as women's rights, supporting prisoners, and civil rights, Chisholm built close alliances with other members of Congress who shared her views on the same issues. For the rights of woman and children, she and US representative Bella Abzug worked together on several pieces of legislation. For example, in May 1971 they introduced a bill to provide federal funding of $5 billion in 1973 for child care services and another $10 billion by 1975. This was the most comprehensive child development bill in history and had the full support of Congress. Abzug compared their bill to some watered-down counterproposals, namely from Representative John Brademas of Illinois and Senator Walter F. Mondale of Minnesota. Chisholm criticized how Mondale's alternative measure would "not even cover the 1,262,400 children under 5 on welfare who will need day care if we pass the family assistance plan."[40] The new comprehensive Child Development Act was vetoed by President Nixon as too expensive and a threat to the institution of the family. His veto was indicative of what Chisholm described as Nixon's "minority government" focused on the wealthy.

Chisholm and her fellow members of the CBC also tackled discrimination in the military. In 1971 ten members of the CBC visited ten military bases to investigate charges of racial discrimination in how Black soldiers were treated. Their one-day trips to army, navy, air force, and marine bases on November 16, 1971, were followed up with three days of Congressional hearings. Chisholm visited Fort Dix, New Jersey, to investigate any "lily-White" justice. Stokes visited Fort Hood in Texas and told reporters he had been "bombarded with letters from servicemen from all over the world, especially Black and other minority servicemen," and Fort Hood was reported as the most discriminatory.[41]

Dellums visited Travis Air Force Base in California to investigate a "disproportionate number of Black G.I.'s confined in military prisons."[42] Additionally, Conyers went to Fort Campbell in Kentucky, George W. Collins and Ralph H. Metcalfe to Naval Station Great Lakes in Illinois, Charles Diggs to Westover Air Reserve Base in Massachusetts, Parren Mitchell to Fort Meade in Maryland, Charles Rangel to Fort Bragg in North Carolina, DC delegate Walter E. Fauntroy to Marine Corps Base Quantico in Virginia, and Charles Knox, the administrative assistant to Representative Augustus F. Hawkins of Los Angeles, to the Marine Corps Base Camp Pendleton in California.

Their findings were disturbing, as Chisholm stated during hearings:

> First of all the somewhat deep pessimism from the parts of some quarters leaves that maybe there is no hope at all, that maybe nothing can actually be done. I do not believe that to be the answer. I think what has to be done is to actually scrap the whole structure as it currently exists. First of all a large number of the persons in the military in the high command level are persons who come from the southern section of our country. This has been a way of life, this has been a career for many of these persons because of a lack of certain other opportunities for these White individuals. Then you have on the other hand, on the opposite side, Black persons in a society where these persons have been relegated for the most part to a nonrelevant and subservient status . . . now being under the control of persons on the other end of the scale who have helped to propagate that theory over the years. Therefore if we are going to do anything about the inherent racism in the military system we are going to have to scrap

the manner and the way in which many of these persons
who are holding the top level command positions in this
country have been controlling the system.[43]

There was other evidence of discrimination, such as a 1963 secret
navy memorandum outlining how Black soldiers were to be excluded
from being deployed to Iceland because their race made them ill suited
for an assignment there. The memo was clear any public divulgence
of this would be disputed. The CBC discussed the issue of racism in
the military for years in Congress after the initial hearing in 1971.

Despite all the good things Chisholm wanted for the American
people, she wasn't always popular for some of the alliances she built.
She caused controversy during the 1970 governor's race supporting Howard J. Samuels for the Democratic nominee versus Arthur
Joseph Goldberg. Goldberg's lieutenant governor running mate was
her longtime ally Basil A. Paterson. She saw Goldberg as a pawn of
the Democratic machine. When accused of not supporting Paterson,
her response was this "is a lot of baloney." She continued, "I'm not
fighting Arthur Goldberg per se. He's a fine jurist, a distinguished
American, but he allowed himself to be used by the bosses, and Basil
almost didn't get on his ticket, as a result. They kept saying to me,
'Three Jews and a Black man. That just won't go over up state.' I told
them, 'O.K.', if that's your problem, take one of the Jews off [in reference to the three Jewish candidates running]."[44] Goldberg won the
primary with 52.16 percent of the vote but lost the general election to
incumbent Nelson Rockefeller, who gained 52.41 percent.

As a backdrop of what was occurring nationally in 1970, Chisholm's
famous biography was released. The book was an honest testament to
what she had experienced throughout her life, her views on key issues,
and a reflection on her experiences as a political figure. She also wrote
an article in the January–February issue of the *Black Scholar* revealing
her views on race and feminism. She spoke of the destructive force

of antifeminism and the need for women to become revolutionaries. Her article was very dark at some points but also uplifting:

> Everywhere we turn today we are confronted with a revolution of some kind. Slogans that range from "You've come a long way, baby" to "All power to the people" have become jaded chants that dribble from the mouths of jaded TV announcers. There is an almost paranoid fear eating at the guts of all Americans. Black-White, Male-Female, Young-Old represent schisms between us. Racial Polarization, the Generation Gap and Virginia Slims are all brand names for products that may become lethal. The Doomsday Criers are amongst us chanting their wares and bemoaning their fate. Vietnam and the Middle East are no longer powder kegs; they are instead sputtering fuses. The campuses and the ghettoes are eruptions of revolutionary acne. The President circles the globe seemingly handing out carte-blanche military commitment credit cards and scientists in Houston dissect dusty rocks in search of other life-forms while humans starve to death—physically, mentally and spiritually—at home and abroad.[45]

Chisholm's quote summed up the feelings of many voters across the country who felt there was a need for change in the government addressing the needs of women, minorities, young people, and other groups whose voices were not being heard. There were movements demanding change while some politicians in power were steadfast in maintaining the status quo to the point of disenfranchising those who disagreed. She also spoke on the need for these groups to use power to fight for their rights, which she espoused in her plan to run for president.

7

OPPOSITION FOR
THE WHITE HOUSE

"I am the candidate of the people of America. And my presence before you, now, symbolizes a new era in American political history."

CHISHOLM'S POLITICAL SUCCESS was remarkable for the times. During the 1950s, '60s, and '70s, she was hampered by what some perceived as a "twofer handicap" of being both a female and Black. There was a perceived hierarchical order in America in terms of how much one could achieve, and even how a person was socially, economically, and politically viewed. This hierarchy, from top (viewed highest) to bottom (viewed lowest), ran as follows: White men, White women, Black men, and then Black women. This was reflected in income data. According to the US Census Bureau, in 1972 the median income of White families was $11,550, compared to $6,860 for "Negro" families. Overall, for men working full-time it was $10,540, compared to $6,050 for women.[1]

Chisholm ran for the presidency at a time when the nation was facing several political challenges. The United States was still involved in the Vietnam War. The country was still mourning the assassinations of John and Robert Kennedy, Dr. King, and Malcolm X, and civil unrest had left many urban centers in ruin. Every year after Dr. King's death Chisholm gave a speech in his memory in recognition of what she saw as his direct action to fight for civil rights. President Nixon was seeking reelection in 1972 and, as later revealed, was using political tactics that included illegal spying and covert smear campaigns against those on his Enemies List. He was deeply unpopular in some segments of a country that felt in many ways disillusioned. It was against this backdrop that the first Black woman would throw in her hat to run for president as a candidate for a major party.

In many ways, a Black candidate for the US presidency was the culmination of the events of the 1950s and '60s. Civil rights had been fought at lunch counters, on buses, and in the streets. Supreme Court rulings, federal legislation, and presidential executive orders had legally struck down racism across the country. A Black candidate symbolized the gains Black people had made but also represented a social and political shift some in the country were fearful of. A Black political candidate also represented the fulfillment of the promises made to the Black populace by the Democratic Party. However, the Democratic Party itself was deeply fractured since the early 1960s. There was no leading Democratic candidate, and the party was divided after President Johnson announced he would not run for election on March 31, 1968, during a televised speech addressing the state of US military forces in Vietnam.

There were already efforts by Black leaders to have a Black candidate run in the 1972 presidential election. In 1970 Black nationalists began working with some Black congressmen to form a Black political party. *Jet* magazine asked their readers to complete a mail-in survey on whether they would support a Black candidate. Chisholm was listed, but all the others in the top ten were Black men. They included

Manhattan borough president Percy Sutton, Carl Burton Stokes (who was then the first Black mayor of a major US city, Cleveland, Ohio), Michigan Congressmen John Conyers and Charles Diggs, Senator Edward W. Brooke III of Massachusetts, Supreme Court Justice Thurgood Marshall, former UN representative Ralph Johnson Bunche, Georgia state representative Horace Julian Bond (who at thirty-one was too young to run), and Nixon appointee to the Department of Labor Arthur Allen Fletcher.

The survey results found 98 percent favored an African American candidate but only 5 percent supported Chisholm. The top two choices were Julian Bond, a leader of the civil rights movement and a founder of the Student Nonviolent Coordinating Committee who gained 30 percent of votes, and Carl Stokes, who gained 27 percent. Bond had no desire to run but did support more Black power in the Democratic Party with the goal of addressing demands of its Black members. He would later outline his support of a "favorite son" strategy where Black voters from each state would support their Democratic candidate with enough votes to influence the party platform. Stokes also had no desire to run but was direct in his views that Black people "do not have to continue to be the unrewarded servants of either major political party."[2] Representative William Clay of Missouri was confident they'd obtain significant concessions.

Preparing to choose a candidate, twenty-five Black leaders met privately in Chicago, Illinois, on May 7, 1971, to discuss a political strategy and possible presidential candidate. It was held at the home of Theodore Roosevelt Mason Howard, a Black physician and civil rights leader. Members of the CBC were invited to the meeting, but only Conyers and Fauntroy attended. At the meeting, Sutton discussed the United States being a democratic country that was ready for a Black candidate and his earnest hope that "White people will vote for a Black man for president. This is audacious thinking and we must get White people to believe this."[3]

The Reverend Calvin Sylvester Morris pointed out that if a White racist such as George Wallace could gain popularity, then a Black candidate could do the same. The group collectively called for a "Third Force," not as the third political party Morris advocated for but rather, as Sutton explained, in the interest of fostering Black unification; with this unification and six hundred Black delegates, Black leaders felt their voices would have to be heard at the 1972 Democratic National Convention.

The names of other possible Black candidates floating across the country included Stokes, Conyers, Senator Richard H. Newhouse Jr. of Illinois, Justice Marshall, and activist and comedian Richard Claxton "Dick" Gregory. Chisholm was upset her name was not mentioned by Black leaders, particularly since she was one of the few Black members of Congress. She knew it was because she was a woman, and Black male leaders didn't want Black women in leadership roles. However, she felt the time called for the idealistic leadership of a woman with sensitivity and determination.

She discussed her desire to run for president with Conrad and Wesley Holder in July 1971. Both gave their support, but pointed out the realities of low funding, lack of national name recognition, and being Black and a woman. Conrad later recalled, "I happily went along with the program because I was used to having a politician in the family. My father [John Chisholm] was in politics. And Shirley was a brilliant woman who wanted to make a point. The point was that anyone could run for president as long as they were thirty-five years old or older and born in America."[4] During another interview he spoke again of his support, stating, "I couldn't do what Shirley Chisholm is doing. So why should I keep her back from doing something so vital to this great country of ours. My father, incidentally, was like my wife. He was born the same date, November 30, and Sagittarians are the same. They fight, they are looked upon as leaders. My father was everything."[5]

By this point, Chisholm had already been prodded to run by sup-porters. As she traveled the country giving speeches, supporters would tell her to run because she was unique in being a woman, Black, and knowledgeable about the issues they cared about. For example, in September 1971 she attended a voter registration rally along with New York City mayor John Lindsay. While the crowd was not receptive of Lindsay, Chisholm's speech was constantly interrupted by cheers, and she even received a standing ovation at the end.

However, Chisholm was not the first woman to run for the pres-idential office as part of a major political party. In 1964 Republican Margaret Chase Smith of Maine, who had served in both the US House and Senate, was the first woman of a major political party to run. Smith described why she ran, and for many of the same reasons Chisholm did, in part stating:

> First, it has been contended that I should run because I have more national office experience than any of the other announced candidates—or the unannounced candidates— with that. Second, it has been contended that regardless of what happened to me, should I become a candidate, it was not really important—but that what was really important was that through me for the first time the women of the United States had an opportunity to break the barrier against women being seriously considered for the Presidency of the United States—to destroy any political bigotry against women on this score just as the late John F. Kennedy had broken the political barrier on religion and destroyed once and for all such political bigotry. This argument contends that I would be pioneering the way for a woman in the future—to make her more acceptable—to make the way easier—for her to be elected President of the United States. Perhaps the point that has impressed me the most on this

argument is that women before me pioneered and smoothed the way for me to be the first woman to be elected to both the House and the Senate—and that I should give back in return that which had been given to me.[6]

Chisholm was also not the first African American to run for president. Her predecessors included Frederick Douglass in 1888, George Edwin Taylor in 1904, Clennon Washington King Jr. in 1960, and Leroy Eldridge Cleaver, Dick Gregory, Channing E. Phillips, and Charlene Mitchell all in 1968. Mitchell was the first Black woman to run for president, under the Communist Party. Of note also is Charlotta A. Bass, who was the first Black woman to run for vice president in 1952.

However, Chisholm differed from her predecessors in several ways besides running as a candidate of a major political party. The focus of her platform was not only focused on rights for African Americans but also for women, Native Americans, members of the LGBT community, the poor, and children. Nor was she a symbol of rebellion against established politics or democracy; rather, she sought unity and integration of political ideas and social views. She also stuck to her principles and refused support from White-run political machines seeking to control her.

A woman running for president was being openly discussed by other national leaders, even if not by most Black leaders. Betty Friedan, who cofounded the National Women's Political Caucus with Chisholm and others, had suggested it in July 1971 during the first meeting of the NWPC, although she suggested it wouldn't happen until five years later. The *Amsterdam News* took a poll from its readers that same month, and there were many responders interested in seeing Chisholm run.

At a press conference in September 1971, Chisholm stated she would "shake up the system" and run if she could raise enough funds, though she didn't have the support of political leaders in Brooklyn.

Out of the four Democratic assembly leaders of Bedford-Stuyvesant, Crown Heights, and Brownsville, three opposed her because she supported women's rights and other issues they believed were not connected with Black rights.

As her 1968 campaign manager, Thomas Fortune, put it, "I was told that it would come back to haunt me. . . . She was spending so much time with women's lib and gay lib that she was forgetting about Black lib right here in Bedford-Stuyvesant."[7] Chisholm knew their positions and went public to fight against them by pointing out that other politicians were just looking to line their pockets at the expense of their constituents. Fortune didn't deny her accusations but rather freely confirmed them: "Hell, it's been going on since time immemorial, you understand, but we just found out where all that patronage was coming from. Now, just when we're getting the door open a little bit, she tells us we shouldn't take it."[8]

Richard G. Hatcher, the first African American mayor of Gary, Indiana, organized (but didn't personally attend) a secret meeting of Black leaders on September 24, 1971, in Northlake, Illinois. The attendees included Coretta Scott King, Jesse Jackson, Willie Brown, Imamu Amiri Baraka, Charles Diggs, Julian Bond, Maynard Jackson, Vernon Jordan, Antonio Harrison, Percy Sutton, John Conyers, and Walter Fauntroy. Chisholm did not attend. With guards posted at the door, the group tried to reach a consensus on a Black political strategy for the upcoming election. Bond discussed his "favorite son" strategy where areas with large populations of Black voters would select the most popular local Black candidate. This would lead to multiple candidates across the country centered in large Black urban areas, forcing White Democratic leaders to make concessions to narrow the field for delegate votes. Sutton argued for a single candidate, while Baraka advocated for a Black political party chosen during a Black political convention. No sole idea was settled on, but rather the participants agreed to mobilize and hold further strategy meetings.

They didn't support Chisholm's bid because they resented her for not asking any Black leaders for permission or even allegiance. There was a collective perception that she expected them to fall in line behind her campaign once she made her intentions public. When asked about the meeting, she responded, "I don't care to get involved in those details. I was invited to the big meeting they had out in Illinois, but they knew I couldn't go because I was in Texas and New Mexico collecting delegate votes. Because I am a woman, because I am Black I've always had to do that work."[9]

By the time the meeting took place, Chisholm was already traveling the country garnering support for her campaign. She gave speeches in Greensboro and to a convention of North Carolina Democratic women, telling them, "I've got organizations working for me in 21 states, and our momentum increases all the time. The male candidates will cancel each other out spending fortunes. I don't have a slick, expensive machine like that. I've got to raise $200,000—and I will. Then I'll make my formal statement New Year's Day about entering five primaries, or more."[10]

The next major Black-led event to select a Democratic candidate took place from September 25 through October 3, 1971, when Operation Breadbasket held its Black Expo '71 in Illinois at the Chicago International Amphitheatre. Operation Breadbasket was formed in Atlanta, Georgia, in 1962 as the economic arm of the SCLC in order to develop strategies to improve the economic conditions of Black communities. The expo featured hundreds of companies, and attendance was estimated to be in the hundreds of thousands. Chisholm was invited to speak and overhead a Black politician remark, "There she is—that little Black matriarch who goes around messing things up,"[11] in reference to her already campaigning for support while Black leaders were still trying to agree on a candidate.

"Black matriarch" had nasty connotations in the Black community—Farmer had already tried to use it against Chisholm—and harked back to the trope of Black women leading Black family households because of the psychological emasculation of Black men during slavery and then a century of institutionalized discrimination. This resulted in Black men turning to crime while unable to succeed in education or employment, leaving the Black woman to run the household. Solving this issue required the Black man to use his patriarchal role to take control of the Black family and community and put Black women back in their place under Black male control. The myth of Black matriarchy has been and continues to be a damaging stereotype of the roles and relationships of Black men and women, and of their relationships as Black mothers and fathers.

In her speech at the expo, Chisholm warned an audience of Black women to have self-confidence or be worn down by sexist and racist comments. She put it plainly: "Black women are not here to compete or fight with you brothers. If we have hangups about male or female, we're not going to be able to use our talents to liberate all our Black people."[12] She was specifically speaking to the Black male leaders who didn't support her run for office.

After the expo, Chisholm continued to publicly outline how her being a woman made her uniquely qualified to understand the needs of young people, and in addressing such problems as family and education. Ron Dellums agreed with her and said he knew he would support her after reading *Unbought and Unbossed*. In November 1971 she was asked her thoughts about the Chicago Strategy, as it was called, developed at a different secret meeting on May 7, 1971. She replied she started her campaign six months earlier and wished those Black leaders developing such a strategy well. When Julian Bond was asked about supporting Chisholm, his view was he and others might do so by default if they couldn't get behind another candidate. Dellums called this doubt others had in Chisholm "psychological genocide," which she wouldn't subscribe to in fighting to build a "coalition" of voters.

There was later a closed session at the expo entitled "National Polit-ical Strategy Sessions for 1972," chaired by Diggs with panel members including Sutton, Hatcher, Imamu Amear Baraka, and Coretta Scott King. Topics discussed were funding a Black candidate, transforming the civil rights movement into a political movement, and holding a Black national convention. Reporters cornered Florida state represen-tative Gwendolyn "Gwen" Sawyer Cherry at the event to ask what she thought of Chisholm's run. Cherry applauded Chisholm making a deci-sion to run while Black male leaders were meeting with little progress in selecting a candidate and replied, "They were standing around peeing on their shoes, so Chisholm finally said the hell with it and got a campaign going. If she hadn't we'd still be without a Black candidate."[13] Exem-plifying the views of other Black leaders who resented her for setting out on her own while they continued to have meetings on a candidate, Julian Bond replied to Cherry's statement, "We may have been peeing on our shoes, but if we were, she wasn't around to get splashed."[14]

Although some Black leaders blamed Chisholm for creating divi-sion among Black Democratic leaders because she made the decision to run on her own, there was already a rift in the Democratic Party that she was trying to seal with a unified political strategy. This rift was not only evidenced by the inability to agree on a candidate with less than a year until the general election but also by private disagreements among leaders that became public. She gave an interview in November 1971 discussing her reasons for running:

> I run because of the need in America for a different kind of candidacy and I am a catalyst for change. I truly believe that change can come about within the system. I am part of the system. I am part of the Establishment. I believe that this system can be made to work, but it's going to need people who have the courage to make some dramatic changes and movements within this system.[15]

Also in 1971, Chisholm gave an interview with the BBC on running for president. She stressed a priority was ending US involvement in Vietnam and using the money to improve services, including revitalizing cities. She said the federal government needed women, Black people, Native Americans, and young people instead of just White people: "America is composed of all kinds of people—part of the difficulty in our nation today is due to the fact that we are not utilizing the abilities and the talents of other brown and Black peoples and females that have something to bring to the creativity and the rejuvenation and the revitalization of this country."[16]

When asked if Americans were ready for a woman president, she responded that it was going to be a challenge, but the women's and Black movements were strong, so the election would show if their demands were rhetoric or action. She spoke on racism being institutionalized, and that Black and White men were the same in their sexist views of women in politics. As an advocate of women's liberation, she stressed women should just be judged on their merits; the pie of America was large enough for everyone to have a slice, and the government should be of, by, and for the people, not in the pockets of large corporations.

Chisholm unofficially announced her intentions to run to 1,300 supporters at the Americana Hotel ballroom in New York City on November 11, 1971. Leading political figures in New York such as Mayor John Lindsay attended the fifty-dollar-a-plate fundraiser dinner, which raised $60,000 for Chisholm's campaign.

Speaking to the crowd, she proclaimed, "I'm here to tell you tonight, yes, I dare to say I'm going to run for the Presidency of the United States of America!" She was out to prove "that other kinds of people can steer the ship of state besides the White men." She continued, "Regardless of the outcome, they will have to remember that a little hundred-pound woman, Shirley Chisholm, shook things up!"

An article in the *Village Voice* included these quotes from her and her opposition, discussing how she proactively established herself as a candidate outside the bargaining and secret meetings being led by Black male leaders:

> In any case, Shirley Chisholm had definitely out-maneuvered her male colleagues, spoiling any chances for multiple Black candidacies, locally based, and embarrassing them by making the rift between her camp and theirs very public. The whole point of their effort was to bring a solid bloc of united Black delegates to the Democratic Convention, to bargain on platform issues of importance to their constituents.[17]

The next major Black political event was the CBC's National Conference of Black Officials at the Sheraton Park Hotel in Washington, DC, on November 18–20, 1971, with over three hundred attendees. It was a contentious event, as the Black leaders made it clear to some attendees they were not going to support her. Some organizers did all they could to ensure Chisholm was not visible when discussions on selecting a candidate were held. Clay chaired a panel session called "The Development of Black Political Power in the Seventies." Chisholm was not on the panel, and her absence was questioned by Gwendolyn Cherry, as Chisholm was currently the only known Black presidential candidate. During a speech later, Chisholm explained she wasn't even told there was such a panel and would have been on it if asked by the CBC, intimating that she was purposely not invited:

> The Caucus asked its members to choose what workshops they would like to take part in during the meeting and I, because of my background as an educator, asked to be included in a workshop on early childhood education. When the meeting got underway, it developed there was also a

workshop on national politics, and I had not been included
in the panel. It seemed clear to me that there had been a
subtle but unmistakable attempt to keep me out of the lime-
light and there was no possibility that I would ever gain the
unified backing of the Caucus.[18]

Chisholm's conflict with the CBC made national news because
of the number of attendees at the event and her being shunned in
such a public and high-profile forum. The next day, it was featured
in an article in the *New York Times* entitled "Mrs. Chisholm Chides
Black Caucus" that discussed how Black male leaders felt Chisholm
running without their approval hampered their ability to bargain with
the White bosses of the Democratic Party:

> Observers regarded the incident as the broadest public airing
> so far of a six-month-old fight between Mrs. Chisholm and
> Black male political leaders who feel that her candidacy for
> the Presidency makes it difficult for other Negroes to bargain
> within the Democratic party.
>   Some male political leaders who would not allow the
> use of their names, contend that a Negro candidate should
> be named to seek the Democratic Presidential nomination
> but that his support should come out of an all-Black political
> planning session.[19]

Black male leaders continued to publicly express anger at
Chisholm's candidacy. A cocktail party was held in the Rayburn building on Capitol Hill on November 18 for visiting Black politicians, and
some attendees made disparaging comments about Chisholm's decision
to run. The reaction from even CBC leaders such as William Clay was
that she needed to know and stay in her place. The CBC collectively
wouldn't endorse her. Indicative of this were Black leaders like Clay,

who sarcastically responded when asked about Chisholm's candidacy by a reporter from the *Village Voice*, "Who's Shirley Chisholm? You don't represent *The Village Voice*, you can't represent *The Village Voice!*"[20] Louis Stokes just laughed and shrugged his shoulders when the reporter asked him the same question.

Chisholm's view was simple: "While they're rapping and snapping, I'm mapping. They think I am trying to take power from them. The Black man must step forward, but that doesn't mean the Black woman must step back. Being a woman is a bigger drawback for me than being Black."[21] Her response was indicative of how Black women were kept out of leadership roles by the Black men who led the civil rights movement.

Even some whom Chisholm had earlier endorsed and considered allies turned against her. On Christmas Eve later that year, Mayor Lindsay invited her to Gracie Mansion, the residence of the mayor of New York City, to talk her out of running. She supported Lindsay in his run for mayor in 1969 over the Democratic candidate.

When he asked if she was serious about running, she asked him how many times she had to repeat herself. When he tried to dissuade her by pointing out the thousands of dollars she would need, she snapped back, "It takes millions, I know that. . . . But I'm the only candidate who's Black and a woman. . . . You're my friend, but I'm so goddamn fed up with all this shit you men keep putting down. You've got the media. You've got the money. I go out and get maybe five, six people to a meeting, and the press reports it. . . . But you got the money to go out and bring people in by the busloads so it looks like you get good crowds all the time."[22] Lindsay was contemplating a run for president himself. When Lindsay complained her run would cut into his vote, she replied, "That's the same thing [George] McGovern told me. But, goddamn it, this is the American Dream—the chance for a Black woman to run for the highest office. If you're so worried about cutting into the progressive vote, why don't you and McGovern get together—and one of you decide to back out?"[23]

Chisholm's Candidacy Announcement for President

Chisholm officially announced her intention to run for President a few months after the CBC's conference on January 25, 1972, at Brooklyn's Concord Baptist Church surrounded by some of the city's prominent Black religious and political leaders. She officially became the first Black person to run as a candidate of a major political party for president, and the first woman for the Democratic Party. In her announcement, she stated:

> I stand before you today as a candidate for the Democratic nomination for the presidency of the United States of America.
>
> I am not the candidate of Black America, although I am Black and proud.
>
> I am not the candidate of the women's movement of this country, although I am a woman and I'm equally proud of that.
>
> I am not the candidate of any political bosses or fat cats or special interests.
>
> I stand here now without endorsements from many big-name politicians or celebrities or any other kind of prop. I do not intend to offer to you the tired and glib clichés, which for too long have been [an] accepted part of our political life.
>
> I am the candidate of the people of America. And my presence before you, now, symbolizes a new era in American political history. I have always earnestly believed in the great potential of America. Our constitutional democracy will soon celebrate its 200th anniversary, effective testimony to the longevity of our cherished Constitution, and its unique Bill of Rights, which continues to give to the world its inspirational message of freedom and liberty.[24]

She outlined her goal of raising $300,000 and the contributions she had already received, and she reiterated the Constitution's eligibility requirements for president, which she met. She ended her speech with her famous V-shaped wave to the crowd. In terms of her full campaign platform, Chisholm didn't name a vice presidential running mate. However, she later stated she would have selected a Black running mate and nominated a man to head the Department of Health, Education, and Welfare and a Native American to the Department of the Interior.

On policy issues, her campaign platform included addressing urban unrest, housing, unions having an open-door policy for opportunities programs, equalitarian policies focused on South Africa and Rhodesia, and a national health insurance program. She sought improvements in education, women's rights, and civil rights, and to reverse the damage of the Nixon administration. For example, she felt military aid should be reduced to regressive regimes in Greece, Portugal, Spain, and Cambodia and that the US should be tackling problems in other countries.

She criticized President Nixon continuing US involvement in Vietnam and, speaking before the National Press Club, described his escalating bombing attacks as "harebrained gibberish"—meaning decisions not driven by logic or analysis. Her views mirrored those of thousands of protestors around the country, particularly young protestors. Other White candidates announcing their intentions to run were just as critical of the president, which he did not receive well. During a television and radio address on February 9, 1972, Nixon spoke on why he hadn't ended US involvement in the war and directly to the presidential candidates that criticized him, including Chisholm:

> I have no complaint over the fact that during this period, when I have been ending a war I did not begin, I have been subjected to vigorous criticism. I do not question

the patriotism or the sincerity of those who disagree with
my policies to bring peace, but as I said in 1968 when I
was a candidate for President, we have only one President
at a time, and only the President can negotiate an end to
the war. There should always be free debate and criticism,
so that our policy will represent the best thinking of our
Nation, but a candidate for President has a higher responsibility than the ordinary critic. A candidate should make
any criticism he believes would contribute to bringing an
honorable peace. But I would hope that anyone seeking the
Presidency would examine his statements carefully to be
sure that nothing he says might give the enemy an incentive
to prolong the war until after the election.[25]

The National Black Political Convention

Just as Black nationalists and politicians had agreed, they held a
Black convention to discuss selecting a candidate and starting a Black
political party. During the National Black Political Convention from
March 10 through March 12, 1972, Chisholm was busy campaigning,
so instead of attending Chisholm sent her aide Thaddeus A. Garrett
Jr., who worked as her senior policy adviser. The event was held in
the West Side High School gymnasium in Gary, Indiana. It was sponsored by the CBC for the purpose of "developing a national Black
agenda and the crystallization of a national Black strategy for 1972 and
beyond" and was "open to all people regardless of party affiliation or
ideology, to reflect the full diversity of interests of 25 million Blacks."[26]

It was organized by convention cochairman Richard Hatcher (who
later would chair Jesse Jackson's campaign in 1984) for the purpose
of "translating the ideas of Black Power into an effective strategy,"[27]
and coconvened by cochairmen Imamu Amear Baraka and Charles
Diggs. Adam Clayton Powell Jr. served as the honorary chairman. The

theme of the event was "Black Politics at the Crossroads," centered on a publication titled "The Black Agenda" based on "an independent Black political movement, an independent Black Political Agenda, and independent Black spirit."[28]

In attendance were three thousand Black delegates representing each state, members of Congress, entertainers, civil rights organizers, and state legislators, all part of the estimated eight thousand to ten thousand attendees. The delegates represented Democrats and Republicans, nationalists and integrationists, conservatives and communists. The leading Black figures of the time attended the convention, including Coretta Scott King, Malcolm X's widow Betty Shabazz, Fannie Lou Hamer, Queen Mother Moore, Muhammad Ali (who served as sergeant at arms over a security force prepared in response to threats against the convention), Dick Gregory (who weighed only ninety pounds because he had been fasting in protest of the Vietnam War), Black Panther Party leader Bobby Seale, Nation of Islam leader Minister Louis Abdul Farrakhan Sr., and entertainers Richard Roundtree, James Brown, Sammy Davis Jr. (who was booed on stage because he endorsed Nixon for reelection), and Harry Belafonte. Speakers on the program included Seale, Farrakhan, Roundtree, Carl Stokes, Louis Stokes, Yvonne Brathwaite (she later changed her last name to Burke when she married William A. Burke in June 1972), Jesse Jackson, Walter Fauntroy, Ronald Dellums, Vincent Harding, Patricia Patterson, Kim Weston, Barbara Jordan, and Julian Bond.

The convention agreed as a group that African Americans should "stand aloof from the entire list of candidates for the Presidency of the United States" and not support candidates who were "only interested in hip pocket politics."[29] This mainly referred to White candidates, but also included any potential Black candidates who met this criteria of running only for financial gains. Richard Hatcher opened the convention by proclaiming neither the Democratic nor Republican Party had kept their promises to African Americans, and now the

Black vote was strong enough to force both parties to listen to Black concerns, a view Chisholm shared. He also made a rousing speech at the convention opening:

> Its destiny will depend on us here at Gary this afternoon. How shall we respond? Will we walk in unity or disperse in a thousand different directions? Will we stand for principle or settle for a mess of potage? Will we maintain our integrity or will we succumb to the man's temptation? Will we act like free Black men or like timid, shivering chattel? Will we do what must be done? These are the questions confronting this convention and we, you and I, are the only ones that can answer them and history will be the judge.[30]

The concerns of Hatcher and the convention leaders were to be spelled out in "The Black Agenda" voters could use to judge politicians. The agenda of action items was extensive, including home rule for the District of Columbia, a national health insurance, and a minimum wage, although attendees weren't able to develop unified strategies to address change for any of them. The attendees were divided on such topics as integration and the recognition of Palestine as an independent state, and issues such as taking over schools versus integration became so heated, some delegates walked out in anger. Upon Baraka's suggestion, William Greaves and his son David filmed the event—with a small crew and no financial support. Greaves turned his film into a documentary entitled *Nationtime*, and it was narrated by Sidney Poitier. (An eighty-minute version of the film was digitally restored in 2020 thanks to funding from actress and activist Jane Fonda and the Hollywood Foreign Press Association.)

The event was criticized by the NAACP for excluding White people and an early push to exclude White media, a move they believed couldn't foster the collaboration needed to bring about the political and social changes African Americans wanted. NAACP President Roy Wilkins saw the convention leaders as separatists and nationalists. Wilkins, who went so far as to the leave the country and not return until after the convention ended, called Stokely Carmichael "a reverse Mississippi, a reverse Hitler, a reverse Ku Klux Klan."[31] Senator Brooke was also critical of the nationalists in general and described them as extremists when Black people needed allies, not adversaries, and he was particularly critical of Carmichael. The NAACP's assistant executive director, Dr. John A. Morsell, attended to keep an eye on the event.

The nationalists were not concerned over criticisms. They were equally critical of Senator Edward Brooke. As one article stated, "Some hotheads in the rights movement virtually accuse him of being an Uncle Tom. To millions of other Negroes, his image is blurred at best. Because of his pale skin, his Episcopalian faith, his reserved New England manner, he is looked upon as what might be described as a 'NASP'—the Negro equivalent of the White Anglo-Saxon Protestant."[32] An important note is Brooke was well respected by Chisholm, members of the CBC, and national leaders such as Jesse Jackson. In 1973 Jackson even stated, "There is no more qualified candidate in the Republican Party than Ed Brooke."[33] In Congress, Black Democrats saw Brooke as an ally to link the interests of the Democratic and Republican parties to address the needs of African Americans. Although Chisholm and Brooke sometimes differed on the means to improve the social and economic condition of African Americans, they agreed on the needed outcome.

Chisholm's aide, Thaddeus, worked hard to get groups at the convention to endorse her. However, a motion was presented and approved during a floor meeting led by Baraka that the convention would not endorse any political candidate for the presidential election. This also upset Black supporters of Hubert Humphrey and George McGovern who tried to get them endorsed as well. Thaddeus reported back to Chisholm that she was not supported mainly because the

Black men felt if she ran, she would do so on behalf of women rather than Black people. One Black leader stated, "She's a militant feminist and she rubs us the wrong way," while another "questioned whether Mrs. Chisholm's prime commitment was to the Negro cause or that of the woman's liberation campaign which is expected to provide much of her campaign financing."[34]

Chisholm didn't expect support from the Black men and was particularly critical of Baraka. In discussing him, she once stated, "Imamu is a separatist. . . . To be consistent, [he] should work outside the existing political structure. . . . He has for some reason never submitted himself to the test of running for office."[35] Other political leaders echoed concerns over Baraka's motivations. For example, Julian Bond summarized the convention in stating, "Much of the disunity was due to different people supporting different candidates, and that started long before Gary. Further, people have different perceptions of what power is. People were saying let's vote for Shirley Chisholm to demonstrate our power, but that did not demonstrate any power. And there was a struggle over who was to be the broker for Blacks. Mrs. Chisholm wanted to eliminate Walter Fauntroy [nonvoting member of the House from the District of Columbia] and others and substitute herself. Some leaders wanted to eliminate her, and Imamu Baraka wanted to eliminate all of them."[36]

8

ON THE CAMPAIGN TRAIL

"You can yell, 'Black Power, here I come!' 'White power!' . . . The only thing those hard-nosed Washington types are going to understand at the convention: 'How many delegates you got?'"

THE LACK OF SUPPORT from the convention for Chisholm was countered by support from women across the country. She was very surprised some women in the South responded just as strongly as women in the North. She was told of White women in Mississippi losing their jobs because of their support, and even Representative Cherry urged Chisholm to visit her hometown in Florida due to her popularity there. Chisholm was officially endorsed by the *Amsterdam News*, and women locally and nationally raised funds. A woman in California went so far as to borrow the funds needed to put Chisholm's name on the ballot in her district.

Chisholm did have the support of some CBC members, including to some degree John Conyers, but most publicly from Ron Dellums and Parren Mitchell. She characterized Conyers's support as half-and-half, as he sometimes wavered. In the words of Sutton in describing how some of her colleagues felt, "She put a number of us on the spot. I found I could not go around the country committed to a Black presidential candidate concept and not support Chisholm. If I joined her, she is accountable to me."[1] Kareem Crayton further explained her lack of support by the CBC:

> A majority of the group, however, expressed concerns about the long-term consequences of bucking the will of the Democratic House leadership in a losing effort. While solidarity remained a key goal on legislative questions, these members emphasized the need to gain policy influence within the eventual presidential nominee's campaign team by showing strong support early.[2]

However, Chisholm had to make compromises to get support from some CBC members. She had to agree not to campaign in cities and states where Black leaders were already making deals for delegates in support of other candidates. This included the District of Columbia, where William Fauntroy was running, and Ohio where Carl and brother Louis Stokes supported uncommitted delegates. She agreed, but complained how late Sutton gave his support, which was not until January 1972, and that she could have used his support earlier in starting her campaign because he was at the time an influencing Black politician nationally and in the Democratic Party.

As the official campaign season began to select a Democratic Party candidate, Chisholm had almost twenty contenders during the course of her campaign. Among those who campaigned at some point were Edmund Muskie, Birch Bayh, William Ramsey Clark, Rupert Vance Hartke, Harold Everett Hughes, George Wallace, Hubert Humphrey, John Lindsay, Fred Roy Harris, Eugene McCarthy, James Terry Sanford, Walter Fauntroy, Edward "Ted" Kennedy, Wayne L. Hays,

McGovern, Patsy Mink, Wilbur Mills, Samuel W. Yorty, and Henry M. "Scoop" Jackson. Many of the hopefuls were much more experienced in politics and better financed than Chisholm. Some benefited from large donors, travel budgets, and professional campaign staffs. Hers was a grassroots campaign against organized politicians accustomed to competing at the national level, and thus the odds were very much stacked against her.

Chisholm's leadings rivals for the upcoming primaries were McGovern, Muskie, Humphrey, Wallace, and Jackson. Humphrey was President Johnson's vice president and ran against Nixon in 1968. Muskie was considered the favorite to win by the Democratic establishment and according to polls. He was the Democratic vice presidential running mate of Humphrey in 1968, and he served as the first Democratic governor of Maine in twenty years from 1955 through 1959 and as a US senator for Maine since 1959. He gained the nickname "Mr. Clean" for his support of environmental policies such as clean air standards.

Muskie did create controversy during a meeting with a group of African American community leaders in the Watts neighborhood of Los Angeles on September 8, 1971. When asked if he would consider an African American vice presidential running mate, he replied that doing so would rule out his chance of winning. When questioned by reporters later, he answered, "I said that in my judgment such a ticket was not electable, that therefore it would not serve the purposes which we were discussing," but to gain the Black vote "what we need to do was to elect a ticket that would be committed to dealing effectively with questions of racial inequality."[3] The comments worried Muskie's aides so much they called Black leaders and liberal Democrats around the country to reassure them that Muskie was firmly committed to civil rights.

McGovern was seen as having an outside chance. He was a World War II hero and earned a PhD in history before serving in the US House representing South Dakota from 1957 through 1961, but he lost his bid for the Senate in 1960. In 1961 and 1962 he served as director of the Food for Peace and Foreign Policy program under President Kennedy, won a Senate seat in 1962, and was reelected in 1968. He was known as a liberal lawmaker, and since he had served President Kennedy was considered one of the "New Frontier senators," in reference to Kennedy's New Frontier programs. The Kennedys were instrumental in McGovern's Senate win in 1962. Beyond serving with John F. Kennedy in Congress, where he also got to know Robert, McGovern attended social functions at their homes. The Kennedys felt their being Catholic was one reason McGovern did not win in 1960 because South Dakota voters were so conservative. However, President Kennedy was very popular in 1962, particularly after resolving the Cuban Missile Crisis, so McGovern's ties to him helped him win the Senate race. He ran a brief campaign for president in 1968 but failed to gain the Democratic nomination.

Of the other candidates, Henry Jackson, from Washington State, had served in the House and Senate, and had been the chair of the Democratic National Committee from July 1960 through January 1961. George Wallace, former governor of Alabama, was known for his past views on racial segregation and trying to block Black students from entering the University of Alabama in 1963. He is famously known for his positional statement "Segregation now, segregation tomorrow and segregation forever."[4] The 1972 race marked his third run for the presidency after his failures in 1964 and 1968.

While Democrats were competing for the nomination, President Nixon feared public criticisms against him from Democrats and was paranoid about winning the upcoming election. Nixon used a host of tactics to confuse Democrats and attack his rivals. He targeted Muskie early in the campaign, and during a meeting on January 12, 1972 told Charles Colson, his chief counsel, to start false rumors that Muskie was against major issues considered patriotically American such as the space race, preserving White schools, and support for criminal justice.

This would split the votes and take away from Muskie being able to win delegates: "We got to get Muskie, you know, out on the limb on some of these critical issues. . . . Now, get a massive mailing in Florida that he's against [FBI Director] J. Edgar Hoover, a massive mailing that he's for busing. Put the necessary funds into getting mailings to every Democrat that he is for busing, that he is against Hoover and he's against the space shuttle." To attack Muskie, he planned to use a fake mailing from Senator Ted Kennedy: "Yeah. Put this down: I would say, a postcard mailing to all Democrats in New Hampshire. Write in Ted Kennedy. . . . Get every Democrat in the state."[5] Kennedy received 954 votes during the New Hampshire primary, even though he wasn't running, but the mass mailings in Florida did little, since by then Muskie was already so low in the polls.

Nixon operatives planted spies in McGovern's campaign, including a reporter who followed all campaign trips, another inside his campaign site in California, a third in McGovern's national headquarters in Washington, DC, and another spying on his headquarters at the Democratic Party National Convention in Miami. The spies provided floor plans down to the air ducts of offices, and the break-in at the Watergate hotel occurred after Nixon spies couldn't bug McGovern's campaign headquarters.

Communications later unclassified revealed just how closely the Nixon administration was watching the Democratic race. One memo from Republican strategist Robert M. Teeter to John N. Mitchell, Nixon's campaign manager and later attorney general, on April 11, 1972, detailed how Democratic candidates could be manipulated: "If possible, we should begin to take whatever steps are necessary to have Shirley Chisholm, Eugene McCarthy and Benjamin Spock on the ballot in all critical states. Chisholm appears to be our best choice of these potential candidates. Consideration should be given to funding the candidacy of one of these persons to permit their filing as a third party candidate in as many states as possible. Similarly, we must make every effort to prevent a conservative third party candidate being used against us."[6]

Chisholm was unaware of the tactics Nixon was using against her and others running at the time. She continued to focus on some congressional issues while campaigning. In February 1972 she outlined concerns about the power of big businesses and the need for more antitrust policies in a letter to citizen advocates Ralph Nader and Mark Green. She provided them with a series of position papers on economic policy, criminal justice reform, and the need for greater penalties for business leaders and large corporations committing white-collar crimes and environmental policy infractions. The closing of the letter exemplified her support of the working man, the unemployed, and consumers of the nation:

> May I close with the comment that I am devoting my political career to turning this country around, to reversing its priorities and ending the unfairness, injustice and inequality which permeates our national life. In dedicating yourselves to the same cause, you give me the confidence to believe that this effort can succeed, despite the enormity of the task. I earnestly hope your letter and related activities will encourage more political figures to begin to challenge the political and economic power of the corporate state, and its ability to impose its will on the Nixon administration and its distorted values on the American people.[7]

While on the campaign trail, the sexist implications within the questions directed at her husband continued as they always had before her presidential run. Conrad spoke on what it was like being married to Chisholm while she was running in an interview that same month of February 1972 with the Associated Press writer Dolores Barclay. He was asked if her run injured his ego, to which he replied, "She's doing something I can't do. Conrad Chisholm does not have the intellect or the charisma or the know-how that Shirley Chisholm has. What he does is play his role to the hilt. As her husband, I have to take care of all her needs—see that she's fed, clothed, eats on time and gets to her appointments."[8]

To fully support her candidacy, Conrad took a leave of absence from work to help his wife, driving and escorting her to events for personal protection, and ensuring that she was in the spotlight whenever they were photographed together by walking just slightly behind her. He continued to explain, "I have no hang-ups about a woman running for president. I hate to get in the spotlight. Shirley's the one out there making it, not me. . . . Shirley Chisholm is the star. If you are a man and a mature man, you do everything to maintain your wife's stardom." He also commented on their personal time spent together: "We both enjoy going to the theater, when we can—especially Shirley. She loves music. She likes to dance. I don't."[9]

The caucus and primary schedule for the 1972 Democratic primaries was grueling for candidates trying to get their names on state ballots. It began with the Iowa caucus on January 24 and continued until the New York primary on June 20. For the caucuses and primaries, Chisholm focused on the March 14 Florida primary after skipping the March 7 New Hampshire primary because Florida had more delegates up for grab, and voters there were more interested in her agenda. At the time, Florida's Black population hovered around 15 percent of the state's overall populace, and voters there also held strong support for the women's rights movement. This was in sharp contrast to New Hampshire, with a population that was over 99 percent White. Only Muskie and McGovern took part in the New Hampshire March 7 primary, with commentators essentially calling the primary in Muskie's favor and conjecturing on just how wide the margin of defeat for McGovern would be.

However, Muskie's lead and public support all but evaporated because of his reaction to a Nixon-orchestrated smear campaign. False reports were published in the *Manchester Union-Leader* that Muskie made disparaging comments about French Canadians and his wife was a drunk who used vulgar language. This letter to the paper is famously known as the "Canuck Letter"—*canuck* being a slang term for Canadians. Muskie broke down and cried during a televised interview with reporters while denying the report. Although he claimed it was melting snowflakes on his face and not tears, since he gave the speech during a winter snowfall outside the newspaper building that published the article, this devastated his public political standing. It was later revealed the Nixon administration was also behind a news release published on Muskie stationery that labeled Democratic candidates Humphrey and Henry Jackson sexual predators.

From that point, the list of contenders quickly reduced to thirteen, and Chisholm's campaign ran into internal challenges. She lacked funding for hired staffers and thus relied on volunteers. Chisholm also worked with grassroots supporters in each state, including James Pitts in Massachusetts, Tashia Young in New Mexico, Roxanne Conlon in Iowa, and Jacqui Hoop in Michigan. She later explained how problematic that was: "There was no alternative to depending on volunteers. . . . We never did lack for eager volunteers, but there was no one who could give clear-cut directions. Some work was duplicated while other chores were left undone."[10] At the same time, Chisholm had hired Gerald Robinson to run her campaign, but he quit after just a month due to "the confused mess of squabbling groups he had to work with."

Nevertheless, Chisholm stayed focused on key issues in the states she visited. One of the primary political issues discussed in Florida was busing Black students to wealthier but predominantly White schools, which the Supreme Court had ruled in favor of to support integration in the 1971 case *Swann v. Charlotte-Mecklenburg Board of Education.* This issue was especially contentious because White schools resisted integrating, and the House of Representatives attempted to pass legislation that same year to end busing. Proposed bills went so far as to call for no federal funding for any programs that included busing, and the issue was tied to the $21.7 billion higher education bill, which upset Chisholm because her life had been spent supporting equality in education.

She and the CBC were even more upset the proposals to end busing were being led by northern House members. Addressing her colleagues who wanted to flatly end busing, she sharply stated, "Where have your voices been for those children through all the years? Now it is the same old pattern, and because it now affects a certain segment that have been the beneficiaries of the status quo in America, it takes on a highly different picture."[11]

Chisholm did not support busing by some states that were supported by White national politicians because she saw it as an artificial solution to solving the larger problem of school segregation. She and most of Black legislators pointed out busing was used for decades in the deeply segregated South. For proof of its ineffectiveness, one just had to look at the fact that only Black children had been bused. As she stated in February 1972, "There would be no busing controversy if local school districts would furnish quality education to all of their children, both Black and White, in good faith. But since they have refused to do so. . . . I support busing as a legitimate temporary means to aid the integration of our public schools."[12]

She only made two trips to Florida because of limited funding and came in seventh in the state's primary. Her campaign suffered from constant infighting between women's rights activists and Black community organizers. One such incident occurred when Betty Friedan, who had volunteered as a delegate for Chisholm in the Harlem/Westside Nineteenth Congressional District, wanted to run a campaign event called "Travelling Watermelon Feast" where she would hand out watermelons. Although she had the best intentions, this insulted Chisholm's Black supporters. Friedan canceled the event, but tensions simmered.

As Chisholm later explained, "The conflict between Blacks and White women appeared to be a competition over which group was going to own me and my candidacy."[13] Chisholm was so fed up with the bickering, she once arrived for a rally at an airport and let a complete stranger drive her to the event. As she got in his car, her Black, White, and female supporters bickered over which of their cars Chisholm would ride in.

Her trying to unify support from the different movements was no easy task. The civil rights and women's rights movements each had their own platform. Their leaders were unwilling to concede their agendas for the sake of others, and each felt their movement was unique and more important. As she later explained, "The women didn't want me to discuss what the Black people were talking about. The Black people didn't want any of the women's programs. I was trying to bring everybody together. It was a hell of a position to be in. I wonder how I got as far as I did during the presidential campaign."[14]

Still, Chisholm forged on, confident in the change she was trying to make. As she once said:

> You know, everybody goes through so much to get this most important position—the pressmen, the buses, the signs, the staff men running back and forth. And there I sit with my little crew, knowing that I'm the only unique candidate out there, thinking in the depths of my heart that I might be the one to decide the nominee. . . . I'm very serious with what I'm doing in this country. . . . If we want change in America, we can't get it by sitting back and letting the traditional things happen.[15]

So she told her campaign workers as a way to coalesce them into one unified force, "You can yell, 'Black Power, here I come!' 'White power!' . . . The only thing those hard-nosed Washington types are going to understand at the convention: 'How many delegates you got?'"[16]

Continuing to attend the scheduled primaries, her campaign leaf-let for the March 21 Illinois Democratic primary outlined that she was the first Black woman elected to Congress, with more than twenty years' political experience, and that the key items on her agenda were based on the same issues she had fought for in Congress, such as the ERA, nationwide day care centers, a minimum wage for families, and criminal justice reforms such as getting rid of no-knock laws.

Disappointingly, Chisholm only received 0.06 percent of primary votes in Illinois. Undeterred, she continued campaigning and outlined the urgency of the election in preparation for the next primaries and caucuses during a fiery speech to supporters on March 29, 1972, while campaigning on her "Chisholm Trail to 1600 Pennsylvania Ave." Her words spoke to the need for change in the Democratic Party and

Shirley Chisholm 1972 Presidential Campaign Poster. *Poster by N.G. Slater Corporation, courtesy of Library of Congress Prints and Photographs Division*

stressed that she felt she was the best candidate because she represented all Americans and not just one group, and because of her
proven record of being a politician with integrity:

> I am not the candidate of Black America, although I am
> Black and proud. I'm not the candidate of the Women's
> Movement of this country, although I am a woman and
> I'm equally proud of that. I am the candidate of the people
> and my presence before you now symbolizes a new era in
> American political history.[17]

As the primaries continued, Chisholm was not treated fairly by
her competitors or the Democratic Party. She was not given the same
press coverage as other candidates, and the Democratic Party didn't
ensure she had equal airtime on television and radio, such as scheduled interviews with leading political analysts or special appearances
at fundraising events. She did make some television appearances, even
though she was excluded from televised debates among the Democratic candidates. She was interviewed by Sherry Henry on *Woman!*,
a CBS show, on March 29, 1972. She spoke before the National Press
Club in Washington on April 20, 1972. She also received international
attention. During her campaign, German filmmaker Peter Lilienthal
shot the documentary film *Shirley Chisholm for President* for German
Television channel ZDF. Filmmakers Robert Denby and Tom Wer-
ner also produced an award-winning documentary, entitled *Shirley
Chisholm: Pursuing the Dream*.

The CBC and Chisholm were still at odds as the primaries continued. Most members gave their support to McGovern because they felt
he could defeat Nixon. Beyond feeling Chisholm had not consulted
with them, they felt she was betraying their focus on Black issues
by trying to establish a coalition of Black people, women, Hispanic
people, White liberals, LGBT people, young people, and the poor.

Highly aware of the lack of men at any of her rallies, she countered this claim by saying they opposed women in politics: "What makes you think Black male politicians are any different from White male politicians? . . . This 'woman thing' is so deep. I've found it out in this campaign if I never knew it before."[18]

She also faced opposition from some of her female colleagues, including those she thought she could count on, most notably her fellow cofounders of the National Women's Political Caucus. Bella Abzug, with whom Chisholm also worked closely with on several pieces of legislation, endorsed McGovern, although she would describe Chisholm's campaign as "an idea whose time has come."[19] Betty Friedan wavered between supporting Chisholm and McCarthy before finally supporting Chisholm. As Chisholm explained, "Betty Friedan was against me because I refused to go out on the picket line to protest a cocktail lounge that refused to admit women. Well, that's a White, middle-class virtue. If men don't want me in their lounges, I don't want to be in them."[20]

During a television interview in Chicago she attended with Chisholm, Gloria Steinem showed her reluctance in supporting a female candidate: "I'm supporting both Chisholm and McGovern. I don't think that's a conflict of interests. I feel he's the best White male candidate."[21] Chisholm was direct in her response: "Gloria, you're supporting either George McGovern or Shirley Chisholm. I don't mind if you are supporting George. If he is your candidate, so be it, but don't do me any favors by giving me this semi-endorsement. I don't need that kind of help."[22]

Overall, Abzug, Friedan, and Steinem supported Chisholm's ambition and felt she was good for the women's rights cause but didn't feel she could win. They were more comfortable backing a pragmatic candidate like McGovern who they felt could defeat Nixon and hopefully support their cause while in office. Some historians point out another issue: although Chisholm was a woman, Abzug and the rest still had an issue contending with the fact that she was also Black. The women's movement was progressive but had yet to become color-blind.

Steinem supported McGovern, even though she remarked in April 1972 she started supporting Chisholm after hearing her at a meeting in her district. She had previously supported him but changed her views due to the surprise in McGovern's voice "at the strength of women's issues in New Hampshire, or that one benefit speech in Florida could bring ten thousand dollars in ticket sales into campaign coffers. He still doesn't understand the women's movement."[23] Although she had brought in McGovern's largest campaign contributor in 1968, in her words, "I had raised as much money and done as much political work as anyone in McGovern's last brief presidential effort and still had been treated like a frivolous pariah by much of McGovern's senate staff, yet I had refused to admit even to myself that this was so."[24] McGovern even removed abortion from his campaign platform, further upsetting Steinem. Steinem would later try to get a woman nominated as McGovern's vice presidential running mate at the 1972 Democratic convention. She would nominate Frances Tarlton "Sissy" Farenthold, who surprisingly started amassing votes until the McGovern team realized what was occurring and pressured delegates to stop voting for her.

Friedan hinted at Chisholm running as McGovern's vice presidential running mate in an introductory speech at a NOW meeting in Bedford–Stuyvesant a few weeks after Chisholm declared her candidacy. While she introduced Chisholm as "the first woman President of the United States," she added, "and will settle for no less than the Vice Presidency."[25] Chisholm's response after she reached the stage was "I want to make unequivocally clear that I am running for the Presidency of the United States. I don't want half-baked endorsements. I want whole-hearted people. If you are going to be with me in a half-hearted fashion, don't come with me at all."[26] Steinem and Friedan eventually served as delegates in New York for Chisholm.

Stereotypes against Chisholm reflected the sexist culture of America, such as women being intellectually and physically inferior to men as well as using emotions to make decisions rather than logic. As she once said, "The emotional, sexual, and psychological stereotyping of females begins when the doctor says: 'It's a girl.'"[27] The day after she made her official campaign announcement, CBS news anchor Walter Cronkite stated, "A new hat—rather, a bonnet—was tossed into the presidential race today. That of Mrs. Shirley Chisholm, the first Black woman to serve in Congress."[28] Cronkite's play on words wasn't meant to be sexist, and he later apologized, but his words were indicative of the inexperience national commentators had with a woman in a high-level political race.

Other comments were more derogatory. Comedian Redd Foxx famously quipped, "I sure as hell prefer Raquel Welch to Shirley Chisholm" in speaking on Chisholm's physical appearance.[29] He also made jokes about her looks in his comedy routine and on his television show *Sandford and Son*, which aired on NBC from 1972 through 1977. An article in the *Wall Street Journal* on February 14, 1972, called her campaign "quixotic" and noted that "few politicians, Black or White, believe it."[30]

Edgar F. Berman, physician and personal friend of presidential candidate Hubert Humphrey, openly criticized any women running for office as unfit for the job because of their menstrual cycles. Berman was on the Democratic Party's platform committee, and, in response to Representative Patsy Mink's call for women's rights to be a part of the party's platform during a session of the Democratic Party's Committee on National Priorities, Berman commented that women have "raging storms of monthly hormonal imbalances." He proposed the following scenario: "Suppose that we had a menopausal woman President who had to make the decision of the Bay of Pigs or the

Russian contretemps with Cuba? All things being equal, I would still rather have had a male JFK make the Cuban missile crisis decisions than a female of similar age."[31]

In response to Berman, endocrinologist and physiologist Estelle Rosemary Ramey wrote condemning letters to the *Washington Evening Star* and *Washington Post* on being "surprised" to learn as an endocrinologist that ovarian hormones were toxic to brain cells. She also reminded readers that during the Cuban Missile Crisis, President Kennedy suffered from a hormonal imbalance due to his Addison's disease, which was an endocrine disorder. She and Berman held a debate sponsored by the Women's National Press Club in which she dominated Berman. When Berman opened the debate by stating he loved women, Ramey replied that was also true of Henry VIII. Chisholm sent a scathing letter to Humphrey demanding Berman resign, as did Mink, while Steinem started a petition, and even Berman's wife made public comments condemning his words. Berman immediately resigned but held firm, commenting that the world was uptight, and women were "different."

Berman's views were shared by some media reporters. An editorial in a Black newspaper, the *Chicago Daily Defender*, accused Chisholm of running a campaign built on "vaginal politics" because she supported women's rights. A columnist in another newspaper commented how voters were doomed to an era of women such as Chisholm meddling in politics. Others focused on her looks rather than her policies, such as one editorialist in a 1972 *Oakland Post* article who wrote, "Mrs. Chisholm . . . speaks with an engaging lisp," and that she was "diminutive and short in knee-high lace-up boots."[32] The Reverend William Jones, acting chief for the SCLC's Operation Breadbasket, dismissed Chisholm's career in Congress as merely symbolic. When asked about the article, Chisholm responded, "I'm looking to no man walking this earth for approval of what I'm doing."[33]

Male Black leaders continued to be split on their support. Jesse Jackson, John Conyers Jr., and Julian Bond supported McGovern. Not only had McGovern supported the CBC being established, but Black leaders also felt if elected he would support the Black agenda. Louis Stokes supported Humphrey, attempting to use his influence as the first Black member of Congress from Ohio to sway other Black voters. Prominent Black leader Alcee L. Hastings (who had failed to win the Democratic primary for his US Senate race in 1970) supported Muskie. Senator Leroy Johnson from Georgia also supported Muskie.

All of this was lobbied at Chisholm while she faced the hurdle of a lack of funding. She launched her campaign with $44,000 and a goal to raise $300,000, but even that goal was far less than what she needed to compete on the national level. In the average presidential campaign, a candidate needed at least $1 million just to run a primary race. Over the course of the 1972 general election, Nixon spent $69.3 million and McGovern $67.3 million. McGovern spent $12 million just to get the Democratic Party nomination, compared to $7 million by Muskie and $4.7 million by Humphrey.[34] Candidates overall spent more during the 1972 general election campaign than any other in history up to that point. Unlike her competitors, Chisholm refused to become politically beholden to large corporate donors and interest groups. An authentic grassroots campaign like hers meant relying on small donors, which necessarily meant a much lower budget.

Another hurdle was Chisholm's staff not being prepared for the demands of a national campaign, which required extensive travel and a unified campaign strategy. Added to all of this was the public scrutiny that accompanies national politics, which can be devastating. During her campaign she endured racially motivated hate mail, death threats, and at least three confirmed assassination attempts.

One assassination attempt was by a man with a knife that had a ten-inch blade who tried to stab her in the back before people near her stopped him. This really bothered Chisholm, and for that reason she shied away from talking about it. Conrad served as her bodyguard until she was able to get US Secret Service protection, which she had before as a congressperson. After the assassination of Robert Kennedy in 1968, Secret Service agents were assigned to high-profile figures (at least for a short time), including Chisholm because she was the first African American woman in Congress and Georgia governor Lester Maddox due to his harsh segregationist stances—he notoriously refused to allow Dr. King to lie in state in the Georgia state capitol after his assassination.

Kennedy's assassination changed the Secret Service, as all major presidential candidates since have been extended this federal protection. One of Chisholm's Secret Service agents was Susan Ann Baker, who later wrote the book *Behind the Shades* about her experiences being one of just five female agents in 1971. Chisholm was upset by the attempt on her life as well as the assassinations of the 1960s, and this violence motivated her to press for increased gun control.

Just before the Michigan and Maryland primaries, George Wallace was also the target of an assassination attempt on May 15, 1972, in Laurel, Maryland, by a twenty-one-year-old busboy named Arthur Bremer. While shaking hands outside with supporters in an estimated crowd of one thousand, Wallace was shot five times, leaving him paralyzed for life from the waist down. After the assassination attempt on Wallace, Secret Service protection was immediately given to Chisholm, Wilbur Mills, and Senator Ted Kennedy, since his two brothers had been assassinated.

The next day, during a speech on May 16, 1972, in San Francisco during the Commonwealth Club's luncheon, while under close guard by the Secret Service, Chisholm questioned how many more assassinations it would take before there was a political will to regulate weapons.

The threats didn't stop her. Robert Gottlieb, an intern in her congressional office when he attended Cornell University and later the student coordinator for her presidential campaign, stated, "She was unafraid of anybody. Her slogan was 'unbought and unbossed.' She was really unbossed." He continued:

> So I'm 21 years old. I'm a senior in college. I'm raring to go. And my first trip was to North Carolina to go to some colleges to try to organize students. And I had to wait until we received the bumper stickers and brochures that we could hand out. Coming from the printer they were in boxes . . . but on the outside of the box you had one bumper sticker. On the other was one brochure, "Chisholm for President." I took a plane to Raleigh, North Carolina. And I go to pick up my bags and the brochures and bumper stickers from the luggage carousel. And scrawled all over it was "go home nigger." That's how the campaign began.[35]

Even with the threats to her life and racism experienced during the May 6 North Carolina primary described by Gottlieb, Chisholm was undeterred and ran on behalf of "women, Blacks, brown, the young, the old, activists for social change, and just people who are tired of reading the election results before the votes are counted."[36] She said her followers were "going to prove that our candidates and our policies and our government are not the exclusive preserve of the financial community, the political establishment, and the opinion polls."[37]

She campaigned nationally and succeeded in getting her name on fourteen primary ballots. She stressed that women needed to stop supporting male candidates out of habit because women didn't need someone to represent them; they could represent themselves. Her campaign song, "Chisholm Trail," written by one of her staffers, summed up what she was fighting for:

> If you're looking for a road to freedom,
> Take the Chisholm Trail

If you're looking for peace and equality
Take the Chisholm Trail
Proposition coalition,
Students, brothers, Black and White
She will get us out Vietnam
She will set our women free
Reach out to the minority.

Chisholm gained support from the marginalized groups she was bringing attention to. For example, she gained support from the Gay Liberation Front in Boston, founded in 1969 by trans activists Marsha P. Johnson and Sylvia Rivera. Both were leaders in the Stonewall Inn uprising for gay rights in 1969, resulting from gay community members protesting homophobic targeting by local New York City police. Chisholm was vocal in her support of gay rights, a conviction Dr. Zinga A. Fraser, director of the Shirley Chisholm Project on Brooklyn Women's Activism at Brooklyn College, once said was ahead of its time and often overlooked by scholars.

As Chisholm's campaign picked up momentum, some of her democratic rivals complained she was taking away their primary votes. She didn't care because she knew their concern was that she was a Black woman being taken seriously, and publicly questioned why it had to always be White males who got the vote. She campaigned in the states she could with her limited finances and small staff, including New York, New Jersey, California, Massachusetts, Minnesota, Michigan, North Carolina, and Tennessee—although sometimes she was only able to visit a state once. For example, she spoke against the Vietnam War at a Detroit, Michigan, rally on May 13, 1972. Just a few days later, on May 18, she spoke to supporters at Laney Community College in Oakland, California. She also addressed students at UCLA on May 22 and discussed being a catalyst for change undaunted by insults, attacks, and cynicism. She emphasized the time for new blood to deal with challenges the country faced. She was sick of being asked if she was serious about her run, as the question was based on her race and sex. The country needed to rely on humanism, she outlined, and she had the best qualifications based on fifteen years of serving the people.

In the midst of all her travels and campaigning, Chisholm's supporters, Wallace's followers, and the media were shocked when she later visited Wallace in the hospital to express her concern and sympathy after his assassination attempt. She explained it was her belief it was not appropriate to impugn the motives or malign the character of her opponents, and to do so would encourage "the same sickness in public life that leads to assassinations."[38]

Reflecting on the visit, she recalled, "Black people in my community crucified me. But why shouldn't I go to visit him? Every other presidential candidate was going to see him. He said to me, 'What are your people going to say?' I said, 'I know what they're going to say. But I wouldn't want what happened to you to happen to anyone.' He cried and cried and cried."[39] She was correct about other visitors, which included Nixon, Vice President Agnew, Muskie, Ted Kennedy, Ethel Kennedy, Humphrey, and McGovern.

As her campaign intern Robert Gottlieb later recalled, "Thinking about it then and now, that says everything you need to know about her. She did not agree with anything Wallace stood for. There's no question about that . . . but she understood that if you really care about the country and you want to affect change, you have to embrace everybody. She was a true human being of sensitivity, commitment. And when he was shot, he was a human being in pain. And she wasn't going to turn her back on him."[40]

House representative Barbara Jean Lee of California, then working on Chisholm's campaign, was flabbergasted at her actions given Wallace's horrible history of supporting segregation. As she later recalled during an interview in addressing "Miss C." when she returned from the hospital visit:

How could you do that? I mean this man. First of all, he's running against you. And secondly, he's running for president. And thirdly, he's a segregationist and he's trying to maintain the status quo that you're trying to change." And once again, she shook her finger at me. She said, "Little girl," she says, "C'mon now, you're working with me in my campaign, helping me," she said. "But sometimes we have to remember we're all human beings, and I may be able to teach him something, to help him regain his humanity, to maybe make him open his eyes to make him see something that he has not seen.[41]

Chisholm's outreach to Wallace did have political repercussions. In North Carolina, opponents touted a vote for Chisholm was a vote for Wallace. As she would later recall, "George Wallace for some strange unknown reason, he liked me. George Wallace came down to Florida and he went all over Florida and he said to the people, 'if you all can't vote for me, don't vote for those oval-headed lizards. Vote for Shirley Chisholm!' And that crashed my votes, because they thought that I was in league with him to get votes. That's what killed me in Florida."[42] She faced such criticism for visiting Wallace she feared she would lose her seat in Congress because Brooklyn voters had such a hatred for Wallace. There was even a poster created based on a parody of the famous 1930 painting *American Gothic* by Grant Wood. Hers and Wallace's faces were spliced onto the iconic farmer and his wife in a photomontage designed by Alfred Gescheidt called *American Gothic—Shirley Chisholm and George Wallace*. Chisholm was upset with the painting and all the dirty politics but concluded these things unfortunately happen in American politics and there was nothing one could do to stop it.

Some of the political attacks on her were more vicious. She was distraught to the point of breaking down in tears from a June 2, 1972, press release describing her as mentally ill and a sexual deviant. The release was typed on the official stationery of Hubert Humphrey, and alleged, among other things, she had been committed to an insane asylum and was schizophrenic, a "transvestite," and prone to bouts of emotional outbursts. It also stated she was still under periodic psychiatric consultation in both Washington, DC, and New York City but had not been formally committed to an institution since 1952. It outlined how the voters of America needed to be aware of a candidate's full record and background to make a meaningful choice, and particularly Black voters, as they were her strongest supporters.

The release was sent to several news outlets, including *Ebony*, *Jet*, and the Associated Press. No news outlet published it because it was so derogatory and widely believed to be false, and it wasn't until 1973 it was revealed the press release was part of a smear campaign by President Nixon's White House, as Chisholm was on Nixon's Enemies List. The revelation was made as part of the FBI investigation of the Watergate scandal. Staffers for Humphrey had reported their Los Angeles office had been broken into and official campaign stationery was stolen from a closet. None of this had an impact on the primaries, however.

What was also revealed years later when the Nixon tapes were unclassified was that Nixon and his aides discussed paying a Black candidate to run for the Democratic nomination as early as September 14, 1971, so that person could take away votes from other Democrats. Their plan included spending up to $1 million on a campaign and perhaps paying the person $10,000 for every 1 percent of the vote he or she was able to garner. One such meeting took place between Nixon, his chief of staff, Harry Robbins "Bob" Haldeman, and his chief counsel, Charles Wendell Colson. They debated about using Chisholm, Jesse Jackson, or Julian Bond, if any could be persuaded. After deciding against them, fearing the Democrats would find out and buy them off, the group toyed with the idea of spending $50 million to start a Black Democratic Party but never implemented any of these ideas.

As more Democratic debates took place on television, Chisholm's campaign submitted a complaint that she was not being given equal airtime by the major television networks, in violation of Federal Communications Commission rules. According to her:

> An important legal precedent was set during my campaign through the work of a young public service lawyer, Tom Asher of the Media Service Project in Washington, D.C. During the weeks just before the California primary, Hubert H. Humphrey had challenged George McGovern to a series of television debates. Somehow (and I am not sure the full story of how it happened ever became public) the three networks—CBS, ABC and NBC—wound up donating their weekly half-hour public affairs interview programs to the two candidates. "Meet the Press," "Face the Nation" and "Issues and Answers" were all stretched to an hour and rescheduled to provide, in effect, three one-hour debates between Humphrey and McGovern during the last full week before the California primary. Tom Asher filed a protest on my behalf with the Federal Communications Commission, citing section 315 of the Federal Communications Act, which says that if any broadcasting station permits itself to be used by any legally qualified candidate for an office, it must permit equal opportunities to all other candidates.[43]

In addition to dealing with challenges from the Nixon administration and her own party, Chisholm had support in her complaint against the networks. The Feminist Party organized protests, captured in a short film called *The Feminist Party Streetwalks*, against the "whiteout" that was limiting Chisholm's coverage. They demonstrated outside the buildings of the *New York Times*, ABC, CBS, NBC, and Time Inc., demanding equal time for Chisholm. They chanted and sang, with one protest song including the lyrics "Give us Chisholm and McGovern / Gotta get rid of Richard Nixon / Gotta get rid of corporate fixers / We've had enough of them."[44]

A leader of these protests was Florynce "Flo" Kennedy, who was a lawyer, civil rights activist, and women's rights champion. Her activism began early in life when she threatened to sue Columbia University for not allowing her admission to its law school. Her threat to sue led to an admission's spot suddenly becoming available. She was famous for her flamboyant outfits, often wearing cowboy hats and boots, and outrageous comments to bring attention to the injustices she fought against. She was aptly described in a 1976 *People* magazine article, "the biggest, loudest and, indisputably, the rudest mouth on the battleground where feminist activists and radical politics join in mostly common cause."[45]

Chisholm's campaign was granted a federal court order for airtime on the major networks and in a televised debate. NBC's *Today* show and other programs with ABC and CBS rushed to get her on the air. In her memoir, *My Life on the Road*, Gloria Steinem recalled being pressed into service as a last-minute speechwriter to help Chisholm:

> My proudest moment was writing a televised speech for Shirley Chisholm in her 1972 run for the U.S. presidency. She was on the ballot in only fourteen states, but she was the first major-party Black presidential candidate and the first woman to run for the Democratic presidential nomination. Single-handedly, she took the "White males only" sign off the White House door. Because she was "Whited out"—as Flo Kennedy put it—of a televised debate before the New York primary, Chisholm and her campaign manager, Ludwig Gelobter, brought a legal action for equal time. She was given a half-hour at the last minute. Ludwig asked me to write

overnight a speech that knit together Chisholm's farsighted positions. Staying up to do it, then watching her deliver it on television, was a high I won't forget.[46]

Chisholm was allowed to participate in the final Democratic debate, which occurred before the June 6 California primary. Humphrey, General Taylor Hardin (a stand-in for Wallace), McGovern, and Los Angeles mayor Sam Yorty were in the ABC studio in California. Chisholm joined from a New York City studio, becoming the first woman to participate in a presidential debate as a candidate. By this time, most polls showed McGovern and Humphrey as the leading contenders for the Democratic Party nomination.

The debate started with a question to the candidates on who would support the final nominee from the upcoming Democratic Party National Convention, their positions on the Vietnam War (including what would happen with prisoners of war), and domestic affairs. McGovern addressed Chisholm participating in the debate by stating, "First of all, I'm grateful for this broadcast today. This is the third one of these discussions we have held. I noticed on all three networks, all the panels have been males, and all the guests have been males, and today for the first time we have a woman, Mrs. Chisholm, and I think it has added an interesting and bright note to our discussion."[47]

Chisholm discussed her opposition to the US continuing its involvement in the Vietnam War after eight years of being involved in an unwinnable war in which Americans soldiers were increasingly being held as prisoners of war. She discussed her support for Palestinians living in the Middle East and how the United States needed to include them in negotiations with Israel to secure peace in the region. She was asked about the court ruling allowing her to be part of the debate, and in part responded, "Unless you can buy, and unless you have the money, people that have ability, creativity, and new solutions to how Government should work are left out."[48]

She spoke on her candidacy not being taken seriously, but she planned to keep candidates and delegates at the Democratic National Convention honest. She cautioned those who planned to use backroom bargaining to determine the final candidate that she would shed light on what they were doing and hold them politically accountable to voters. Chisholm was asked if she would support McGovern or Humphrey if they won, and she replied she would need to see what they offered in terms of their vice presidential selections, as well as their policies. The moderator then asked if she was now considering being a vice president, and Chisholm responded that she was running to be president, not vice president, and could do it, "believe it or not."

After the televised debate, the next state primary was California, the most populous Democratic stronghold with the largest number of delegates. McGovern and Humphrey were most concerned about Chisholm running in this primary because the state had a large Black population. Although she couldn't win the entire state due to the competitiveness of her opponents, she could take Black votes away from other candidates and cause them to lose. However, they were united against false smear campaigns then raging against all of them—again, as was later revealed, being perpetrated by the Nixon administration. The Humphrey campaign issued an urgent press release on June 5, 1972, including a reference to Chisholm:

> Bogus news releases on Humphrey for President letterheads appeared throughout California today in an apparent last-minute effort to confuse voters and the news media. Humphrey for President Campaign Manager Jack Chestnut denounced the two bogus releases as the "lowest kind of dirty politics."
>
> One release purported to signify Humphrey support for Proposition 9, an antipollution proposition on the June 6 ballot.

"Senator Humphrey has not spoken for or against Proposition 9, nor has anyone in his campaign organization,"
said Chestnut. "We have put out no news release. What has
appeared on the editors' desks this morning is bogus and
does not emanate from the Humphrey campaign."

The other release mentioned Congresswoman Shirley Chisholm, who is also in the Democratic Presidential
Primary ballot, in a derogatory manner. "This release is
completely false. It does not come from the Humphrey campaign," Chestnut said. "Like the other release, it is spurious
and bogus."

Chestnut noted that the mimeograph paper supply cabinet in the Humphrey campaign headquarters has been rifled
during the evening of June 4 and that several reams of news
release paper had apparently been stolen.[49]

Chisholm's supporters were energized in California because they
were finally working together and had greater support from voters
there. She even had the endorsement of the Black Panther Party
because of her past backing of laws supporting Black communities,
her past speeches supporting all coalitions, including those associated
with the Black Power movement, and her denouncing the federal
government's tactics against such organizations. She openly welcomed,
instead of disavowing, their endorsement, as some would have hoped.
She characterized them as yet another oppressed group who suffered
from the "meaningless platforms and empty promises" of other
political leaders. When asked by a reporter if she felt accepting their
endorsement would be politically damaging, she replied, "First of all,
there are a lot of people who are not going to vote for me anyhow.
Secondly, you should say, hallelujah. Hallelujah because they're saying
that they're going to try now to use electoral politics. They're coming
back home."[50] The Black Panthers even had registration drives and

hosted fashion shows, dinners, and nightclub activities to increase her support.

McGovern won California by a slim margin—but he had chaired the Commission on Party Structure and Delegate Selection (later known as the McGovern Commission) before he ran for president, and the rules the commission put in place were instrumental in his victory. This commission's goal was to reform such issues as delegate selection and seating after the fiasco of the 1968 Democratic Convention and to reunite the Democratic Party after Humphrey lost the 1968 presidential election to Nixon. In the past, Democratic bosses handpicked convention delegates rather than electors, candidates could attend without winning any primaries (such as Humphrey in 1968), and women and minorities were barely represented as delegates.

The California primary was a winner-take-all event, so McGovern initially took them all by the slimmest of margins. This was legally challenged, and the Democratic Convention's Credentials Committee reversed the party's rules. This led to California's delegate votes being split among all candidates, with McGovern receiving 120, Humphrey 106, Wallace 16 as a write-in candidate, Chisholm 12, Muskie 6, Yorty 4, McCarthy 3, Jackson 2, and Lindsay 2. Despite coming in fourth, she had her greatest voting success in California of all the primaries, receiving over 157,435 votes.

Just before the Democratic National Convention, Congressman Walter Fauntroy from Washington, DC, held a press conference to announce 96¾ Black delegates who were uncommitted were now supporting McGovern. This was upsetting to Chisholm, because Fauntroy was a fellow CBC member and there was never a prior discussion in the Democratic Party about having uncommitted delegates. This further diluted the leverage Black voters would have at the Democratic Convention. Fauntroy was criticized for seeking personal power rather than caring about Black issues. The Black leaders had previously agreed to maintain all uncommitted delegates until the Democratic

National Convention to use as leverage in getting support for the Black agenda from whichever candidate was in the lead.

Chisholm obtained votes in fourteen state primaries, receiving her largest share in California (4.4 percent) and North Carolina (7.5 percent), and garnered forty-eight delegates from a total of 430,703 votes. This may seem small, but it was impressive for a previously unknown national candidate. It was particularly impressive since hers was a grassroots campaign that relied on building a coalition of disenfranchised voters and coalesced around trying to gain equal rights for those who were overlooked by politicians.

As a result, she appeared on *Meet the Press* on July 9, 1972, along with McGovern, Humphrey, Muskie, and Jackson to discuss their platforms and agenda for the convention. Frank McGee, the host, asked her, "Mrs. Chisholm, how do you account for the fact that no more Blacks than half have come to your cause in this primary process and now at the convention?" Chisholm responded:

> Well, I think you have to recognize, first of all, gentlemen, you have to really recognize I'm doing something in this country that has never really been done before. It's a question of inculcation, reorientation and education. Never before in this country, ever since the inception of the republic, have you had a woman seriously running for the presidency. I'm not talking about someone nominating someone at the convention as a mere gesture of symbolism and tokenism. I'm talking about someone that has been going out on the highways and byways for the past seven and a half months and saying to the American people that indeed this is a multifaceted society, that Mrs. Chisholm also can be considered a person that can run for the presidency of this country.
>
> I was breaking the tradition, a tradition on which only White males have only been the gentlemen in this country

that have guided the ship of state. So you don't expect people Black, White, men or women to suddenly overcome a tradition that has been steeped ever since the inception of this republic. So I understand that. I've broken the ice.[51]

The 1972 Democratic National Convention

The Democratic National Convention was held in Miami Beach, Florida from July 10 to 13, 1972, with its largest participation of Black delegates. While they only constituted 2.2 percent of delegates during the 1964 Democratic Convention and 5.5 percent in 1968, they reached 15 percent in 1972. Because of this, Black leaders had planned to attend with a twelve-point bill of rights, including such demands as an end to US involvement in Vietnam, increased employment opportunities for Black people, and education reform. They intended to make it clear the Black vote in the November election would go to the candidate who most supported these demands. The convention also included a record number of young people and women, in particular, who accounted for 39 percent of delegates compared to only 13 percent during the 1968 convention.

The proposed party's platform included a fifteen-point rights of women plank thanks to the NWPC, which Chisholm, Friedan, Steinem, Abzug, and others cofounded. The plank included support for the Equal Rights Amendment, eliminating discrimination in job and public accommodations, equal access to education as well as tenure and promotions for female instructors, higher salaries for women, maternity benefits, and the appointment of women to top-level positions in the federal government. One item not included because it was defeated during delegation votes was abortion. Chisholm's delegates to the convention were Gloria Steinem, Flo Kennedy, Brenda Feigen Fasteau, Stephen Berger, Sandra Hochman, Marc Fasteau, Ellen Roberts, and

Arturo Santiago. Alternate delegates were Rona Feit, Richard Feigen, and Mary Vasiliades.

By the opening of the convention, many candidates had withdrawn, including Muskie, McCarthy, and Lindsay, leaving six in the running, including Chisholm. The event has been described as a disastrous start to the general election campaign for Democrats and was fraught with controversy. The convention commission had drastically changed party rules, such as that relating to the seating of delegates. Jimmy Carter, who was then governor of Georgia, led a "Stop McGovern" campaign in opposition to the McGovern Commission rules manipulating delegate seating while also trying to become McGovern's vice presidential running mate. The McGovern Commission rules rewrote the procedures to nominate a presidential candidate, determined how many minorities could be delegates (basically setting a quota), and limited the number of young people in each state's convention delegation.

Demonstrations for Shirley Chisholm and George Wallace at the 1972 Democratic National Convention. *Photo by Thomas J. O'Halloran, courtesy of Library of Congress Prints and Photographs Division*

The final convention platform included women's rights, desegregation, welfare reform, and the "Right to be different." This latter issue was added as a compromise to tone down a call for gay rights being added. It was spearheaded by James "Jim" Foster, political chairman of the Society for Individual Rights, and fellow delegate Madeline Davis, vice president of the Mattachine Society of the Niagara Frontier, the first openly LGBT people ever to address a national party convention. The original plank was worded as "We do not come to you begging your understanding or pleading your tolerance. We come to you affirming our pride in our lifestyle, affirming the validity of our right to seek and to maintain meaningful emotional relationships and affirming our right to participate in the life of this country on an equal basis with every citizen."[52] Foster, Davis, and Mattachine were pleased at the opportunity to discuss gay rights on prime-time television before national media as it signaled the concerns of the gay community were finally making it onto the national political scene.

McGovern was the primary competitor to beat for the party nomination, nicknamed the "Triple-A" candidate of "amnesty, abortion and acid"[53] by opposers because of his support for forgiving draft dodgers, allowing the states to decide abortion rights, and decriminalizing marijuana. He wanted to change the personal tax law and give a large tax exemption to every American and reduce the bureaucracy of the welfare system. Even some Democrat leaders felt he was too liberal. He used grassroots support to combat establishment opposition to his nomination as the Democratic candidate. This created a swell of convention delegates who were successful in controlling the seating of delegates and reducing the number of women and minorities who were seated. They limited participation to the point the mayors of Los Angeles, Chicago, San Francisco, Boston, Detroit, and Philadelphia were not allowed to attend the convention.

Chisholm delivered several speeches at the convention trying to rally support for her nomination, but also to keep the delegates focused on platform issues rather than on being used by those making backroom deals. During a luncheon, she addressed the women in attendance and celebrated their presence. She acknowledged there were different agendas within the movement, but they were still a unified cause. She also addressed the CBC and their supporters at a separate event and tried to persuade them to unify Black delegate votes by forcefully and eloquently stating, "My brothers and sisters let me tell it to you this afternoon like it really is. There's only one thing that you my brothers and sisters have going—the only thing you have going is your one vote. Don't sell that vote out! The Black people of America are watching us. Find out what these candidates who need our votes to get across the top are going to do for us concretely and not rhetorically."[54] Her message was misunderstood by some. Congressman Clay gave a press conference speaking against her and for the responsibility of the delegates to reject Chisholm and vote for whomever they were sent there to vote for. He didn't understand her speech was focused on telling the Black delegates to make sure the candidate they voted for would support the Black community.

Chisholm was disgusted at her colleagues making backroom deals with White candidates using delegate votes as leverage. She was direct in speaking to a group of Black delegates on her lack of support from Black men while they cut these deals: "I'm the only one in here who has the balls to work for Black people."[55]

Dellums was supposed to nominate Chisholm as the Democratic candidate, but at the last minute endorsed McGovern instead. He told reporters he could not "sit quietly while diabolical and cynical efforts are being made to stop McGovern's nomination" and urged all uncommitted Black, Chicano, and women delegates to support McGovern.[56] He later justified this as the most pragmatic political decision, but Chisholm viewed this as another backroom deal cut by a politician looking for power. McGovern had endorsed Dellums for Congress in 1970 and warned Dellums he would be politically punished and primaried if he endorsed her. Chisholm was blunt about this threat: "It is incomprehensible to me, the fear that can affect men in political offices. It is shocking the way they submit to forces they know are wrong and fail to stand up for what they believe. Can their jobs be so important to them, their prestige, their power, their privileges so important that they will cooperate in the degradation of our society just to hang on to those jobs?"[57]

On Wednesday night of the convention, July 12, 1972, Percy Sutton gave a passionate speech in support of Chisholm as the party's nominee:

> This candidate, in her candidacy, has outspokenly unmasked hypocritical authority, self-righteousness, and callousness, which feed the wrongs of our society. She has challenged irresolution and drift, deceit and conformity. And she has challenged it forcefully and articulately.
>
> This candidate, this lady of determination—in the course of her candidacy, and often in the face of scorn and ridicule from many sides—resolutely continued in her passionate demand for freedom of spirit and human dignity—for all Americans, of all conditions of life. This candidate's candor has made many Americans look deep within their hearts and souls for that which is generous, honest, and noble.
>
> In taking on and sharing the deepest passions of the distressed and forgotten or ignored Americans, this candidate, this lady of valor, has won the love and admiration of millions of people around the world.
>
> This candidate, this lady of unusual ability, by her candidacy has opened a new and dramatic phase in the struggle for racial equality. But . . . my fellow Democrats . . . in addition to her unshakeable resolve to help to heal the long lingering open sores of our American society, this candidate has, in the course of her candidacy, dared to raise and discuss many issues to which other candidates have not yet addressed themselves.
>
> This candidate, this unbought and unbossed lady, has, by her candidacy, invited the locked-outs, the left-outs and

the dropped-outs to recognize that they too have a stake in political and social reform in this nation and they too, the disenchanted of the system, ought to work together for responsible and sweeping change.[58]

Sutton's nomination and his motion were seconded by James Charles Evers, the Black mayor of Fayette, Mississippi, and brother of Medgar Wiley Evers. With this, Shirley Chisholm officially became the first African American and first woman nominated for president within a major political party. One surprise to her was the delegation from Alabama, the home state of George Wallace, screamed in joy at her nomination. They celebrated with approval even louder than the delegation from her home state of New York.

Shirley Chisholm addressing the 1972 Democratic National Convention. *Photo by Thomas J. O'Halloran, courtesy of Library of Congress Prints and Photographs Division*

After convention voting, Chisholm received 151.95 delegate votes (10 percent of the total), a combination of those she received campaigning and those Black delegate votes released to her as a symbolic gesture when Humphrey knew he was going to lose the nomination. She had tried to get more after both Humphreys and Muskie withdrew, and persuade Black and female delegates that McGovern would not look out for their interests. Her efforts were countered by the likes of Julian Bond and California assemblyman Willie Brown who brokered deals with McGovern. Bond questioned why Chisholm felt she could be the chief broker for Blacks.

The final results from the Democratic primaries won were McGovern (10), Humphrey (4), Wallace (5), and Chisholm (1). Chisholm only won New Jersey, where she and Terry Sanford were the only two running, but Sanford had already withdrawn from the race. However, her run and getting to the Democratic convention was a monumental effort, given all those who never made it as far and because she was Black and a woman. She achieved this with a limited budget based on individual rather than corporate donations, a lack of support from Black male leaders, having to forgo some primaries for lack of funding, and running as a Black woman at a time when that demographic was politically disenfranchised in voting and holding public office.

Chisholm's delegate votes were the most for any female candidate until Hillary Clinton in her 2008 presidential bid. Her votes also showed that her message resonated with hundreds of thousands of Americans. Even if she didn't win the Democratic nomination, she had hoped to influence the party's political agenda to garner support for women, the poor, and other important issues. She did later speak on her disappointment in not winning the nomination: "See, if it was a Black man that was running, I think it would be different. If it was a White woman that was running, I think that would be different. But here, a woman and a Black person running, it just couldn't come together."[59] Still, she gave words of unity in her concession speech at the end of the convention.

McGovern never made any firm commitments to addressing Black people's concerns after he won the party's nomination, just as Chisholm feared when Black leaders were making backroom deals with him. However, true to her word, Chisholm campaigned on his behalf after the convention. She told voters if they did not participate in the electoral process and vote, they deserved what they would get with Nixon. Nixon and McGovern were very different in their political views. Nixon accused McGovern of supporting socialist policies stifling free enterprise, and McGovern accused him of economic policies only benefiting the rich.

McGovern lost by a landslide in the general election, Nixon garnering 520 electoral votes and carrying 49 states, compared to 17 electoral votes for McGovern, who only carried the District of Columbia and Massachusetts. Nixon only received 13 percent of the non-White vote. McGovern was bitter about his loss and decades later would blame Wallace for not supporting his campaign—even though, McGovern claimed, Wallace went to his grave believing that Nixon's people set up his getting shot.

After the election, the Nixon administration still focused on their "enemies" and falsely charged Chisholm with mishandling campaign contributions. She knew this accusation of mishandling $686 was just a further attempt to discredit her. When asked how she felt about the investigation, she replied how unfortunate it was that those who were honest in politics were being dragged into the paranoia-controlled national politics. She was cleared of all charges a year later by the Department of Justice. She also knew racism and sexism still played a role in how others viewed her. She was making more than any other member of Congress from speaking engagements (approximately $30,000 in 1972), and some were quick to describe her and Conrad's second home in the Virgin Islands as "lavish" and negatively comment on how well she dressed.

Chisholm didn't get nominated not only because she was a long-shot candidate but also because those in power used collusion to ensure they remained in power. This included members of her own CBC who felt their decisions would suit their political careers. She wrote an article in October 1972 speaking to the role of power in politics and general society. She discussed continued efforts in American society to keep people in segregated classes according to race, gender, and sexual orientation. She felt these actions were deliberate by those who sought to maintain power, resulting in mediocre men being in top public and private positions that "have wrecked our economy, involved us in civil wars abroad, and divided us at home—to hold onto their power by limiting the corps of potential competitors."[60] She felt for America to succeed, "We must work to create a climate in which Americans are allowed to move up in the system solely on the basis of their intellect, perseverance, and physical ability."[61]

The next year, in 1973, Chisholm wrote her second book, *The Good Fight*, discussing her run for president. She reflected on how her run would pave the way for others: "The next time a woman runs, or a Black, or a Jew or anyone from a group that the country is 'not ready' to elect to the highest office, I believe he or she will be taken seriously from the start."[62] She also addressed the challenges she faced when racism and sexism were still part of the American fabric: "I never blamed anyone for doubting. The Presidency is for White males. No one was ready to take a Black woman seriously as a candidate. It was not time for a Black to run, let alone a woman, and certainly not for someone who was both."[63]

After her loss, she shrugged off the idea of her campaign as being mainly symbolic. She had the goal of both winning the nomination because she knew she could make a real difference in politics and also opening the doors for other Black candidates to run for offices at every level of government. She once stated, "The United States was said not to be ready to elect a Catholic to the Presidency when Al Smith ran

in the 1920's. But Smith's nomination may have helped pave the way
for the successful campaign John F. Kennedy waged in 1960. Who
can tell? What I hope most is that now there will be others who will
feel themselves as capable of running for high political office as any
wealthy, good-looking White male."[64]

During a speech to the NWPC Convention in Houston, Texas,
in 1973, she further talked about her campaign being a turning point
for women in politics:

> As I look back on the past year and a half, I think my cam-
> paign did help to break the barrier against women seeking the
> presidency and other elective offices, but my experience also
> made me acutely aware of some of the problems women can-
> didates face as well as particular problems which the women's
> movement, and especially the National Women's Political
> Caucus, must face up to. One of my biggest problems was
> that my campaign was viewed as a symbolic gesture.[65]

As far as support from women, Chisholm recognized there was a
divide between White and Black women. While some of her White wom-
en's rights peers waffled, the support from Black women was steadfast.
On the latter's support, she stated, "They did not have the one problem
with my candidacy that many White women did; the Whites knew I
couldn't be elected, and so their support, even when it was given, seemed
a little tentative, because they felt they were fighting for a lost cause. But
women like Fannie Lou [Hamer], Lupe [Anguiano] and the rest, having
been long active in the civil rights movement and other minority causes,
were used to taking up seemingly impossible challenges."[66]

Chisholm also felt her run was not just for Black people. As she
later explained, "My potential support went beyond the Black community. It could come from the women's movement, from young
voters, and even from a growing number of older White voters who

had reached the end of their patience with the programs and candidates of the two major parties."[67] She also knew what she had done would pave the way for the future of African Americans as well as women running for president. She would later reflect, "I ran because somebody had to do it first. In this country everybody is supposed to be able to run for President, but that's never been really true. I ran because most people think the country is not ready for a Black candidate, not ready for a woman candidate. Someday . . ."[68]

Her impact on national politics coupled with the Black Power movement led to African Americans winning significant gains in politics. In 1973, just one year after Chisholm's run, Thomas "Tom" Bradley was elected the first Black mayor of Los Angeles, Coleman Alexander Young as the first Black mayor in Detroit, and Maynard Holbrook Jackson as the first in Atlanta, Georgia, at the age of thirty-five. Other Black mayors elected were Clarence Everett Lightner in Raleigh, North Carolina; Richard D. Hill in Greenville, Georgia; Doris A. Davis in Compton, California; and Lyman Parks in Grand Rapids, Michigan. Lelia Foley was elected in Taft, Oklahoma, becoming the first African American woman ever elected as a mayor in the United States, and in 1975 Walter E. Washington was elected the first Black mayor of Washington, DC.

After the 1972 election cycle, Democratic Party leadership knew it had to improve relationships among the factions in the party. There was great concern that George Wallace was able to gain such popularity, and this was a signal that racist, old guard southern Democrats were grappling to retake control over the party. Chisholm's run symbolized the new political power of African Americans, women, and the other groups she represented, while McGovern's loss to Nixon reflected how the overall party needed to change its national strategy.

9

BACK IN CONGRESS

"Service is the rent we pay for the privilege of living on this earth."

ALTHOUGH CHISHOLM DIDN'T WIN the Democratic nomination, this by no means damaged her politically in New York or Congress, but rather made her more of a popular national figure. She mended her relationships with members of the CBC to continue focusing on their joint agenda and the congressional work they had to do. When she ran for congressional reelection in 1972, she won almost 88 percent of the vote against rivals Republican John Coleman, Conservative Martin S. Shepherd Jr., and Socialist Worker Party candidate John Hawkins. She was lauded as one of the *Ladies' Home Journal* Women of Year 1973 for "proving that any individual with the capacity for leadership can rise above both sex and racial labels."[1]

In 1974 a Gallup poll of the most-admired women listed her in the top ten, tied at sixth place with Indian prime minister Indira Gandhi and ahead of Jacqueline Kennedy Onassis and Coretta Scott King. She began making speeches across the country due to her increased popularity. With the $30,000 a year she was making from speaking engagements and her $42,500 congressional salary, she and Conrad were able to afford a second home in the Virgin Islands. However, her time away running for president resulted in her having the lowest congressional attendance record of any delegate from New York, which was normal for a member of Congress running for president.

As evidence of her popularity, Chisholm again easily won reelection in 1974, getting 80.19 percent of the vote against Republican Francis J. "Frank" Voyticky, Conservative Martin S. Shepherd Jr., Workers League Teresa Delgado, and Socialist Workers Party member Maxine Williams. The diversity in the candidacy in terms of party showed how much the political landscape of Brooklyn was changing. This resulted from dissatisfaction with the major two parties, as well as the Liberal Party not representing their interests and citizens joining fringe political parties or starting their own.

Part of the reason for these fringe parties was that while Bedford-Stuyvesant was continuing to diversify, it was also suffering from urban decay. As explained in *America's Changing Neighborhoods*, edited by Reed Ueda, "Racial segregation persisted throughout the greater New York area and particularly in Bed-Stuy, where 85 percent of the population was Black, accounting for 60 percent of all African Americans in Brooklyn. The Puerto Rican population grew as well, to as much as 12 percent of the neighborhood's total during the 1970s. At the same time, racist attitudes mixed with sensational newspaper headlines to create a popular image of Bed-Stuy as seedy, violent, and frightening. For example, a *New York Times* article conjured images from Charles Dickens when it described Bedford-Stuyvesant as a place 'of decay and degradation—of drug dens, crumbling tenements and ragged urchins romping in rubbish strewn lots.'"[2]

The United States was trying to heal from two executive branch scandals. Nixon's vice president Spiro Theodore Agnew had resigned in October 1973 after pleading no contest to a felony charge of tax evasion. After his resignation, Gerald Ford was nominated to succeed him. Nixon nominated Ford because he had a reputation for being honest and was most likely the only Republican the Democrats in Congress would confirm. Ford was nominated on October 12, 1973, and confirmed by a Senate vote of 92 to 3 on November 27. He was confirmed by the House by a vote of 387 to 35 in December 1973. His appointment was the first time the Twenty-Fifth Amendment to the Constitution was used.

Subsequently, Nixon resigned on August 9, 1974, before he could be impeached for his role in the Watergate scandal, and was succeeded by President Ford, who then gave Nixon an unconditional presidential pardon on September 8, 1974. Chisholm felt President Ford's pardon of Nixon exemplified the double standard of the justice system, stating, "My first reaction would be that it sets a double standard of justice in this country. The fact that the new President could give a pardon to the last President with all the evidence indicating quite clearly that he was involved in the Watergate situation, is a very clear indication of one type of law for the privileged and one type of law for the masses."[3] She went on to say President Ford should pardon those who evaded the draft and were dishonorably discharged. Chisholm believed that those who refused to participate in the Vietnam War because they it believed it to be unjust "committed an act of consciousness."

President Ford's first administrative action was to select a vice president. He was considering several appointees, including New York governor Nelson Rockefeller, former congressman and US ambassador to NATO Donald Henry Rumsfeld, Tennessee senator Howard Henry Baker Jr., and former Republican Committee chairman George H. W. Bush. Chisholm wrote to President Ford on August 12, 1974, with her recommendation that he select either Edward Brooke, Bush, or Rockefeller because "any one of these three men would offer a refreshing type of leadership which the American people so want and deserve."[4] President Ford chose Rockefeller because he was considered a liberal Republican and could help Ford win reelection in 1976. There were still conservatives, both Republican and Democrat, who didn't support Rockefeller. However, he was highly regarded by African Americans for his family's support of civil rights. His grandfather, John D. Rockefeller, was the founder of Standard Oil and became a philanthropist who funded the historically Black Spelman and Morehouse Colleges and the rebuilding of southern Black churches bombed by racists. Nelson Rockefeller supported Dr. King and the efforts of the SCLC while serving as governor.

Chisholm sent a letter to her fellow House members urging them to "strongly support the nomination of Nelson Rockefeller with a clear conscience because he is one of the best-qualified men in the nation to assume the Vice-Presidency," ignore unproven rumors he had squandered his fortune, which was estimated to be over $1 billion, and support him because, "on balance, his tenure as Governor of my state clearly demonstrates his record of human and social concern."[5] She also submitted supporting statements to the Senate Rules and House Judiciary Committees, each of which were to hold hearings on Rockefeller's qualifications, citing, "We are living in critical and uncertain times. The call and need for strong, fair, and experienced leadership in this nation is greater than ever before. Accordingly, this is not a time for petty partisanship—but rather a time for national unity."[6] Rockefeller was confirmed by the Senate on December 10, 1974, by a vote of 90 to 7, and the House gave its approval on December 19 by a vote of 287 to 128.

Unlike Nixon, President Ford welcomed the CBC to the White House, assuring them the Oval Office would always be open and that he would appoint more Black Americans to key positions. Members of the CBC publicly stated they were cautiously optimistic at Ford's promises and would wait to see what policies materialized. President Ford kept parts of his promises, appointing William Thaddeus "Bill" Coleman as the nation's first Black secretary of transportation on March 7, 1975, although he was the only Black cabinet member. He also expanded the Voting Rights Act of 1965 to permanently forbid literacy tests, and Black History Month was celebrated for the first time nationally in 1976. However, he was criticized by Black leaders for failures to end the recession, tackle unemployment, and support federal programs such as welfare benefiting Black Americans, and for his support of a slow approach to end school segregation.

One achievement for the women's movement under President Nixon was the issuance of Proclamation 4147 designating August 26, 1972, Women's Rights Day. Congress approved H.J. Res 52 on August 16, 1973, in recognition of women being given the right to vote on August 26, 1920. The law passed, and Chisholm attended the signing by President Ford on August 22, 1974, along with other representatives.

The 1972 elections resulted in Congress having three more Black women added to its ranks. Barbara Jordan, from Texas, became the first Black woman elected to the House from the South, and Yvonne Brathwaite Burke the first African American woman from California and the first woman to give birth and be granted maternity leave in Congress. Jordan's addition was particularly great for Chisholm, as she would no longer be the sole Black feminist. These two, along with Chisholm, would form the Congressional Women's Caucus in 1977.

The third was Cardiss Hortense Collins of Illinois, who was elected during a special election on June 5, 1973, after her husband, George Washington Collins, was killed in a plane crash a month after being elected to his second term. She became the first African American woman to represent Illinois and continued to serve until January 1997. During the 1973 to 1975 ninety-third session of Congress, there were sixteen women legislators, and they were all in the House. The Senate would not have a female member until 1977. However, 1972 was a historic year with an unprecedented seventeen Black Americans elected or reelected.

During the 1975–1977 congressional session, nineteen women served in the House. Diversity changes were being seen across the

President Gerald R. Ford seated at the Cabinet Room table signing a proclamation on Women's Equality Day 1974. Standing behind President Ford are Representatives Yvonne Brathwaite Burke (D-California), Barbara Jordan (D-Texas), Elizabeth Holtzman (D-New York), Marjorie S. Holt (R-Maryland), Leonor K. Sullivan (D-Missouri), Cardiss Collins (D -Illinois), Corinne C. Boggs (D-Louisiana), Margaret M. Heckler (R-Massachusetts), Bella S. Abzug (D-New York), and Shirley Chisholm (D-New York). *Courtesy of White House Photographic Office Collection (Ford Administration), National Archives*

country. In 1974, 2,991 Black people held elective office in forty-five states and the District of Columbia, compared to 1,185 in 1969. The percentage gain was seen in the South (led by Texas, Georgia, and Arkansas) and in the North (in New Jersey and New York). The states with the largest number of elected Black people were Michigan (194), Mississippi (191), New York (174), New Jersey (152), Illinois (152), Arkansas (150), Louisiana (149), Alabama (149), and Ohio (139).[7]

During this time of change, Chisholm fought unfounded attacks on her colleagues, including those in the Republican Party. For example, Edward Brooke continued to be a target as a Black Republican representing Massachusetts, and Chisholm supported him for a number of reasons. He cowrote parts of the Civil Rights Act of 1968, criticized President Nixon, supported legalized abortion and affirmative action, was awarded the Spingarn Medal by the NAACP, was an advocate against housing discrimination, and fought for equality in education. Yet in 1975 an NBC *Today* show host claimed Brooke had "never met another Black person in his life," meaning he "acted White." Chisholm came to his defense and sent a letter to NBC's chairman stating the claim "libels his character and his record in Congress. I know the Senator and I know that he has worked long and hard to improve the education and employment opportunities of Blacks, and indeed, all underprivileged people."[8]

Although Black people and women were increasing their representation in Congress and local elected offices, the 1970s saw the beginnings of a political attack on liberal programs established in the 1960s. President Nixon and conservatives tried to dismantle programs implemented under President Johnson's Great Society that sought to improve education, medical care, and urban development for all Americans—but particularly for the poor, minorities, and the elderly. When programs couldn't be dismantled through legislation, Republican presidents would appoint directors and other leaders who would intentionally weaken an agency's power through cutting funding, staff, or full program implementation. While President Ford wasn't as aggressive as Nixon, this attack on liberal policies and politicians would intensify later under President Reagan. This is the environment in which Chisholm returned to Congress, and it's these events that informed the issues she supported. There were, of course, many topics and causes she championed, but of these myriad issues, there are a few that stand out both because of her level of support and because they were the primary issues of the time for Congress and the presidents in office.

Support of Palestinians and Israel

Chisholm often championed struggles around the world similar to those Black people, women, and the poor faced in the United States. In her view, a struggle for equality anywhere in the world where the United States was directly involved should be addressed. In 1972 she made international news for her views that Palestinians should be included in peace negotiations in the Middle East, and its people should not be forced to live in ghettos because of Israelis' growing control of the region. Speaking on the Palestinian refugees who had left Israel in 1948 and 1967, she stated, "In the midst of rejoicing at the creation of a national homeland for the Jews, the world overlooked the hardship and misery created for the Palestinians. The Palestinians have been forced to live in wretched refugee camps, their homes gone, many of them stateless, living on U.N. relief supplies."[9]

This was a provocative view in light of the United States' open allegiance with Israel. It also stood apart from the position of the Black leaders who drafted a "Gary resolution" in March 1972 during the National Black Political Convention, condemning Israel for the suffering of Palestinians in their struggle for self-determination and alleging Israel committed war crimes in violation of the Geneva Convention. In addressing this and being careful not to take a unilateral position against Israel, Chisholm explained, "While the Gary Convention resolution called for the dismantling of Israel, I have not and will not ever take such a radical and absurd position. I have always and will continue to stand firmly in favor of the right of existence for the State of Israel, and wish to be fully disassociated from the Gary position."[10]

Chisholm's views were shared by the other members of the CBC. On March 21, 1972, the CBC issued a unanimous statement in defense of Israel and in repudiation of the Gary resolution. This was controversial, since the CBC had sponsored and attended the Black National Convention where the stance against Israel was adopted as part of its political platform, called "The Black Agenda." Chairman Louis Stokes stated the CBC's position succinctly:

> As the Black elected officials to the U.S. Congress, we affirm our position that we fully respect the right of the Jewish people to have their own state in their historical national homeland. We vigorously oppose the efforts of any group that would seek to weaken or undermine Israel's right to existence. . . . We pledge our continued support to the concept that Israel has the right to exist in peace as a nation.[11]

That same year Chisholm gave a speech during the Washington, DC, Association of Arab-American University Graduates (AAUG) chapter's annual banquet. Addressing the audience of two hundred, she spoke on the "treadmill of fruitless talks and new outbreaks of violence"[12] characteristic of American relations with Arab nations and people. She tied this to African Americans gaining true equality through a revolution, to applause by the audience: "We are now entering an epoch that could bring the liberation of oppressed and deprived people of the world. There is now a social revolution in progress in this country. Black Power, Red Power, La Causa and La Huelga; and yes, Arab Power—these are a few of the slogans of that revolution."[13]

In October 1973 the majority of the CBC sponsored a House resolution calling for "mutual recognition of Israeli and Palestinian rights," consistent with the caucus's belief that "Israel must recognize that the Palestinian question is essentially a political one. The avoidance of the question of providing for a homeland for displaced Palestinians can only lead to another war," and also that "on the Palestinian side, the notion of replacing Israel with a secular state must be completely abandoned."[14] Chisholm felt the United States and the Soviet Union each needed to stop sending weapons to the region and allow for Israeli-Arab negotiations that included Palestine. She felt the United States had "allowed the Soviet Union to posture as the real friend of the poor in the Middle East. While courageous governments in Libya, Egypt and the Sudan, for example, struggle to maintain their freedom and independence from Soviet influence, we have been sidetracked into forgetting about the Palestine problem and simply engaging in endless maneuvering with the Soviet Union."[15] Leaders of the National Black Political Convention would later soften their stance against Israel as well because it was a strategic ally to the United States in the Middle East and many Americans had both familial and religious ties to Israel.

In 1975 Arab nations attempted to lead an effort to suspend Israel from the UN General Assembly. On August 1 Chisholm and nine others of the then seventeen members of the CBC issued a statement condemning the Arab efforts, concluding, "The U.S. and many other nations will be forced to reassess the basis of their membership in the United Nations."[16] The statement was drafted by Charles Rangel (D-NY) and outlined "the similarities between the position of the people of Israel and that of the oppressed Black peoples of South Africa." Additionally, "as we oppose the business interests whose political influence make U.S. policy toward Africa dependent upon economic rather than moral considerations, we oppose the same interests who seek to weaken our support for Israel because of Arab oil."[17] In addition to the CBC, 243 House members signed a resolution that any successful attempt to remove Israel would lead to the United States reassessing its membership in the United Nations. Israel was not suspended, but tensions in the region continued without a resolution for long-term peace.

Minimum Wages and Welfare Reform

Chisholm continued to fight for equal pay, improved working conditions, and the very existence of the Office of Economic Opportunity, which was formed to ensure employment equality. Once back in Congress full-time, she used her alliances to push legislation, and in 1974 she was vying for congressional support for a bill to extend minimum wage legislation to domestic workers. Facing opposition from members from southern states, she called George Wallace, who helped her gain their support. President Nixon had been an obstacle to gaining success for many programs Chisholm pushed for, including a minimum wage law. When both the House and Senate approved increasing the minimum wage with almost full bipartisan agreement from $1.60 to $2.60 an hour and extended coverage for the first time to domestic workers, the bill was vetoed by Nixon on the basis it would lead to unemployment. He also vetoed a bill that would have provided state-subsidized day care for working parents on the grounds it would promote "communal approaches" to rearing children and "Sovietize America's children."[18] Congress did not have the two-thirds votes required to override his vetoes. This didn't deter Chisholm, and she continued to push for a minimum wage increase, which successfully passed into law through Congress and the president later that same year. As she had done in the New York State Legislature, she ensured the new federal law also applied to domestic workers.

Welfare reform was another part of her agenda. Years earlier, on May 26, 1969, she made a statement in the House while introducing a bill to amend the Public Assistance titles under the Social Security Act. She was clear on why this bill was needed: "Shortsighted and unjust public and private policies have drained the disadvantaged poor into cities, but the weight of social service costs is too great for our cities, or even our States, to carry. Their shrinking tax bases and obsolescent property taxes are inadequate to withstand the strain. As a consequence, the Nation's cities are staggering under the costs of responding to their citizens' needs."[19]

She emphasized that federal support was needed because a Supreme Court ruling had struck down residency requirements for assistance, which would increase poverty levels in northern and western parts of the country, and because current law limited the number of children per family eligible for support. She made an impassioned statement for welfare reform again before the House on February 22, 1973, citing inequality in the country and the failures of the Nixon administration, highlighting how "the inheritors of that caste system are with us today and are still being denied the right to earn a living with dignity and self-respect. They want that right. They need that right. They must have that right with all the privileges that go with it."[20]

Welfare reform under Presidents Nixon and Ford was minimal due to their continued attacks on President Johnson's Great Society program. Nixon did expand the food stamp program from three million to fifteen million people by 1974 through implementing a national eligibility standard and easing enrollment barriers. It was estimated that appropriations increased from $610 million in 1970 to $2.5 billion in 1973. He also signed the Social Security Amendments of 1972, creating Supplemental Security Income under a federal standard rather than disparate state programs to support retirees, the disabled, or the blind. However, Chisholm didn't think this was enough in comparison to how much was spent on the Vietnam War and other initiatives, and she felt the programs started under President Johnson should have been greatly expanded.

Chisholm also fought for increased support for the elderly. The Older Americans Act was originally passed in 1965 as part of President Johnson's Great Society program, recognizing a growing percent of elderly in poverty. The law created the Administration on Aging to support the elderly with funding, meals, counseling, transportation support, health promotion, and a range of other resources. She and other congressional members were concerned over President Nixon's attack on Johnson's Great Society programs, including such programs as Medicare and Medicaid. According to Chisholm, "The predicament of the elderly in our nation must be dramatically brought to the attention of all citizens. It is now apparent that the elderly must be added to the list of groups abandoned by the Nixon Administration. My judgment is based on what I have seen the President do, not on what I have heard him say. The proposed increases in Medicare cost-sharing, the suggested new restrictions on social services, and the threatened veto of the Older Americans Act, are all indicative of the present Administration's disregard for the needs of our senior citizens."[21]

Chisholm was one of the cosponsors of a House resolution (H.R. 3922) proposed as "An Act to amend the Older Americans Act of 1965 to establish certain social services programs for older Americans and to extend the authorizations of appropriations contained in such Act, to prohibit discrimination on the basis of age, and for other purposes." It provided a range of increased support to the elderly themselves and also to the states and nonprofit agencies. It passed in Congress and was signed by President Ford on November 28, 1975.

Ban on Rhodesian Imports

In 1973 Chisholm and the CBC were fighting against the Nixon administration's decision to import chrome from Rhodesia, in line with their express opposition to the United States forging relationships with countries controlled by White suppressive governments. The issue with Rhodesia was part of a larger problem Chisholm and the CBC noted: legislative issues supporting African independence were not being supported by White southern congressmen, particularly those who represented states and districts with large Black populations. During the 1960s, when many African nations successfully fought to end European rule, the White population of Rhodesia established government control to stop a Black-led government from being established. This led to a civil war and international condemnation. The United Nations issued economic sanctions against the White minority regime, so it was concerning the United States would include in the Military Procurement Act of 1971 a section to allow importation of chrome, ferrochrome, and nickel from the country, material used to make stainless steel and castings. This was added by what was known as the Byrd Amendment, as it was sponsored by Senator Harry F. Byrd Jr. of Virginia, a known racist and supporter of segregation in the United States.

Members of Congress, including Chisholm, cosponsored a bill to amend the UN Participation Act of 1945 to stop US dealings with Rhodesia. As Representative Donald M. Fraser from Minnesota put it:

> It has placed the United States in open violation of international law. It has weakened the United Nations and strengthened the position of an oppressive and openly racist regime in Rhodesia. It has contributed to unemployment in the United States. It has eroded our credibility as a Nation which supports self-determination and majority rule. It can endanger the business and investment opportunities for the United States in Black Africa, where we now have some $3 billion in investments. On the other hand some business and industrial interests assert that they need free access to Rhodesian imports.[22]

President Ford would not end the imports from Rhodesia, and by the time he left office, 17 percent of US imports of chrome were from Rhodesia. Chisholm cosponsored additional legislation again in 1975 and 1977 led by Representative Fraser. The House agreed to a resolution she sponsored on March 14, 1977, to end the imports, and President Carter officially repealed the Byrd Amendment that month. The loss of US support significantly degraded the morale and economic standing of Rhodesia's White government. It showed the US no longer supported Rhodesia's racist stance toward its Black population, which led to the country gaining its independence from Britain in April 1980 and changing its name to the Republic of Zimbabwe. Open elections led to the installment of Robert Gabriel Mugabe as prime minister, ending White minority rule.

School Desegregation

Just as she had fought for in the New York State Legislature, in the US Congress Chisholm continued to fight for school desegregation and was frustrated at how there continued to be such resistance across the country. In 1974, twenty years after the Supreme Court ruled in *Brown v. Board of Education*, many schools throughout the country were still segregated because of their failure (unintentional or deliberate) to adhere to federal desegregation mandates. There were continual court battles over this issue, and some states did not fully integrate their school systems until the late 1980s. The Civil Rights Division of the Department of Justice and the NAACP Legal Defense Fund had already won court cases against many individual school districts. These lawsuits were based on counties, cities, and even states that were slow to address how they were going to desegregate schools, or just outright resisted it in defiance of even the Supreme Court. In *Green v. County School Board of New Kent County*, the Supreme Court ruled schools had to formulate plans and steps to ensure a desegregated school system, and in *Alexander v. Holmes County Board of Education* the court's decision mandated the immediate desegregation of public schools in the South.

This was something even President Nixon had aggressively supported. On February 16, 1970, he established the Cabinet Committee on Education as an informal cabinet-level working group to examine how the federal government could assist school districts in immediately desegregating schools. He passed the Emergency School Aid Act to help school districts deal with the costs of desegregation. When he took office in 1968, 68 percent of Black children in the South were attending all-Black schools. By the end of 1970, that rate had fallen to 18.5 percent, and then to 8 percent by 1974. Still, there were areas of segregated schools in the North, and busing failed to remedy the issue.

As previously mentioned, Chisholm considered busing an artificial solution and felt reforms in the housing market were needed to achieve racially diverse neighborhoods that would then lead to integrated schools. She also knew there was too much focus on southern schools at a time when most segregated schools were located in northern states. She spoke on the issue of segregated schools in the US House on May 14, 1974, in a lengthy statement, and the below are excerpts on her concern that very little progress had been made in desegregating schools since the Brown decision and in all parts of the country, not just the South:

> It was two decades ago . . . a full 20 long and difficult years . . . that the Supreme Court in what seemed at the time to be one of its most compelling and momentous decisions, found that racially separate schools were unconstitutional. As I take stock and look around me today and ask, "what is the actual progress we have made in achieving the specific mandate of the Brown decision?" I am saddened and shocked by the answer. The answer is that in spite of courageous efforts—heroic efforts by attorneys in the litigation of desegregation suits and of Black children facing mobs of angry White bigots and their parents brave enough to send those children out to become the psychological and sometimes physical victims of those bigots—in spite of all this, the US Department of Health, Education and Welfare can still report to us that two-thirds of the nation's Black students are still attending schools that are overwhelmingly Black. And this does not include the large numbers of minority children from other non-White backgrounds who remain isolated

from their White counterparts. The latest Federal Government figures show that in 1972 in the 32 northern and western States, 72 percent of non-White pupils attended public schools having a majority of non-Whites. For the nation as a whole, the picture is somewhat brighter, for the south has made some progress. Only 54 percent of the non-White children in southern States are in non-White majority schools. But the national figure for non-White children attending what might be called integrated schools—that is, schools whose enrollment is half White—is still only 36 percent.[23]

Chisholm continued and pointed out school desegregation was tied to a larger issue of inequality in housing and employment that was segregating many parts of the country along economic and racial lines. By this point in her career, the organized groups that fought this issue in the 1960s had disappeared, and Black voters were less politically active, so she called for more political activism in the Black community and among its local leaders.

The problem of segregated schools did not improve. Busing was not successful because parents with the financial means enrolled their children in private schools that were predominantly if not all White. It was further degraded as a strategy when the Supreme Court ruled in *Milliken v. Bradley* in 1974 that school systems did not have to employ steps to end segregated schools unless those schools had actually implemented segregation policies in the past—for instance, by intentionally drawing school district borders along racial lines.[24] As White people migrated to the suburbs and inner cities became predominantly Black and Hispanic, the percentage of segregated schools increased even without such deliberate policies. Segregation also resulted from poor families living in areas separated from middle- and upper-class families. Though the percentage of Black students attending majority White schools nationwide increased from 9 percent in 1954 to over

30 percent in 1970, and to an all-time high of 43.5 percent in 1988, these changes took decades. A report by the Civil Rights Project outlined the following as their key research findings:

- Black and Latino students are an increasingly large percentage of suburban enrollments, particularly in larger metropolitan areas, and they are moving to schools with relatively few White students.
- Latino people are now significantly more segregated than Black people in suburban America.
- Black and Latino students tend to be in schools with a substantial majority of poor children, while White and Asian students typically attend middle-class schools.
- Segregation for Black people is the highest in the Northeast, a region with extremely high district fragmentation.
- Segregation is by far the most common in the central cities of the largest metropolitan areas; the states of New York, Illinois, and California are the worst in terms of isolating Black students.
- California is the state in which Latino students are most segregated.[25]

Although Chisholm continued to fight hard on this issue, it has lasted far beyond her tenure in Congress. Almost forty years later, President Barack Obama issued an executive order on July 25, 2012, entitled White House Initiative on Educational Excellence for African Americans. The result of continued unequal access to education was outlined in the order:

Substantial obstacles to equal educational opportunity still remain in America's educational system. African Americans lack equal access to highly effective teachers and principals, safe schools, and challenging college-preparatory classes, and they disproportionately experience school discipline and referrals to special education. African American student achievement not only lags behind that of their domestic peers by an average of two grade levels, but also behind students in almost every other developed nation. Over a third of African American students do not graduate from high school on time with a regular high school diploma, and only four percent of African American high school graduates interested in college are college-ready across a range of subjects. An even greater number of African American males do not graduate with a regular high school diploma, and African American males also experience disparate rates of incarceration.[26]

Crime

Chisholm particularly focused on juvenile crime during a hearing of the House Committee on Education and Labor in early 1974. Just as she had seen in Brooklyn, juvenile crime across the country was increasing, yet federal and state policies focused on punishment rather than rehabilitation. As a member of the Subcommittee on Equal Opportunities, she raised questions on how federal funds should be used to support "juveniles who have been just cast aside at the bottom of everybody's priorities because they are not a real power group in the sense of the word to be reckoned with in our country in terms of moneys and grants."[27] She addressed youths being forced out of school without any follow-up, today known as the school-to-prison pipeline.

The hearing led to the passage of the Juvenile Justice and Delinquency Prevention Act of 1974. It not only provided funding for states to comply with standards but also removed juveniles from adult correctional facilities. It later created the Office of Juvenile Justice and Delinquency Prevention (OJJDP) in the Department of Justice to support local and state efforts to prevent delinquency and improve the juvenile justice system.

Chisholm's fight for the new law didn't stop once it was passed. At a hearing discussing the progress of the OJJDP in 1982, she was very direct to the chairman of the Subcommittee on Human Resources for the Justice Department about her concerns of personnel in the office being indiscriminately moved and thus weakening its effectiveness by getting rid of experts who had experience working with juveniles. She also felt that this move signaled an end to Congress's focus on reforming the criminal justice system for the protection and rehabilitation of juvenile offenders. She declared:

> We have already seen in some of the other area of bumping going on in other departments that people, square pegs are being put into round holes and vice versa, and that the persons are not necessarily prepared to undertake the kind of responsibility that is very important with respect to certain programs. Of course, we're in a sense, moving people around like pieces on a chess board, and we're not taking into consideration the human factors that are very, very important with respect to the development of certain kinds of programs. I'm deeply concerned about that on the basis of experiences that have gone on in other departments already.[28]

As a testament to Chisholm's focus and dedication, the program and office did survive, and the act has continually been reauthorized in Congress since its passage.

President Jimmy Carter, the CBC, and the Haitian Refugee Crisis

Chisholm won her 1976 reelection with 87.05 percent of the vote against Republican Horace L. Morancic and Conservative Martin S. Shepherd Jr., and the next year was a hopeful one for Democrats with the election of President James "Jimmy" Earl Carter Jr. He supported civil rights as governor of Georgia, and now as president, he placed several Black Americans in high-level positions. Patricia Robert Harris was appointed secretary of the Department of Housing and Urban Development, making her the first African American female presidential cabinet member. Drew S. Days III became the first African American division head in the Department of Justice, serving as assistant attorney general for civil rights. Wade H. McCree was appointed solicitor general, John B. Slaughter as director of the National Science Foundation, Eleanor Holmes Norton as chair of the Equal Employment Opportunity Commission, Franklin Delano Raines as assistant director of the White House Domestic Policy Staff, and Mary Berry as assistant secretary for education in the Department of Health, Education, and Welfare. Later, Clifford Leopold Alexander Jr. became the first African American secretary of the US Army on February 14, 1977, and Andrew Jackson Young Jr. the first African American US ambassador to the United Nations.

Young was sworn in on January 30, 1977, by Supreme Court justice Thurgood Marshall. However, Carter removed Young in 1979 for his meeting with Palestinians, which violated the agreement the US had with Israel. Chisholm and other Black leaders were upset that Young had been forced to resign, which Chisholm characterized as Carter using Young as a scapegoat for the entire "muddled mess in the Middle East."[29] She knew Carter when he was running for the presidency, and Andrew Young arranged for Carter to meet with her in 1975. Young was then in the House and a member of

the CBC. Carter sent the following handwritten note to Young on
July 17, 1975:

> To Andrew Young
> I enjoyed being with you and really appreciate the tremen-
> dous help you gave me on my trip to Washington. Just being
> with you was a fine boost. I was able to see about 50 mem-
> bers of Congress (and their staffs) and the visits were all
> pleasant and productive. My favorite was Shirley Chisholm,
> who gave me some excellent advice and encouragement.
> Tomorrow morning I'm off to Missouri and Illinois.
> Thanks again for your friendship.
> Jimmy[30]

The relationship between Chisholm and President Carter was
cordial, but she would not agree with many of his policies. They met
several times on such issues as helping urban areas continuing to suffer economic and social decay, but President Carter was ineffective in
addressing this issue. In October 1977 he walked through the streets
of Bronx, New York, to observe its condition, but many dismissed his
visit as a mere symbolic gesture. Chisholm's and other Black leaders'
perceptions were confirmed when President Carter concluded policies in
place were enough to deal with urban decay. He felt increasing welfare
spending would somehow work its way to improving the inner cities,
which proved to be wrong. He proposed a host of initiatives such as
strengthening urban economies, expanding job opportunity and job
mobility, promoting fiscal stability, expanding opportunity for those
disadvantaged by discrimination and low income, and encouraging
energy-efficient and environmentally sound urban development pat-
terns.[31] However, these policies predictably failed to produce concrete
results because they were not targeted to specific communities, the initiatives competed with one another for resources, and he didn't forge

strong relationships with Democrats in Congress such as Chisholm and members of the CBC. Chisholm also did not support his policies on funding for education, public funding for abortion, and reducing the military.

One major issue Chisholm and President Carter disagreed on was support for Haitian refugees fleeing poverty, natural disaster, and crime for asylum in the United States. She fought for Haitian refugees and urged President Carter to admit ten thousand people stranded in Florida for seven years just as he had admitted 230,000 boat people from Asia. A statement signed by Chisholm, Senator Richard "Dick" Bernard Stone, Senator Moynihan, William Lehman, Cardiss Collins, Mickey Leland, Fauntroy, John Conyers, Melvin Evans, William Gray, Dellums, Frederick Richmond, Robert Garcia, Vernon Jordan, Sol Chick Chaikin, Bayard Rustin, Andrew Young, and others was sent to President Carter on April 2, 1980. They outlined their commitment to protecting human rights and the Asian refugees admitted but wanted equal treatment for the Haitians fleeing oppression in their home country and migrating to the US since 1972. They called the Haitians America's "boat people" who deserved "humane and equal treatment [that] is fundamental to our laws and other national conscience. Giving them assurance of a haven is long overdue. Also overdue is federal assumption of some responsibility for providing needed social services to the refugees, a responsibility which the churches, Florida and Dade County have borne alone. Exercise of the parole authority would best resolve these critical matters."[32]

They requested President Carter take action before April 21, 1980. Chisholm's congressional office also released a press release headlined POLITICAL REPRESSION CONTINUES IN HAITI:

> The Congressional Black Caucus Task Force on Haitian Refugees today sponsored a briefing for Caucus members and other interested Congressional offices. The primary speakers

at the briefing were Mr. Paul Dejean, Director of the Bureau of the Haitian Cristian [sic] Community of Montreal and Mr. Jean Louis Edouard of Miami.

Messrs. Dejean and Edouard presented evidence of the continued existence of political prisoners in Haiti, including the detention and occasional execution of Haitian asylum claimants deported from the U.S., based on standing orders signed by Luc Desir, a top ranking military official in the Duvalier government.

According to Messrs. Dejean and Edouard the infamous political prison, Fort Dimanche, is, despite Haitian and U.S. government claims to the contrary, still functioning. The Haitian government engaged in a purposeful effort to mislead the OAS Human Rights Commission on prison conditions generally during their August, 1978 mission.

Rep. Chisholm, Chairperson of the CBC Task Force, stated, "In 1976, Amnesty International described Haitian prisons as having 'perhaps the highest mortality rate of any prisons in the world.' It appears that not only do these conditions continue to exist, but the U.S. government is very possibly subject to charges of violation of international law by having forcibly returned Haitian asylum claimants from the U.S. without providing them an opportunity to properly present their claims, thereby condemning them to the horrors of imprisonment, torture and death."

Reiterating the position taken by the Task Force within the last month, Rep. Chisholm declared, "The only moral, humane and practical solution to the plight of these more than 8,000 Haitian refugees in the U.S. is for the president to direct the Attorney General to exercise his authority to grant parole political asylum to those Haitians currently in the U.S. and to ensure that those who come in the future are granted the due process treatment our Constitution prescribes for all regardless of race, class or the ideology of their homeland."

"In the past few months, we have seen an upsurge in support for the Haitian refugees as increasing numbers of our constituents in Florida, labor, civil rights and religious leaders around the country have become informed and have consequently added their voices to those calling for equal justice and asylum for these Black boat people for Haiti." The Congresswoman added, "The CBC Task Force on Haitian Refugees, which includes my colleagues, Reps. Conyers, Evans, Fauntroy, and Leland, will continue to work towards asylum for these people. We also hope that the passage of the Refugee Act, H.R. 2816, will be the beginning of a new attitude in this country toward refugees from all parts of the world."

CONTACT PERSON: BRENDA PILLORS[33]

The Carter administration then allowed in Cuban refugees but not Haitian, leading to accusations the federal government was biased. This led to marches in Miami, New York, and the District of Columbia; hunger strikes; condemnation by the CBC; and hearings by the Senate Judiciary Committee focused on Carter's ambassador for refugee affairs, Victor Palmieri. Chisholm and Fauntroy formed the CBC Task Force on Haitian Refugees to address the issue, renamed the Congressional Task Force on Haiti in 1981 to recognize members outside the CBC and a broader platform addressing US relations with Haiti. Congress passed the Refugee Act to ensure standard and unbiased admissions criteria for refugees as part of special humanitarian concerns. President Carter finally gave the Haitian refugees temporary status for six months in the summer of 1980, and they were not expelled after their temporary status ended. However, within weeks of the law passing over one hundred thousand refugees entered the US from Cuba and Haiti. Amendments to the Refugee Act and dealing with the crisis would continue into the Reagan administration.

Chisholm later criticized the Reagan administration's Task Force on Immigration Policy's plan to implement immigration sanctions. In her view, "Legal sanctions against employers hiring illegal aliens will result in mass forgery of identification documents. Worse, Hispanics and others who might appear foreign will be discriminated against by employers fearing federal investigation."[34] On the Reagan administration's lack of a plan to support refugees, she stated, "At the same time that we are encouraging Southeast Asian countries to accept Indochinese refugees, we are turning away Black refugees from Haiti on the word of a government which has been known to persecute persons who are returned to Haiti."[35] The US has used different policies to address Haitian refugees from those seeking refuge from other countries. Lindskoog explains the US using biased policies: "Policies were specifically designed to deter Haitians from coming in. These policies became the prototype for what became a global system of migrant incarceration."[36]

Chisholm Versus Carter on Education

Chisholm's life was devoted to education, so she opposed President Carter's announcement of creating a new executive department, the Department of Education, by transferring all educational functions from the Department of Health, Education, and Welfare (HEW) and other specific education related functions from other departments such as Defense, Justice, and Agriculture. The remaining HEW functions would be transferred to the Department of Health and Human Services as part of this Department of Education Organization Act. Chisholm was adamant in her opposition to this proposal because she felt it would eliminate the focus on equal educational opportunities for all Americans.

A hearing was held on August 1, 1978, before the Subcommittee on Legislation and National Security of the House Government Operations Committee. Chisholm stated her intent to "forcefully and vociferously voice my opposition to the establishment of a cabinet-level Department of Education. I believe there are many compelling arguments that support opposition to such a proposal; however, I must emphasize that chief among my concerns is the proposed department's obvious inability to ensure equal educational opportunity for all Americans through effective and efficient enforcement of the civil rights laws passed by Congress."[37]

She accused President Carter of playing politics with this new $175.5 billion department, leaving a number of youth service and training programs scattered across the federal government. She highlighted how this move would have particularly negative impacts on minorities due to lost attention on many schools suffering from violence and vandalism and an increased shortage of financial resources. This move would not transfer the civil rights responsibilities from HEW to the new department. In her view,

> Many unknown and unanswered questions associated with transfer of education programs to a new Education Department far outweigh the definitive statements we have received on aspects of this proposed reorganization. The proponents of this bill have yet to articulate a rationale which explains precisely how this new department will expand access to quality instruction for children such as those attending public schools in my district in Brooklyn. Frankly, I am appalled by the rush of some members of Congress to create this department despite the lack of information available about the actual impact of these structural changes. In my opinion, H.R. 13343 represents a $17 bill shot in the dark.[38]

Chisholm felt President Carter's proposal lacked sound planning and would further harm America's public education system with a massive bureaucratic structure that couldn't possibly be effective. She had also supported coalitions to tackle the country's biggest issues such as crime and discrimination and felt this new department would destroy educational coalitions already in place such as labor unions, teachers' groups, parents' groups, and school systems themselves. Further, the new proposal did not have sufficient guarantees that federal laws prohibiting discrimination in education would be enforced.

Republicans in Congress also did not support the president's proposal. They argued he overstepped his constitutional barriers, as education was not an area under his control in the Constitution. Still, the law passed the Senate with a vote of 69 to 22 and the House with a vote of 215 to 201, and President Carter signed the law on October 17, 1979. This move has been controversial ever since, with arguments on the power of the states to have foremost control over public education decisions since they provide the majority of funding. Some argue even today that the federal government can only apply a one-size-fits-all model with education policies, while being too far removed from the day-to-day needs of teachers, students, and parents.

10

CHISHOLM'S FINAL YEARS IN CONGRESS

"Some fine men are in Congress, too few, trying to do a responsible job. But they are surrounded and almost neutralized by a greater number whose instinct is to make a deal before they make a decision."

N 1976 CHISHOLM FACED a strong challenge for reelection from her long-time rival New York City councilman Samuel D. Wright. Born and raised in Bedford-Stuyvesant, he criticized her for being so absent from Congress while she ran for president and argued she had lost her connection with the people of her district because she was focused more on national issues than on those specific to her district. One of his supporters, state senator Vander L. Beatty, said Chisholm had to be defeated or resign. Chisholm countered that her role in Congress had broken new ground: "I can talk with legislators from the South, the West, all over. They view me as a national figure and that makes me more acceptable."[1] During the Democratic primary, she defeated both Wright and Hispanic political activist Luz Vega by winning 53.33 percent of the vote compared to 37.04 percent for Wright and Vega's 9.63 percent. She won the general election by 87.05 percent.

This opposition in no way kept her from being effective. In Congress she served on the Committee on Education and Labor and the Committee on Organization Study and Review, also known as the Hansen Committee. In 1976 her New York delegation supported her running for the chair of the House Democratic Caucus. Representative Herman Badillo, representing the Bronx, nominated her to run against Thomas S. Foley of Washington, then serving as chairman on the Agriculture Committee. Chisholm accepted the nomination, but Foley had already gotten too much support, receiving 194 votes compared to her 96. She then assumed the position of secretary of the Democratic Caucus, later renamed the vice chair, and served from 1977 through 1981. In this position, she was preceded by Patsy Mink (served 1975–1977) and succeeded by Geraldine Ferraro (served 1981–1985). The position was reserved for a female leader until it was eliminated in 1987.

The years 1976–1977 saw renewed congressional interest in the assassinations of the Kennedys and Dr. King. Congressman Henry B. Gonzalez of Texas, who was in President Kennedy's motorcade when he was assassinated in Dallas, Texas, on November 22, 1963, issued a resolution for a seven-member congressional study of political assassinations to reopen the assassination cases and the shooting of George Wallace, arguing there were unanswered questions and a possibility they were connected.

The resolution was cosponsored by many members of the House, including Chisholm, and led to the establishment of the United States House Select Committee on Assassinations in 1976 with Thomas N. Downing as its chair. Gonzalez became chair in 1977 but withdrew the same year due to internal committee struggles. The committee issued its final report in 1979 and concluded Kennedy's death was the

result of a conspiracy by possibly the mafia or Cubans who opposed
Fidel Castro. The Department of Justice stated it found no evidence
of a conspiracy.

At the same time, Chisholm and the CBC continued fighting
for improvements to fair housing laws and amendments to the Fair
Housing Act in 1977, as she explained on the floor of the House on
May 16, 1979:

> The legislation before you carries with it the potential for the
> ultimate realization of the Nation's objectives, set down in
> Title VIII of the Civil Rights Act of 1968, to ensure that all
> Americans have an equal opportunity to get decent housing
> and reside in the neighborhood they choose. Although there
> have been improvements in the area of housing discrimi-
> nation through the fair housing law, for the past 11 years
> Title VIII has remained a statement of goals rather than an
> active force against discrimination in the housing market.
>
> Housing discrimination continues to be an all-pervading
> factor against the evolution of an equal and integrated Amer-
> ican society. All Americans suffer from the ills of segregated
> housing which deny to all of us the opportunity to break
> down prevailing racial barriers and impacts upon the edu-
> cational and employment opportunities of the victims of
> discrimination.
>
> I believe it is important to begin to assess in human
> terms the real impact of the legacy of generations of discrim-
> inatory treatment against certain groups in our society. As
> a professional educator, I know only too well that discrimi-
> nation in our public schools is closely intertwined with the
> evils of bias in the housing market.
>
> Housing discrimination lies at the root of our segre-
> gated educational system. When we survey the patterns of

segregated housing in this country, it is no wonder that much of the Nation's public school system continues to suffer the issues of racial segregation, 25 years after its unconstitutionality was declared.[2]

Their proposed amendment continued to be debated in 1979 and would have granted the Department of Housing and Urban Development the power to hear cases of housing discrimination through administrative law judges. It passed in the House but died in the Senate because it was calendared for later consideration.

While Chisholm continued to fight for issues she had supported her entire political career, she was very disturbed at new attacks on equality in education that began to take place in the courts. The late 1970s began attacks on affirmative action programs nationwide, particularly in higher education, where race was one of several factors considered in college admissions. Affirmative action ensured Black students were given the chance to attend the most prestigious universities after hundreds of years of White colleges and universities excluding minority students. The first case to reach the Supreme Court was *Regents of the University of California v. Bakke* in 1978.[3] The defendant, Allan P. Bakke, was denied admission to the University of California, Davis, School of Medicine because he was too old. However, his lawsuit claimed it was because he was White and the university had a quota that sixteen out of one hundred admissions be set aside for Black students.

While affirmative action had been supported by Presidents Johnson, Nixon, and Ford, the CBC sent a letter to President Carter on September 8, 1977, urging his support of the University of California after the Department of Justice took the position that affirmative action caused discrimination because it excluded others from seats set aside for Black students. As stated in one part of the letter, "We urge the Administration to reconsider and reverse its reported decision to support Allan Bakke's position in this case. As indicated in the memorandum left with you at our meeting on Wednesday, we believe that future generations would come to regard a government brief supporting Bakke's position in the way the nation would now view a government brief in support of segregation in *Brown v. Board of Education*. A government brief opposing affirmative action programs would be a statement to the Black community indicating the government's reversal of its commitment to civil rights in this country."[4]

The Supreme Court ordered the school to admit Bakke but also ruled the use of race as an admissions' criterion was constitutionally permissible as one of several admissions criteria. President Carter praised the ruling as being consistent with the Civil Rights Act of 1964 and the Constitution. In private, leading members of the Carter administration were concerned about the ruling and about challenges to the use of quotas in noneducation areas for different racial and ethnic groups, and the issue of affirmative action was causing a racial divide. Affirmative action programs would remain in place until the election of Ronald Reagan.

Chisholm made history again in 1977 by becoming the second woman and first Black woman to serve on the House Committee on Rules. Before her appointment, the most common committee assignments for women were Education and Labor and Government Operations, followed by Interior and Insular Affairs, Banking and Currency, District of Columbia, Public Works, Post Office and Civil Service, and Veterans Affairs. The House Committee on Rules is highly influential as it sets rules under which any bill regardless of policy area will be presented to the House. When asked why she was chosen by Democratic leadership, she answered, "I think it was because of my ability to work with different groups and because I'm articulate and rather persuasive. So somebody said, 'Let's put the gal on.'"[5] Although she and some colleagues were concerned she would be leaving the Education and Labor committee, Chisholm knew being on the Rules Committee would give her more clout to bring legislation to the floor "having to do with people who've been rather voiceless and powerless."[6]

Also in 1977, the Food Stamp Act was passed—now called the Supplemental Nutrition Assistance Program (SNAP)—another example of how Chisholm remained effective and focused on her key issues. This bipartisan legislation was pushed by Chisholm, McGovern, Bob Dole of Kansas, and Tom Foley. This was an impressive coalition since McGovern and Dole had previously clashed on the issue of the Vietnam War in 1970, creating bad blood between the two. The act permanently amended the Food Stamp Act of 1964 by simplifying eligibility requirements. According to the Department of Agriculture, the law was passed "to strengthen the agricultural economy; to help to achieve a fuller and more effective use of food abundances; to provide for improved levels of nutrition among low-income households through a cooperative Federal-State program of food assistance to be operated through normal channels of trade; and for other purposes."[7] President Jimmy Carter signed the law on September 29, 1977.

Chisholm received another recognition outside Congress when the *World Almanac* announced its list of America's twenty-five most influential women based on a panel of newspaper editors, social commentators, university presidents, and writers. Chisholm was fourth on the list:

> Bella Abzug—Democratic Congresswoman from New York
> Anne Armstrong—U. S. Ambassador to Great Britain
> Helen Gurley Brown—editor of *Cosmopolitan*
> Shirley Chisholm—Democratic Congresswoman from New York
> Joan Ganz Cooney—head of the Children's Television Workshop
> Charlotte Curtis—Op-Ed page editor of the *New York Times*

Betty Ford—First Lady

Betty Friedan—feminist and author

Katherine Graham—publisher of the *Washington Post*

Ella Grasso—Democratic Governor of Connecticut

Nancy Hanks—chairman of the National Endowment for the
    Arts and National Council for the Arts

Lenore Hershey—editor of the *Ladies' Home Journal*

Carla Anderson Hills—secretary of Housing and Urban
    Development

Lady Bird Johnson—former First Lady

Barbara Jordan—Democratic Congresswoman from Texas

Billie Jean King—tennis star

Coretta King—civil rights leader[8]

Unfortunately, earlier that same year, in February 1977, Chisholm and Conrad divorced. She had always maintained a very private life, so she never publicly spoke of the exact reason for their divorce. Rumors of their split began at least a year before, but she refused to let rumors affect her congressional duties. Her only comments were "I think my constituents should only be interested in the job I do for them and the results I get. I don't discuss my personal life and it's not the concern of anyone, but I am running for reelection in November. If I ever do decide to divorce Conrad, it can't be hidden and it must become a matter of public record. As of now, it isn't contemplated."[9] It was then confirmed she and Conrad were selling their $100,000 home in Brooklyn. The stress of being referred to as "Mr. Shirley Chisholm" or "Shirley Chisholm's wife" was a factor in their divorce, along with her busy schedule in Congress. Their divorce was amicable, and he moved to the Virgin Islands. Conrad would live to ninety-three years old and pass away in 2009.

In typical Shirley Chisholm style, she remained undaunted. On July 4, 1977, Chisholm was engaged to businessman and architectural designer Arthur D. Hardwick Jr., who she worked with while serving in the New York State Assembly. The two caused gossip in Washington two years earlier when they attended the Gala White House Party together. Her office responded to questioning, with *Jet* reporting, "Mrs. Chisholm's office explained her husband was not social minded and did not enjoy the hectic life of the nation's capital. So, as a result, Mrs. Chisholm, who normally does not frequent the Washington social circuit, selected an escort for the year's political social finale, Hardwick, a man she has known for years while in the political arena—dating back to the time when she served as the first Black female member of the New York State Assembly."[10]

He was married previously but his first wife passed away. Born in Augusta, Georgia, Hardwick was a World War II veteran and the owner of Sportman's Liquor Store in Buffalo. He was a former New York State legislator at the same time Chisholm was, and the first African American from Erie County to serve as a state legislator. He was elected to the assembly in 1964 representing the 143rd District of Buffalo, where he served two terms before he was defeated by Assemblyman Arthur O. Eve. He served on the Ways and Means, Military Affairs, and Commerce and Industry committees, and was cochairman of the Joint Legislative Committee on Migrant Labor. Hardwick worked with Attorney General Robert Kennedy on exposing the working conditions of migrant workers and wrote the first worker's compensation bill to become law. One of his political focus areas was civic pride. He and Chisholm were among the founders of the New York State Black, Puerto Rican, Hispanic, and Asian Legislative Caucus. Other founding members included Sutton, Bertram Baker, Basil Paterson, William Thompson, and Samuel Wright. The caucus's initial meeting was dubbed "the Midnight Walk" due to it taking place so late at night.[11]

Hardwick and Chisholm were married on Thanksgiving Day, November 26, 1977, in a short ceremony at the Sheraton Inn in

Cheektowaga, New York, followed by a reception of several hundred guests. The marriage ceremony was officiated by her former congressional aide Thaddeus Garrett. Mr. and Mrs. Albert H. Jarrett served as the best man and maid of honor, and wedding arrangements were made by Buffalo City councilman Delmar L. Mitchell. Chisholm was fifty-six, and Hardwick was sixty-one.

By 1978 Chisholm was thinking of leaving Congress at the same time there were forces in New York trying to defeat her reelection. The *Amsterdam News* supported her early career but issued a special preelection editorial called "The Shirley Chisholm Issue" in which the editors stated their intention to hold her accountable to a higher standard of political wisdom or mount an effort to replace her. This came after Chisholm didn't support Bella Abzug in two congressional primary campaigns in the 1970s, nor Sutton in his run for mayor of New York in 1977 but instead Abraham "Abe" Beame, and later Ed Koch over Mario M. Cuomo in the Democratic gubernatorial primary, even though Cuomo had greater Black voter support. She also campaigned against Arthur Eve, an African American, in his failed campaign for mayor of Buffalo. In all these cases, she supported the candidate she felt would best serve the voters rather than toeing the party line.

Andrew Cooper wrote a scathing article in the *Village Voice* on October 30, 1978, titled "Chisholm's Compromise: Politics and the Art of Self-Interest." In part, he stated:

> Those of us who know Shirley Chisholm's politics know that the woman who described herself as "unbought and unbossed" in a 1970 autobiography has in fact made a career of compromise. Since her election to Congress in 1968, she has sat out most of the critical and state races, refusing to back any of the leading Black, female or reform candidates. In this year's Democratic primary, she backed organization candidates

against every Black independent in Brooklyn. In recent years, she supported White candidates for seats created by the courts to increase minority representation.

Her district in central Brooklyn is populated by the largest concentration of Black people in the country, a pivotal resource for the building of Black political power. But Chisholm's brand of politics has divided and contained it.

Her endorsements this September so provoked the *Amsterdam News*, that it departed from its usual news approach to Chisholm and published an extraordinary pre-election editorial entitled: "The Shirley Chisholm Issue." The *Amsterdam News* concluded: "One of the dissonant notes in the campaign has been the role played by Congresswoman Shirley Chisholm. . . . At some point we are all going to have to deal with the troublesome Mrs. Chisholm to make her accountable to a higher standard of political wisdom and loyalty, or to mount a serious effort to remove her. . . . She must lead at a level higher than the petty politics of a single district.[12]

Still, during the 1978 general election, Chisholm received 87.77 percent of the vote against Republican contender Charles Gibbs. In 1980 she won the Democratic primary with 62 percent of votes against Louis Fernandez and David P. Miller, and then the general election with 87.11 percent of votes against Republican Charles Gibbs, Conservative Ralph J. Carrano, and Right to Life candidate Joseph Caesar.

In addition to dissenters in her home district, in Washington, DC, conservatives were pushing policies against almost everything Chisholm had fought for. She was criticized by some Democrats for making compromises with conservative Republicans, such as in her efforts to get minimum wage laws passed, and was accused of having become a part of the political machine. She explained why she needed to work with Republicans as well as Democrats: "I'm a pragmatic politician. We still have to engage in compromises, the highest of all arts. Blacks can't do things on their own, nor can Whites. When you have Black racists and White racists it is very difficult to build bridges between communities. People say: 'Get Whitey!' Oh, it's so frightening."[13]

Muriel Morisey, a constituent caseworker, press secretary, and senior legislative assistant for Chisholm, recalled during a 2017 interview an example of how Chisholm's reaching across the aisle was a successful strategy to get legislation passed:

> Oh, yes, I think it was widely known and understood. She was a great believer in working across the aisle. She was a great believer in finding common ground with Republicans. I remember particularly Congressman Al [Albert Harold] Quie from Minnesota, who I think was probably the ranking Republican on the House Education and Labor Committee, and he had a staff member, a guy named Bob Andringa. Congressman Quie and Congresswoman Chisholm basically told us—it was a particular project, I forget what it was. But they told us to get together and work something out, because if Congressman Quie endorsed it, the Republicans would see it as a good idea. And if Shirley Chisholm endorsed it, the Democrats would see it as a good idea. So they decided our staffs could get together and get it done, because those two endorsements were going to make that thing fly. I can't remember the specific proposal, but I remember working with [Bob Andringa], and all of us, under strict orders: "We're going to make this happen. Congressman Quie and Congresswoman Chisholm are counting on us to get it done."[14]

A double standard at this time was being placed on Chisholm, however. During her presidential run, Abzug didn't endorse her, yet Chisholm was criticized for supporting Moynihan when Abzug ran against him for the Senate. Part of this stemmed from the legacy of his "Moynihan Report." Chisholm responded asking why the media and others didn't question Abzug about her lack of support back in 1972. She argued Black people shouldn't just support Democratic candidates blindly but rather those from any party who would serve their interests. She stressed this in a speech given on June 24, 1978, to the Independent Black Women's Caucus entitled "Vote for the Individual, Not the Political Party: Whatever Is Given to Us Is Almost Always a Trap." She began:

> While I am a Democrat, most of the time—as you all know quite well—I act, think, and vote independently. And though I am a Democrat, I will no longer ask my brothers and sisters to vote for any man or any woman because of the party designation that attaches to their name. In view of the current status of Black folks in this country we need to reevaluate into which basket we put our eggs—and how many. For we have found that the fox gets into the henhouse whenever we look away. Now we've been taken—for granted and otherwise—far too often. We've been drawn in by big words and promises and more promises. Yet the only time we see many of our elected officials is when they come around at election time.[15]

She went on to discuss the history of the two primary political parties, how Black people still faced such issues as unemployment despite presidential campaign promises from both parties, and the need for citizens to drive for change against those trying to deny it. She spoke to the denial of equality for Black people and women even by the Democrat Party. She concluded:

The time has come for us to turn away from the packaging and labeling and sloganisms which have been thrust upon us. The time has come for us to deal with the political fact that there are no longer any substitutes for success and fulfillment in this life. Because it is no longer comforting to believe that failure down here below will be rewarded somehow up above. The time has come . . . and let the word go forth . . . that the sleeping giant has awakened . . . that we are going to flex our muscles . . . that people of color, be they Republicans, Democrats or independent thinkers . . . that we will no longer look only to the label or party designation. We are looking for any party and any person who will work to meet our needs. Because, my friends, for all too many Americans, freedom is just another word for nothing left to lose.[16]

Her rift with some leaders of the women's rights movement was also more apparent by this time in her career because Chisholm was more focused on rights for all women, regardless of color or socioeconomic status. NOW led a boycott of states not ratifying the ERA, specifically boycotting conferences and other major events in an effort to force their hand economically. In April 1978 NOW scheduled its Ninth Annual Women in Law Conference in Atlanta, Georgia. While many NOW leaders did not attend in support of their own boycott, Chisholm did. She attacked the women's rights movement as a "White women's luxury" in response to the protestors outside, given Black women were struggling for survival in raising their children and supporting their families.

The rift between Black and White women continued in 1979 during their annual election of officers when a Black candidate, Sharon Parker, was running for secretary for the second consecutive year and lost. All the leaders selected were White. Aileen Hernandez, who was Black, became NOW's president in 1970 after Betty Friedan stepped down. She had previously stated the organization was not addressing racial inequality, and called for all non-White members to resign after the election in 1979. Many scholars pointed to this fallout between the races as the end of the ERA. This was coupled with the infighting over lesbian women joining, with other members fearing the lesbian members would take control of the movement with their own agenda.

As Chisholm neared the end of her political career, she was already busy planning the next phase of her life. She had several outside interests, such as being the only female member on the initial board of advisers of *Black Enterprise* magazine, which launched in August 1970. Other board members included William Hudgins (president of Freedom National Bank), Julian Bond, Edward Brooke, Charles Evers (mayor of Fayette, Mississippi), Thomas A. Johnson (staff writer for the *New York Times*), Henry Parks (chairman of the board at H. G. Parks), and John Robert Lewis. The goal of the board members and *Black Enterprise* founder and president Earl G. Graves was to build Black wealth and give Black Americans more economic power.

She was also active with her passion of speaking with students. Concerned about the apathy of young people in getting involved in social and political movements, she recalled youth activism during the 1960s in the civil rights and women's movements, and against Vietnam. She recognized this apathy developing after the assassination of such leaders as Dr. King and the Kennedys, the political parties ignoring youth concerns, and the shift to conservative policies beginning under President Nixon. Still, she expressed the need for youth activism during her commencement address to the graduating class of 1981 at Mount Holyoke College in South Hadley, Massachusetts, on May 24, 1981:

> I ask that you ponder just how you will wear the mantle of responsibility which accompanies the achievements we are celebrating here today. You will do your best when you set the highest standards and goals and then make every effort

to do what the Greek philosophers admonished us to do centuries ago. That is to tame the savageness of all men and to make gentle the life of the world. Use the knowledge and the God-given intelligence you have to learn as much as you can about what is going on, not just in this country but throughout the world. Ask questions, demand answers, do not just tend your garden, collect your paycheck, bolt the door and deplore what you see on television.[17]

When President Carter ran for reelection in 1980, Chisholm, Steinem, and Abzug were among those who supported his Democratic primary opponent, Ted Kennedy of Massachusetts. The CBC also declined to support Carter, with Cardiss Collins saying, "He has nothing to say,"[18] which symbolized Chisholm and others' feeling that he had no solid political agenda to appeal to voters and his term as president was a series of dismal failures. This also reflected how the Black community felt Carter had disappointed them. Kennedy sought to capitalize on the atmosphere of discontent, as well as the popularity of his brothers John and Robert. Carter won thirty-six states during the Democratic Convention and gained 51 percent of primary votes, compared to twelve states for Kennedy and 37 percent of votes. This was partly thanks to endorsements by some Black mayors and the Reverend Dr. Martin Luther King Sr. During the general election Carter gained only 49 electoral votes, compared to 489 for Ronald Reagan.

President Reagan came into office in January 1981. He appointed just one African American cabinet member, Samuel R. Pierce Jr., as secretary of the Department of Housing and Urban Development. Pierce was called "Silent Sam" on any issues related to African Americans. Reagan appointed no women to his cabinet. He did place Clarence M. Pendleton as chair of the US Civil Rights Commission. Pendleton was African American but called affirmative action "immoral" and opposed equal pay for men and women. Reagan packed his cabinet and other high-level government positions with conservatives. The few Black people appointed were unknown to Black Americans and did not support their issues. Reagan's conservative appointments to the Supreme Court included William Rehnquist's promotion to chief justice in 1986, Sandra Day O'Connor (the first woman to serve on the court) in 1981, and Antonin Scalia in 1986. His conservative stance was labeled racist when Reagan became the only president since Andrew Jackson to veto a civil rights act, on March 16, 1988, though his veto was overridden by Congress.

Chisholm was concerned about the lack of diversity in President Reagan's cabinet, which couldn't possibly address the needs of Black Americans, women, and young people. As she once explained, "Our government, if [it] indeed is a democratic form of government, must be representative of the different segments of the American society. I feel that the cabinet and the department heads of this country must have women, must have Blacks, must have Indians, must have younger people, and not be completely and totally controlled constantly by White males."[19]

The CBC shared her concerns over the Reagan presidency. In 1982 they stated, "At the 1981 CBC Dinner Weekend, we highlighted the opening of the Reagan Era, an era which we warned would bring America and the Black community record unemployment, record business failures and an unprecedented assault on programs that have improved the quality of life for Black Americans. With unemployment among Black workers now at record levels of 18.5 percent overall and 60 percent among our teenagers, those predictions have come to pass."[20]

One of President Reagan's earliest actions in office was to lift a restriction on tax exemptions implemented under President Nixon to private schools practicing segregation. This allowed these schools to pay no federal, unemployment, or social security taxes. Chisholm spoke on her despair over this and other, similar policies while attending services memorializing Dr. King in Richmond, Virginia, in January 1982: "The dreams of the 60's and 70's have turned into the shrinking reality of the 80's. . . . We [Black people] must realize that the gains made during the past 15 years are being taken away one by one."[21] President Reagan also criticized affirmative action as reverse discrimination against White people.

Democrats maintained diminished control of the House, but Republicans gained control of the Senate in 1981 for the first time since 1953. One of the last pieces of legislation Chisholm unsuccessfully tried to get passed was protection for agricultural migrant workers. Dubbed the Farmworkers Bill of Rights, the bill sought to guarantee unemployment insurance, workers compensation, social security coverage, overtime pay, health insurance, drinking and washing water in the field, toilet facilities, health and safety rights, and a range of other protections.

After this, in February 1982 Chisholm announced she would not seek reelection. She told a reporter for the *Christian Science Monitor*, "Shirley Chisholm would like to have a little life of her own."[22] She revealed her husband had also been in an automobile accident on April 23, 1981, causing him to spend a year and a half in the hospital, nine months in a wheelchair, and six months in therapy. She later explained, "I had been so consumed by my life in politics. I had no time for privacy, no time for my husband, no time to play my beautiful grand piano. After he recovered, I decided to make some changes in my life. I truly believe God had a message for me."[23]

The official press release from Chisholm's congressional office announcing her retirement was written by her press secretary Bob Frishman and dated February 11, 1982:

CHISHOLM TO LEAVE CONGRESS
Congresswoman Shirley Chisholm, seven-term Democrat from Brooklyn, today issued the following statement about her plans for the future.

"I have decided not to seek reelection to the United States House of Representatives.

From the time I first became active in politics twenty-three years ago, I vowed that the remainder of my productive and creative life would not be consumed by politics. I promised myself that I would pursue other careers, that I would eventually return to a more private existence, and that my energy and spirit would not stay chained to the political millstone beyond the time that I still had the strength and wisdom to break those chains.

Today, in good health at age fifty-seven, my energy remains high and my spirit needs new outlets. It would be unfair to myself, and it would be wrong to the people I represent, if I were to remain at a job that for me has become tedious and frustrating.

It has become increasingly difficult to carry the tragic messages back from Washington to the jobless, homeless and hopeless Brooklynites. How can I, as a member of a political and racial minority in today's Congress, hope to put an end to poverty, unemployment and discrimination in Brooklyn and throughout this nation in the face of an administration that is canceling the past fifty years of human progress in America. A stimulative compassionate role for the federal government is being replaced by a philosophy of individualistic selfishness which scorns or ignores the disadvantaged. The tree of hope, planted by Franklin Roosevelt and nourished over the years with investments in our people and in our future, is now withering from icy winds of callousness, militarism and despair.

My public service and leadership role for over twenty years in New York's 12th Congressional District and on the national level has been rewarding and difficult. I have been willing to stand on the cutting edge of public opinion at times. I have fought for Blacks and Whites, and in the process have met both White and Black racists. Indeed it has been a thorny path, but at this point in my life, I can say that I am proud of my achievements. My efforts on behalf of Black colleges, compensatory education, minimum wage for domestics, numerous amendments to bills affecting the Indians, the Haitians, and the poor have all been a part of my philosophy of equitability and opportunity for all people.

I am proud of my role as a leader and a symbol. I am proud of all my friends and supporters in the nation who have never stopped being my friends and supporters. And I am proud of my country, honored to have had the opportunity to serve, and still confident that the bright sun of full equality and justice will someday shine on everyone living under our flag.

It has been said that 'One of the greatest delusions in the world is the hope that the evils of this world can be cured by legislation.' I agree, and I know that in most cases legislation merely reflects the state of mind of the citizenry. By writing, by teaching, by lecturing and by traveling around this land, I hope to help create a new national state of mind that demands change for the better.

This is not my funeral, nor is it my retirement. It is a transitory phase in my life. Out of the political stranglehold, and on my own terms, I will continue to fight the 'good fight.' Freed from the wheel-spinning confines of the Congressional cloisters, I will make even louder appeals to the good sense and conscience of the American people."[24]

Chisholm later admitted to a reporter she was leaving due to the new political climate: "We have an Administration that is not responsive to our constituency. The constituency is going to be more voluble and demanding, and I find myself in a position where I can't help them."[25] Her inability to help was driven by the Reagan administration and conservative Republican control of Congress, which diminished her ability to pass any legislation for issues she had long fought for. But Chisholm promised, "My voice will still be heard, but not as an elected official" and "this is not a funeral, politically."[26]

For her achievements in Congress, the CBC awarded Chisholm the prestigious William L. Dawson Award in 1982, as well as for her unique leadership in the development of legislation addressing the needs of minorities in the United States:

> For her outstanding legislative achievements, the Congressional Black Caucus Foundation is presenting the 1982 Dawson Award to Congresswoman Shirley A. Chisholm.
>
> Mrs. Chisholm was first elected in 1968 to the 91st Congress of the United States. She brought with her an interest in and a commitment to the provision of a quality education for all Americans. In keeping with this commitment, she worked to amend the Elementary and Secondary Education Act of 1978 to establish the Bio-Medical Services Program. Today, this program supports 12 projects nationally which encourage junior high school students to pursue careers in the medical profession.
>
> In 1980, Congresswoman Chisholm responded to the financial needs of Black Colleges and Universities by introducing her own Higher Education legislation. Unlike the Education and Labor Committee bill, Mrs. Chisholm's bill provided "Challenge Grants" to Black, higher educational institutions to allow the establishment of their own endowment funds. Although her entire bill was not passed by the Congress, the "Challenge Grant" component was adopted

and provides an important mechanism for financial assistance to Black institutions.

Mrs. Chisholm has similarly been a major spokesperson and effective legislator in support of: Title IX of the 1982 Education Amendments, which guarantees sex equity in education; juvenile delinquents, by establishing both the Alternative Education and Serious Youth Offenders Special Emphasis Programs within the Office of Juvenile Justice and Delinquent Prevention; and domestic workers by helping to establish a national minimum wage.

Most recently, Congresswoman Chisholm's legislative efforts have also included initiatives in the foreign policy area. As Chair of the Congressional Black Caucus Task Force on Haitian Refugees, Mrs. Chisholm brought national attention to the plight of Haitians seeking political asylum in the United States. The Congresswoman speaking on behalf of the Caucus, testified before the House Judiciary Subcommittee on Immigration, Refugees and International Law on the blatant discriminatory treatment received by Haitian asylum applicants. The Administration, in response to charges of racist refugee policies, finally agreed to change their policy of quick expulsion for Haitians and allow them to remain in this Country as part of the Cuban-Haitian entrant program. Despite this significant change in policy, Mrs. Chisholm continues to press for full recognition of Haitians as political refugees and federal reimbursement to states and localities that have been impacted by the influx of Haitians and Cubans. She has authored legislation, H.R. 3602 which would grant refugee status to Cubans and Haitians and H.R. 6071 which would create an independent asylum review board.

Congresswoman Chisholm's legislative contributions as the Representative of the 12th Congressional District in the

State of New York have been an asset to the Congress and the Nation during her years of service. It is in recognition of these and other legislative achievements that we honor her with this award.[27]

She gave an interview in June 1982 to Jacqueline Trescott of the *Washington Post* discussing her feelings on leaving Congress and political life. When asked about some who felt she was deserting the impoverished and others she had fought for, she spoke of the great demands of having constituents with such diverse needs while having so little time for her own well-being, as some constituents acted as if her entire life belonged to politics:

> One 90-year-old man came in here, and said, "Mrs. Chisholm, you have to recognize that the only thing that belongs to you is your body, you belong to America." I jokingly said I am not too sure my body belongs to me at this point. . . . When people say, "you are deserting me," that makes me tremble.[28]

When asked if she was leaving feeling battered and broken, she responded:

> Broken, no, not at all. I am leaving saddened, somewhat saddened, because I didn't realize fully how people felt about me legislatively. People interpret because I am leaving at a time when, I guess, voices like mine are needed more than ever, that I have selected the wrong time to leave, never taking into account that I have always indicated that I do not want to spend my entire time in the political arena. . . . I am not mad, I am not sad. It's very difficult. . . . This is not my funeral. It is a transitional phase.

Chisholm was asked about any regrets on past decisions, and particularly on her support for Rockefeller and her visit to Wallace when he was in the hospital. She responded, "I don't take one incident of a person's total life and hang the person with it forever." She added Rockefeller supported her when she was in the New York Assembly, outweighing any reservations she had about him. On her visit to Wallace, she explained, "Just like George Wallace standing in the door of the University of Alabama preventing Black young people from attending. . . . I went to the hospital when he was shot in 1972, and later he was the man who helped get the votes on minimum wages for Black women. . . . I believe there is good in everybody, maybe that's a weakness I have."[29]

Later in life, when Chisholm was asked why she left Congress, she was clear in just one word: "Reagan!" She had seen programs she cared about deteriorating or being completely eliminated via the maneuverings and decisions of his administration. The Reagan administration attacked welfare programs, affirmative action, civil rights, voting rights, and women's rights. Chisholm was not the only Black leader disillusioned. Supreme Court justice Thurgood Marshall retired in 1991, and when asked if he would have accepted a Supreme Court appointment from Reagan, Marshall replied, "I wouldn't do the job of a dogcatcher for Ronald Reagan."[30]

It is very ironic that once Reagan left office he was shocked and upset he was seen as being "on the other side" of the civil rights movement. However, his personal views speak to his position. In October 1971 as governor of California he made a call to President Nixon to voice his concern with African countries opposing US approval of the United Nations formally recognizing the People's Republic of China. During this call to voice his anger he stated, "To see those, those monkeys from those African countries—damn them, they're still uncomfortable wearing shoes!" Nixon replied with a huge laugh.[31]

Chisholm gave an interview in November 1992 in which she expressed her frustration with both the male-dominated power structure of Capitol Hill as well the policies of the Reagan administration. She discussed the "scarcity of people in power who are sensitive to the needs, hopes, and aspirations of the various segments of our multifaceted society. We have become too plastic; we have become too theoretical. . . . We need individuals who are compassionate, concerned, committed."[32]

After she retired from Congress, Major R. Owens won Chisholm's Twelfth Congressional District seat, and served the Eleventh and Twelfth Districts until 2007. Thomas Fortune, Chisholm's 1968 campaign manager, led Owens's campaign. Owens retired at the end of his term in January 2007, and the district was represented by Nydia Margarita Velázquez Serrano and then Carolyn Bosher Maloney (as of 2020). The district including Bedford-Stuyvesant was remapped in 1993 to be part of the district representing parts of Brooklyn, Manhattan, and Queens. Bedford-Stuyvesant, as of 2021, was part of the Eighth Congressional District represented by Hakeem Sekou Jeffries, and he was proceeded by Edolphus "Ed" Towns Jr.

When Chisholm entered Congress in January 1969, she was among ten African American members in the US House and Senate. The year after she retired that number had doubled to twenty-two. Those in 1983 included four who were also in Congress in 1969: William Lacy Clay Sr., John Conyers Jr., Augustus Freeman "Gus" Hawkins, and Louis Stokes.

11

LIFE AFTER CONGRESS

"What we will do is to do our best deed, think our best thought, looking only to God—whoever your God is—and to your consciences for approval."

HISHOLM'S LIFE AFTER CONGRESS continued to reflect her dedication to education and fighting for equality. She had amassed a lifetime of wisdom and experiences that she wanted to share with young people, to both educate them and motivate them to be active in their communities. Since she had just left Congress, some of her lectures and speeches served as reflections and warnings on where the country was moving in order to motivate students on the importance of being socially and politically active. One of her constant warnings was on the dangers of complacency. Chisholm was not complacent after retiring from Congress but would continue fighting for national as well as international equal rights.

She immediately sought to reenter the field of education, using her extensive leadership skills. She had made enemies over her political career, and they were vindictive once she left Congress. Medgar Evers

College of the City University of New York was founded in 1970 in Brooklyn, New York, and Chisholm wanted to be its president. Her political opponents blocked her from consideration. The position was vacant when she retired, as the president of the college in 1982 was moved to another college after students took over his office in protest of his poor performance. It was remarkable Chisholm wasn't appointed given she was one of the leading politicians involved in the college being founded, along with state senator William Thompson and Assemblymen Sam Wright and Waldaba Stewart.

In 1978 New York mayor Ed Koch asked her if she would consider being chancellor of the New York City Public Schools. Albert Shanker, president of the American Federation of Teachers and New York United Federation of Teachers, threatened to veto Koch's education bills if he appointed her. Shanker was still upset over Chisholm's support of Black parents during the Ocean Hill–Brownsville governing board dispute, and her other enemies included the most progressive White and Black people. Chisholm withdrew her candidacy.

She moved to Williamsville, New York (a suburb of Buffalo), and taught at Mount Holyoke College in Massachusetts from 1983 until 1987. She was named professor to the prestigious Purington Chair at the college, a post held earlier by the likes of poet W. H. Auden, Nobel Laureate Bertrand Russell, and writer-librarian Arna Bontemps. Chisholm taught a variety of courses focusing on minorities and women in politics, while also giving speeches at college campuses around the country. She taught the students how to be social activists and on the need for White and Black students to work together. Some of her lectures focused on fighting against polarization and hostility, and she cautioned, "If you don't accept others who are different it means nothing that you've learned calculus."[1]

One of her students spoke on what it was like being taught by Chisholm, remembering how she took a 4:00 AM flight from New York to teach an 8:35 AM class:

She would show up every day in a suit, made up, ready to go, on task. After maybe the second week of us showing up in our sweats, I remember there being a change, a conscious decision to get up to put on real clothes, out of respect. She made a commitment to us, and that made an impact on how we showed up for her. She was so well-respected. She listened, and that's a trait we don't often find in our leaders, unfortunately.[2]

She had spoken at over 150 colleges and universities over the twenty previous years. In speaking on her teaching students, Chisholm explained, "I think it's important for them to learn to have different viewpoints and different approaches without feeling intimidated by a professor."[3] In reflecting on how she spoke on campuses around the country, she laughed at how she would be approached by politicians thinking she was up to something when she visited their districts or states. She jokingly recalled one southern legislator who approached her. In an imitated southern drawl, she said he asked her, "Chisholm, I saw in my newspapers that you were down in my state recently. What are you up to?" She simply replied, "Why, I'm just teaching these days."[4] When she wasn't teaching or lecturing, she spent time with Hardwick and read biographies in her extensive home library.

One of her speeches to students was given at Greenfield High School in Greenfield, Massachusetts, on October 3, 1983. She spoke on the history of equality in the United States, how some in the country were trying to revive racial discrimination by pulling what she described as the "lid off the coffin" in reviving old racist tactics, and was blunt about her disdain of the conservative policies of President Reagan. She also warned the audience of the dangers of complacency in being active in social and political change, which contributed to the ills of Reagan's presidency:

I don't blame our president at all. I really don't. The reason I don't blame our president is because America has gone to sleep. We are a bunch of Rip Van Winkles, quiescent. Everybody is quiet, only wringing their hands and wondering what is going to happen to us in the future. Where is our energy? Where is our spirit? In the 60s and the 70s in this country, the people rallied, the people moved. This country is the only country on the face of the planet called Earth where people can redress their grievances without any real fear of repercussions.[5]

One of the efforts Chisholm had helped fight for while in Congress that came to fruition in 1983 was the observance of Dr. Martin Luther King Jr.'s birthday as a federal holiday. The effort to have a federal holiday was spearheaded by the National Citizens Committee formed in 1968 by Howard Bennett. Four days after Dr. King was assassinated in 1968, Representative Conyers and members of the CBC introduced a bill for a King holiday. It did not initially pass, and six million people signed a petition in 1970 to recognize Dr. King's birthday. Conyers and Chisholm submitted legislation every year for the next fifteen years from 1968 until it was finally made a holiday by President Reagan on November 3, 1983, with Coretta Scott King and members of the CBC in attendance at the signing ceremony.

It was well known that President Reagan really didn't support the holiday, and he once told a conservative backer, "I have the reservations you have but there the perception of too many people is based on an image, not reality."[6] In reality, he was concerned that if he had not signed the law, his veto would have been overridden in Congress, as the bill had passed with broad bipartisan support. The passage of the legislation was also pushed by a march on the Lincoln Memorial on August 27, 1983, to commemorate the twentieth anniversary of King's March on Washington, with more than two hundred thousand attendees. Dr. King's holiday was first nationally recognized on January 20, 1986.

On June 4, 1984, Chisholm gave the commencement address at the Massachusetts Institute of Technology in Cambridge, Massachusetts. In her speech she not only spoke on past issues she'd fought for, such as minority and women's equality, but also current issues that concerned her, such as President Reagan's policies that were supporting the wealthy at the expense of the rest the county:

> I must say to you that fewer events in my life have been more difficult for me to watch than the Reagan's administration's replacement of compassionate egalitarian government, with government pledged to greed and selfishness and the ascendancy of the rich and the advantaged in this nation, and that is all that I had better say on that subject [applause] because once I get started it might be time to order a pizza and settle in for a tirade. I will spare you, however. I am sure that my opposition to the President's policies is no secret to anyone here.[7]

True to her word, Chisholm remained active in politics by establishing coalitions and supporting political candidates as she had done while in Congress. She helped form the National Black Women's Political Caucus (NBWPC; originally called the National Political Congress of Black Women) in 1984 along with Cynthia Delores Tucker. The original fifty members included leading women in the fields of politics, journalism, labor, fraternal organizations, education and civil rights. Tucker is an icon of the civil rights movement and is well known for her fight against profane and misogynistic language in hip-hop and rap music in the 1990s. She was the first female African American secretary of state in the nation, serving the Commonwealth of Pennsylvania from 1971 to 1977.

The caucus's founding was historically significant when established, given Geraldine Ferraro was then running as the Democratic vice presidential candidate alongside presidential candidate Walter Mondale (noteworthy, Chisholm came in second as the Democratic vice presidential nominee to Ferraro during the Democratic National Convention, even though she wasn't running or seeking the position).

Chisholm also campaigned for Reverend Jesse Jackson's presidential nomination in 1984 and 1988, and the NBWPC was actually formed out of the frustration Black women experienced trying to support either Mondale or Jesse Jackson during their runs for the presidency. Organizations such as NOW held closed-door sessions where they supported Mondale and Ferraro without considering Jackson, prompting Chisholm to act because she had experienced the results of backroom dealmaking when she ran for president. In 1988 the NBWPC had grown to over eight thousand members across thirty-six states, and they sent a delegation of one hundred women to the 1988 Democratic National Convention to demand civil rights and improvements to social programs.

Chisholm was a speaker at the Democratic convention, and outlined how Jackson was the only candidate who addressed grassroots issues such as women's rights. She touted him as the voice of the poor, disenchanted, and disillusioned, just as she was when in office. Jackson did not win either race, but his showing was impressive. He surprised detractors in 1984 when he came in third place after the Democratic primaries behind Senator Gary Hart and the winner, Carter's former vice president, Walter Mondale. In 1988 he was more well known, better organized, and better financed. Michael S. Dukakis of Massachusetts won the Democratic Party nomination with 1,792 delegates, but Jackson did receive 1,023 compared to 374 for Albert Arnold "Al" Gore Jr.

Chisholm's husband, Arthur, died on August 17, 1986. She continued to teach until the next year, focusing her life on speaking and giving interviews, while remaining politically active after getting Hard-wick's home, personal effects, and other affairs finalized.

In 1988 she voiced her concerns about candidates in the presidential campaign race. Televangelist Pat Robertson was seeking the Republican Party nominee against contenders George H. W. Bush and Senator Bob Dole. Robertson was a conservative leader of the religious right whose views were particularly damaging to minorities and women. Of concern to many was his growing popularity, as even Bush trailed him in the Iowa caucus. Chisholm was stern in her judgment of Robertson, calling his campaign "astute, but frightening [because it] appeals to people who do not care about issues, only about bringing morality back to America. These people believe America has become another Sodom and Gomorrah, and that's why we have AIDS, teen pregnancy, and dropouts. They don't care about his stance on nuclear weapons, they want a Messiah."[8]

She discussed the issues of racism tied to his popularity: "Racism is imbedded in this country's bloodstream. None of the minorities have come here with a brass spoon in their mouths, but the blood and the sweat of the Black people has been in the soil of this country longer than any other minority."[9] Bush won the Republican primary by 67.9 percent, compared to 19.2 percent for Dole and only 9 percent for Robertson. Bush defeated Dukakis in the general election with 53.4 percent of the popular vote and 426 of the 537 electoral votes.

Chisholm was very concerned about the rise of conservatism that began in the 1970s and exploded in the 1980s, as evidenced by the popularity of Reagan and Robertson. Driven by a Republican agenda of a smaller federal government and reducing taxes on the wealthy, such leaders were trying to erase over twenty years of racial and gender equality policies.

At this same time, Chisholm was also still focused on abortion. In 1990 African American Women for Reproductive Freedom was formed to support abortion rights, and one of its focus areas was eliminating the stigma of abortion faced by Black women. A year before the group was officially formed, sixteen Black women and one man released a declaration brochure outlining their support for pro-choice and equal access to abortions. Entitled "African-American Women Are for Reproductive Freedom," it was signed by Chisholm as a member of the National Political Congress of Black Women.

Chisholm retired to Palm Coast, Florida, in 1991 and later moved to Halifax Plantation in Ormond Beach, Florida, in 2003 to live next door to her best friends. She was even godmother to their daughter, Maria Bosley. She was a part-time lecturer and wrote op-ed pieces as well as speeches for some members of Congress, but she would never reveal who they were. In 1991 she was the commencement speaker at East Stroudsburg University (ESU) in Pennsylvania, where she was conferred their first-ever honorary doctorate, and an annual ESU student award was created in her honor.

She had received other honorary degrees for her life's work. In 1974 she was awarded an honorary doctor of laws degree by Aquinas College and was their commencement speaker, and the very next year she was awarded an honorary doctor of laws degree from Smith College. In 1996 she received another honorary doctor of laws degree from Stetson University, in Deland, Florida, and her thirty-eighth honorary degree in 1999 from San Diego State University College of Health and Human Services. She received her fortieth from Rutgers University in 2002. Over her life she received honorary doctorate degrees from colleges and universities all over the world.

She gave a speech addressing NOW on July 11, 1991, in Washington, DC, during their Twentieth Anniversary Gala. This event celebrated the history of the caucus and its founders and outlined their agenda for the future. Each founding member spoke on their experiences with founding the caucus. Chisholm spoke on the daring of creating the organization so women could control their destinies, and the challenges she personally faced in politics.

She told the story of one of her first experiences in Congress with the Georgia congressman who was upset she sat at his delegation's table as a lesson for young women and men to understand "the depths of discrimination and feeling against a person at that time who is female and Black and dared to move out."[10] She saluted her fellow founders seated on the stage with her: "To the best of our abilities, in spite of all the adversities, in spite of the snide remarks, in spite of the vile epithets that were uttered at us from time to time, we knew that we were about the business of attempting to bequeath a legacy for future generations to come. And you are here today to carry on that legacy."[11] Other speakers included Linda Ellerbee, Patricia P. Bailey, Sharon Pratt Dixon Kelly, Mary Louise Smith, Jill Ruckelshaus, Betty Friedan, Gloria Steinem, Patsy Mink, Bella Abzug, Geraldine Ferraro, and Maxine Waters.

Chisholm was still widely respected in politics after she retired, and in 1993 President Bill Clinton offered Chisholm the post of ambassador to Jamaica, stating in his announcement, "Shirley Chisholm is a true pioneer of American politics, whose passion for social justice is unparalleled. I am honored that she will be my Ambassador to Jamaica, and confident that she will do an outstanding job in that position."[12] She was honored to be nominated and met with President Clinton at the White House. However, she declined due to ill health. The White House Office of the Press Secretary issued another press release on October 13, 1993:

> With regret, Mrs. Shirley Chisholm has asked that her name be withdrawn as President Clinton's prospective nominee for the position of Ambassador to Jamaica. Mrs. Chisholm has been suffering a progressive eye disorder in recent months which has significantly affected her vision. Her concern over this problem and its potential effect on her ability to carry out the normal duties of the U.S. Ambassador in Jamaica

has led her to conclude that her interest and those of the U.S. Government would be best served by the withdrawal of her candidacy.[13]

Also in 1993 Chisholm was recognized with the honor of being inducted into the National Women's Hall of Fame:

Shirley Chisholm, the first Black woman elected to the U.S. Congress, was a passionate and effective advocate for the needs of minorities, women and children. Chisholm changed the nation's perception about the capabilities of women and Black Americans.

A New York City educator and child care manager, Chisholm saw the problems of the poor every day, and in the 1950s this led her to run for and win a seat in the New York State Legislature. In 1968, she was elected to Congress from the new 12th District. There she supported improved employment and education programs, expansion of day care, income support and other programs to improve inner city life and opportunity. She advocated for the end of the military draft and reduced defense spending. In 1970, she published her first book, *Unbossed and Unbought*. She served in Congress until 1982 and in 1972 entered several Democratic presidential primaries, receiving 151 delegate votes for the presidential nomination. Her second book, *The Good Fight*, was published in 1973.

She continued to be recognized for her legislative prowess in those years, when powerful committee assignments were not available to women and persons of color. Her legacy is alive at the Shirley Chisholm Center for Research on Women at Brooklyn College.[14]

After these accolades and after the turn of the century, Chisholm's accomplishments remained popular. During an interview with *PBS* talk show host Tavis Smiley in 2003, he asked her what was the greater obstacle during her political career, being Black or a woman. She replied, "I met far more discrimination being a woman than being Black when I moved out into the political arena. . . . All kinds of meetings and all kinds of groups got together in order to stop me from moving out [into politics]. Because I was very outspoken and very articulate and didn't take guff off anybody."[15]

Shortly after this interview, Filmmaker Shola Lynch completed an award-winning documentary chronicling Chisholm's campaign for the presidency. Called *Chisholm '72: Unbought and Unbossed*, it screened at the Sundance Film Festival in 2004, was shown at the 2004 Democratic National Convention, and aired on PBS stations in 2005. It won a Peabody Award "for documenting an historic presidential campaign and reminding us what sort of candidates we have a right to demand."[16]

In the film, Lynch asked Chisholm how she wanted to be remembered. She replied:

> When I die, I want to be remembered as a woman who lived in the twentieth century and who dared to be a catalyst of change. I don't want to be remembered as the first Black woman who went to Congress. And I don't even want to be remembered as the first woman who happened to be Black to make a bid for the Presidency. I want to be remembered as a woman who fought for change in the twentieth century. That's what I want.[17]

Shirley Chisholm died on New Year's Day 2005 in Ormond Beach, Florida, at the age of eighty. She had been ill and suffered from several strokes. She was buried at Forest Lawn Cemetery's Birchwood Mausoleum in Buffalo, New York, with her late husband, Arthur. The inscription on her crypt reads "Unbought and Unbossed." She was survived by her sister, Muriel.

William "Bill" R. Howard, her longtime campaign treasurer, was the spokesperson who announced her death, and he expressed his sentiments stating, "Anyone that came in contact with her, they had a feeling of a careness, and they felt that she was very much a part of each individual as she represented her district."[18]

Howard once recalled how working for Chisholm changed his life beginning in 1965: "I was secretary of the old Metropolitan Savings Bank. There was an article in the *Amsterdam News* about me, that I had become secretary of the bank at 23-years old and was from the community. Chisholm and Wesley Holder came in to see me and indicated they were putting together a team and they would like for me to be on that team."

He continued, "I met four presidents through Mrs. Chisholm; both Bushes, President Jimmy Carter and President Clinton. Robert Kennedy, the entire US Supreme Court, anyone who was anybody in Washington, D.C., came by to shake Chisholm's hand. Mrs. Chisholm was not a selfish person. She would have us stand in the receiving line with her and would say 'just remember this day, remember this day and never forget the abandoned people as you go up the ladder.'"[19]

On January 3, 2005, the *New York Times* printed an obituary:

> Mrs. Chisholm was an outspoken, steely educator-turned-politician who shattered racial and gender barriers as she became a national symbol of liberal politics in the 1960's and 1970's. Over the years, she also had a way of making statements that angered the establishment, as in 1974, when she asserted that "there is an undercurrent of resistance" to integration "among many Blacks in areas of concentrated poverty and discrimination"—including in her own district in Brooklyn.[20]

When he heard of Chisholm's passing, Robert E. Williams, president of the NAACP in Flagler County, Florida, told the Associated Press, "She was our Moses that opened the Red Sea for us."[21] Other leaders of the Black community spoke well of her achievements. Jesse Jackson called her a "woman of great courage" and continued, "She was an activist, and she never stopped fighting. She refused to accept the ordinary, and she had high expectations for herself and all people around her."[22] Al Sharpton stated, "She broke the barrier down for Black women in the highest circles of power in Washington and she did it with dignity and did it effectively and did it with no fear."[23]

An outpouring of grief and admiration came from leaders across the country, and especially from Black people in politics. Representative Maxine Waters of California recalled, "Shirley Chisholm was truly 'unbought and unbossed.' Shirley Chisholm came to Washington as the first Black woman elected to Congress and changed the terms of the debate. She created a platform to discuss issues that had never been a part of the 'old boys' agenda."[24]

President George H. W. Bush called Chisholm "a fine lady, a pioneer in education and public service,"[25] and New York assemblyman N. Nick Perry from the Fifty-Eighth District went as far as introducing a bill to make her birthday, November 30, Shirley Chisholm Day in New York State.

A memorial service was held on January 8, 2005, in Palm Coast, Florida, at the First AME Church of Palm Coast and was attended by over 150 mourners. Mourners gave condolences to Chisholm's last surviving sister, Muriel, and she was presented with the American flag by former representative Annette Rainwater. Chisholm's mother died in 1991; her sister Selma followed in 1986; and Odessa in 2004.

A separate service was held in the US House of Representatives on February 15, 2005. The service was hosted by the CBC and cochaired by Representatives Edolphus Towns and Barbara Lee. Chisholm was hailed as a trailblazer for women and minorities, and for the barriers she broke down for others. She was also cited for her legacy in education, social justice, and the doors she opened for the twenty-three Black women who served in Congress since Chisholm entered and until her passing. Barbara Callender, Chisholm's cousin, spoke on Chisholm's father understanding her in ways others couldn't and how she had the ability to draw people where they needed to go even when they didn't know it. Callender also eulogized how Chisholm never saw anyone as a threat and always looked for the good in people. Current and former members of the House gave tributes, including Nancy Patricia Pelosi, Charles Ellis "Chuck" Schumer, Walter Fauntroy, Hillary Rodham Clinton, Ron Dellums, and Charles Rangel.

That same day, Senator Hillary Clinton introduced a resolution honoring Chisholm during the 109th US Senate, and it was approved without amendment and with a preamble by unanimous consent. It was "a resolution honoring Shirley Chisholm for her service to the Nation and expressing condolences to her family, friends, and supporters on her death," and it honored all her achievements in life and her "work to improve the lives of women and minorities, her steadfast commitment to demonstrating the power of compassion, and her dedication to justice and equality."[26]

That next August, Congress designated the facility of the US Postal Service located at 1915 Fulton Street in Brooklyn, New York, as the "Congresswoman Shirley A. Chisholm Post Office Building."[27]

12

THE LEGACY OF SHIRLEY CHISHOLM

"When I die, I want to be remembered as a woman who lived in the twentieth century and who dared to be a catalyst of change."

SHIRLEY CHISHOLM'S IMPACT on politics is immeasurable. Without her, there would not have been a Hillary Clinton, Barack Obama, or Kamala Harris. There are so many others in lower levels of government who achieved their success directly because of her impact. They exemplified her never being concerned about how things were but rather acting to make things the way they should be. They followed her example of never cowering to discrimination and stereotypes. As Chisholm once said, "We must reject not only the stereotypes that others hold of us, but also the stereotypes that we hold of ourselves."[1]

She entered politics at a time when the votes of Black people and women were being suppressed by intimidation. That all changed with Chisholm, as stated by Brooklyn congressman Major Owens: "We had been suspicious of elected officials, because they didn't want to stir people up and get involved. But all that eventually changed as a result of [Chisholm's] efforts."[2] Chisholm not only changed politics in Brooklyn but across the entire country. She left a lasting impact on millions of everyday people who benefited from the many issues she fought for. For this reason, the legacy of Shirley Chisholm is the change she fostered reshaping American politics into one of the people. She galvanized Black and Latino people, women, and the poor along with White people, men, and the wealthy. Hers was a political life that didn't just recognize those faces we see every day in the streets or at work, but the faces we never see or try to ignore.

History has remembered Chisholm as she wished, and as she once stated: "I want history to remember me not just as the first Black woman to be elected to Congress, not as the first Black woman to have made a bid for the presidency of the United States, but as a Black woman who lived in the 20th century and dared to be herself."[3] Beyond her paving the way in being a "first" in so many political capacities, she is remembered as a daring legislator. This is evidenced by the scope of legislations she introduced or cosponsored in Congress, and Chisholm's congressional record reflects her achievement. In descending order, the category of bills she sponsored most frequently were social welfare, health, government operations and politics, taxation, Congressional reforms, international affairs, armed forces and national security, education, labor and employment, energy, and crime and law enforcement. She sponsored sixty-four pieces of legislation and cosponsored 1,783 others. Fifty-five of these bills became law, the majority of which she cosponsored.

Those who knew Chisholm best spoke of her lasting impact. Fellow CBC member Ron Dellums reflected on her during a 2005 interview. One of the first questions he was asked was about her run for Congress. On the topic of her uphill battle to get elected, he responded:

> Shirley was an independent person with a tremendous heart
> and great courage. And, you know, she wasn't a person that

was handpicked by anyone. Shirley stood up on her own, she was a self-starter, and I think in that regard, you know, someone was always challenging her, but the reality was that she always won. And once she won, she felt that the people were on her side and that if she did a good job and she spoke out and stayed true to her convictions that she would be reelected.[4]

Since Chisholm's 1972 run for president, there have been other Black women who have dared to do the same. Some campaigned openly acknowledging Chisholm's influence, including Peta Lindsay during her 2012 campaign: "My campaign stands in the tradition of Shirley Chisholm—knocking down barriers, demanding inclusion, refusing to be put 'in our place.' I don't meet the criteria of the 'typical' candidate in a lot of obvious ways, and like Chisholm, I know the political and media establishment will use that to ignore or discredit my campaign. . . . Considering all the racist attacks she faced, including assassination attempts, I bet her advice to me would be: 'Don't let the odds intimidate you, don't be turned away, ignore the haters.'"[5]

Chisholm exemplified just how much women can achieve if they galvanize support. Her efforts became a blueprint for organized activism, pushing political change from within the system, and breaking down stereotypes and historical barriers formed to exclude voices that threatened male dominance. Women who followed her had a greater understanding of gender in politics, a topic that before Chisholm was taboo to speak on. Her accomplishments as a legislator revealed the contributions women can make in the highest offices of the nation when barriers are broken.

Chisholm's efforts also changed how the country looked backward to reckon with its history of racism, and how it looked forward in how it would fully recognize the rights of women, Black people, LGBTQIA+ people, and those disenfranchised by political, economic, social, and criminal justice forces. She forced dialogue on both fronts through purposeful action and direct dialogue, never cowering to the pressures to remain silent just because she was a woman or Black. She was a vocal legislative powerhouse when fighting for new laws to combat the ills of the country.

To recognize her contributions, on March 3, 2009, a portrait of Chisholm was unveiled in the US Capitol. This was a high honor, as a Capitol portrait is normally reserved for political party leaders such as Speakers of the House and congressional committee chairs. The striking portrait, painted by renowned author, painter, and illustrator Kadir Nelson, features Chisholm standing with her arms crossed, the US Capitol in the background. Attendees at the portrait's unveiling ceremony included House Speaker Nancy Pelosi, Representative Yvette Clarke of New York, CBC chairwoman Barbara Lee, and other members of the CBC.

Among so many lasting achievements, one with a lasting political impact was Chisholm's founding of the CBC along with Charles C. Digg Jr., Louis Stokes, and William L. Clay. Her actions as a member helped make it an institution in American government by exemplifying the collective power of representation and unity. One of the most touching tributes to her was released on September 25, 2009, by the African American Voices in Congress (AVOICE), a project of the CBC Foundation: "Dear Representative Shirley Chisholm . . . An AVOICE Issue Forum Honoring Her Historic Leadership." It contains individual letters from prominent members of Congress addressed to Chisholm and recalling their admiration for her life and accomplishments. Among the letters were those written by Congresspersons John Conyers Jr., Charles B. Rangel, Edolphus "Ed" Towns, John Lewis, Eleanor Holmes Norton, Bobby L. Rush, Jesse L. Jackson Jr., Barbara Lee, Marcia L. Fudge, and Roland W. Burris. It also contains tributes from five of her former staffers: Muriel Morisey, Andrea "Tracy" Simmons Holmes, Laura W. Murphy, Shirley Downs, and Mia Cole.

Chisholm's legacy is felt in Washington and her home state of New York. She is the reason the SEEK program has benefited thousands of students. As outlined in the Hechinger Report, "Some 420,000 students have been through the program over the course of its 50-year history," and economists found, "SEEK students earned more money as adults in their late 20s and early 30s than academically similar students from higher-income families."[6] Thanks to Chisholm's activism in the New York Assembly, New York domestic workers have benefited from unemployment benefits, female professors no longer lose tenure after taking maternity leave, and agricultural workers benefit from unemployment and social security benefits.

Given her many contributions to the citizens of Bedford-Stuyvesant and the state of New York, on October 4, 2010, New York governor David A. Paterson renamed the thirteen-story state office building at 55 Hanson Place in Brooklyn the Shirley A. Chisholm State Office Building. Per his dedication, "Shirley Chisholm was a lifelong leader who worked tirelessly to better the lives of those in her community and across this country. Her ability to inspire action in others is a gift that continues to resonate today. Naming this building in her honor will recognize her legacy in perpetuity and serve as a constant reminder of her dedication to positive change."[7]

A host of dignitaries were in attendance for the ceremony. Among them was Bill Howard, former senior administrative assistant to Chisholm in Congress, who represented the Chisholm family. He remarked, "Shirley's work can be seen today on the streets of America. Her life's work centered around a better quality of life for all people, especially our youth."

The legislation to rename the building was sponsored by Senator Velmanette Montgomery of the Eighteenth Senate District and Assemblyman Hakeem Jeffries of the Fifty-Seventh District. Assemblyman Jeffries remarked:

> Shirley Chisholm blazed a trail from the streets of Brooklyn in 1972 to the White House in 2008 with the election of Barack Obama. We all owe Shirley Chisholm a debt of gratitude for her dogged spirit and indomitable strength

that changed the very social fabric of our nation forever. As America looks forward to a brighter future, we must never forget to honor those like Ms. Chisholm who helped pave the way and inspire a generation of leaders to seek justice and equality on behalf of the most vulnerable among us. Indeed, she casts a shadow far larger than this building.[8]

In 2014 Chisholm was featured on a US postal stamp designed by art director Ethel Kessler. The special dedication ceremony for the thirty-seventh Black Heritage Forever Stamp was held at Brooklyn Borough Hall in Brooklyn, New York, on January 31. Deputy Postmaster General Ronald Stroman stated, "Shirley Chisholm was a courageous and pioneering woman whose legacy lives on with the issuance of this special stamp. We are proud to honor this great American who shattered barriers of race and gender. Shirley Chisholm fought for the rights of women and the poor as a true champion for justice and equality for all."[9] Stroman was joined by federal, state, and local officials, including Andrew Young.

Chisholm joined the ranks of the special Black Heritage Series that has featured other leaders, starting with a Harriet Tubman stamp, followed by Sojourner Truth, Paul Robeson, W. E. B. Du Bois, Dr. King Jr., Roy Wilkins, Thurgood Marshall, Jackie Robinson, Madam C. J. Walker, Ella Fitzgerald, Marian Anderson, Barbara Jordan, Langston Hughes, Mary McLeod Bethune, John Johnson, and Althea Gibson.

As stated previously, Chisholm is the reason so many Black people and women could be politically successful. When she entered Congress in January 1969, she was the only Black female and one of only ten African American members in the US House and Senate. Decades later, in 2008 the top two Democratic Party primary presidential nominees were Barack H. Obama and Hillary R. Clinton. Chisholm's achievement paved the wave for both.

Recognizing the impact of her legacy, on November 24, 2015, President Obama posthumously awarded Chisholm the Presidential

Medal of Freedom. The award was accepted by her grandnephew, Andre Dubois. Also in attendance were her niece, Valerie Dubois, and her goddaughter, Maria Bosley. President Obama stated the following in his presentation:

> There are people in our country's history who don't look left or right—they just look straight ahead. Shirley Chisholm was one of those people. Driven by a profound commitment to justice, she became the first African-American congresswoman—the first African-American woman from a major political party—to run for President. When Shirley was assigned to the House Agricultural Committee—despite the fact that her district was from New York City she said, "Apparently all they know here in Washington about Brooklyn is that a tree grew there." But she made the most of her new role, helping to create the supplemental nutrition program that feeds poor mothers and their children. Shirley Chisholm's example transcends her life. And when asked how she'd like to be remembered, she had an answer: "I'd like them to say that Shirley Chisholm had guts." And I'm proud to say it: Shirley Chisholm had guts.[10]

Chisholm's greatest legacy is how she inspired others to excel in public service. This is evidenced by those who served as her staffers and continued their achievements, exemplifying the words of Chisholm when she said, "Don't listen to those who say YOU CAN'T. Listen to the voice inside yourself that says, I CAN."[11]

Marion Humphrey served as one of her research assistants while attending Princeton University. He became a circuit judge for the Sixth Judicial District in Arkansas.

Bevan Dufty was a summer intern from Berkeley, then Chisholm's legislative assistant, before becoming the chief legislative director to

Representative Julian C. Dixon of California and then member of the board of supervisors in San Francisco, California.

Chisholm's senior policy adviser, Thaddeus Garrett, served as Chairman of the Howard University Board of Trustees, staff member for President Gerald Ford, special adviser to the Bob Dole–Jack Kemp presidential campaign in 1996, special adviser to former vice president Nelson Rockefeller, and as a senior political adviser to George W. Bush's presidential campaign.

Andrea "Tracy" Simmons Holmes went on to serve as chief of staff to Representative Julian C. Dixon of California.

Brenda Pillors became a CBC fellow before serving as Chisholm's legislative assistant and then legislative director. After Chisholm's retirement from Congress, Pillors served as legislative director for Representative Edolphus Towns and then as his chief of staff.

Laura W. Murphy worked for Representative Parren J. Mitchell of Maryland, California State Assembly Speaker Willie L. Brown, and Washington, DC, mayor Sharon Pratt Kelly, and became director of the American Civil Liberties Union's Washington Legislative Office.

Patsy Fleming was deputy assistant secretary during President Carter's administration, a top aide for Representative Red Weiss of New York, and an investigator for the US House of Representatives.

Edolphus "Ed" Towns Jr. worked on Chisholm's presidential campaign. He served in the US House of Representatives from 1983 to 2013.

On November 5, 2018, the fiftieth anniversary of Chisholm's election to Congress, Congresswoman Barbara Lee released a statement. In it, she recalled meeting Chisholm, "her mentor and lifelong friend," as a college student. The two first met when Lee served as the president of the Black Student Union at Mills College and invited Chisholm to speak on campus. Lee was also a community worker with the Black Panther Party, and a single mother of two on public assistance. She recalled she was willing to flunk a class because the instructor assigned students to work for a presidential campaign and she didn't want to complete it because she felt politicians never supported real social change. Lee didn't know Chisholm was running for president when she invited her to the campus to speak.

As Lee later recalled, "I went up to her and talked to her and told her about this class that I was about to flunk. She said, 'Little girl, are you registered to vote?' And I said, 'No, I'm not going to.' And she really let me have it about the importance of voting."[12]

Lee then joined Chisholm's presidential campaign and served as her delegate at the 1972 Democratic National Convention. Lee continued, "Congresswoman Chisholm is often remembered for being the first. But she should also be remembered for what she accomplished during her tenure in Congress. She used her office to fight for low-income families, hungry school kids, single moms and immigrants. She was instrumental in creating the national school lunch program, expanding the food stamp program, and establishing the Special Supplemental Nutrition Program for Women, Infants and Children, commonly known as WIC. She made this country a better place."[13]

In 2018 New York City first lady Chirlane McCray and deputy mayor Alicia Glen announced the "She Built NY" program to recognize only five of the 150 statues of historical figures in the city were women. In November of that year, on the ninety-fourth anniversary of Chisholm's birthday and the fiftieth anniversary of her election to Congress, they announced she would be the first woman honored in Brooklyn with a statue. Per McCray, "Congresswoman Shirley Chisholm's legacy of leadership and activism has paved the way for thousands of women to seek public office. She is exactly the kind of New York woman whose contributions should be honored with representation in our public spaces, and that is now being realized with She Built NYC."[14] The monument at the Parkside entrance to Prospect Park was designed by artists Amanda Williams and Olalekan Jeyifous. It features a silhouette of Chisholm intertwined with the dome of the US Capitol.

2018 was called the Year of the Woman because so many women were elected to Congress. Chisholm was credited with helping pave the way for the election records set. This was outlined by a statement issued by NOW on November 5, 2018, called "An Inspiration to Women Candidates in 2018: Remembering Shirley Chisholm," which stated:

> Chisholm's achievements were historic and paved the way for more people living at the intersections of several identities to find the courage to run for office. She is emblematic of the power that can be found in giving a voice to a diversity of people. We can honor Chisholm's memory this election season by exercising our right to vote and supporting progressive candidates who, like Chisholm, want to create a better future by empowering women, people of color, LGBTQ people, low-income people, and immigrants.[15]

Decades after Chisholm left Congress, members were still trying to have her formally recognized for her contributions. On November 15, 2018, Senate minority leader Chuck Schumer of New York submitted Senate Resolution 689, entitled "Acknowledging the 50th Anniversary of the Election to the House of Representatives of Shirley Anita St. Hill Chisholm, the First African-American Woman in Congress." The resolution never made it out of the Committee on the Judiciary. Attitudes still lingered in Congress by some who didn't want Chisholm recognized as an idol to others. However, the resolution was historically symbolic.

The resolution not passing didn't stop some members of Congress. The next year, on March 7, Senator Kamala Harris of California and Congresswoman Yvette Clarke of New York reintroduced a bill to commission a statue of Chisholm to be displayed in the US Capitol. A bill had already been introduced by Harris, Kirsten Gillibrand of New York, Cory Booker of New Jersey, and eleven senators in February 2018.

At the time of the bill's reintroduction, there were just four statues and busts honoring African Americans in the Capitol: Rosa Parks, Frederick Douglass, Dr. Martin Luther King Jr., and Sojourner Truth. Harris stated, "Chisholm's legacy inspires us to continue our fight to give a voice to the voiceless and pursue justice and equality for every American. Her legacy deserves to stand tall in the United States Capitol," and Clark explained, "Shirley Chisholm used the authority of her experience to create nutrition assistance programs, expand health care services for parents and children, increase the minimum wage, support the veterans of our Armed Forces, and provide opportunities for women in college, graduate school, and collegiate and professional sports with the enactment of Title IX. For this and countless other reasons, Congress should honor Chisholm's life and living legacy and her contribution to advancing civil and human rights among other defining figures in our nation's history."[16] The bill is still pending congressional approval as of 2023.

Representative Hakeem Jeffries of New York introduced "House Resolution 1968—Shirley Chisholm Congressional Gold Medal Act" on March 28, 2019, to posthumously award a Congressional gold medal to recognize her activism, independence, achievements in politics, election as the first African American woman in the Congress, and run for president. Although supported by 218 cosponsors, it was not approved. This was the fourth time a bill was introduced in the House for this recognition. The first was in January 2007, then March 2011, then February 2013, each time introduced by Charles Rangel.

While Congress was collectively slow to recognize Chisholm, political leaders in New York were not, and tributes to her legacy continued. On July 2, 2019, New York governor Andrew M. Cuomo announced the construction of the 407-acre Shirley Chisholm State Park along the shores of Jamaica Bay, Long Island. In the announcement Cuomo stated, "Today we add another gem to our treasure trove of state parks, transforming what was once a blemish on the South Brooklyn community into exquisite open space. Shirley Chisholm fought to improve the health and wellness of underserved communities, a legacy we are carrying on through the Vital Brooklyn Initiative, so we are proud to dedicate this park in memory of her leadership and accomplishments."[17] Members of Chisholm's family attended the dedication ceremony, including Valarie Bacon, Monique Foster, Chisholm Foster, Lawrence Dubois, Wesley Maloney, and Althea Maloney.

As part of Governor Cuomo's Vital Brooklyn Initiative, the state committed to spending $20 million in both phases one and two of the park. Many New York representatives responded to the governor's announcement. Jeffries stated, "Shirley Chisholm famously said to bring a folding chair if they don't give you a seat at the table and that's what she did all her life. Whether it was her groundbreaking election to Congress in 1968, or her historic run for President, she never stopped fighting to make sure every voice was heard. Governor Cuomo is to be commended for this important effort to honor Shirley Chisholm's legacy."[18]

Beyond the awards are the people Chisholm forever changed. Shelia Y. Oliver credits her success to being inspired by Chisholm. Oliver became lieutenant governor of New Jersey in 2018. Ayanna Soyini Pressley was also inspired by her, as well as Barbara Jordan. Pressley began serving in the US House of Representatives in 2019. Senator Kamala Harris of California was selected by Democratic Presidential Candidate Joseph R. Biden to be his vice presidential running mate for the 2020 presidential election. Harris had sought the Democratic Party nomination for president and credited Chisholm as being her inspiration, even patterning her campaign after Chisholm with the campaign slogan "For the People."

In a February 2019 interview Harris observed, "She reminds me of the many sayings of my mother and that is, 'Don't let anybody tell you who you are. You tell them who you are.' That was Shirley Chisholm, unbought and unbossed. I stand as so many of us do on her shoulders."[19]

In November 2020 Biden won the general election, thus making Harris the first Black, the first Indian, and the first woman to become vice president of the United States. They beat their election rival, incumbent Donald Trump, by over seven million votes, and received the greatest number of votes in US history—over eighty-one million. In many ways, the election of Biden and Harris reflected a renewed hope for America as a country respecting the diversity of its citizens.

Chisholm once mused how she wanted nothing more than the country to embrace its diversity with inclusiveness:

> America is a wonderful land. It's no question about it. That is why every group from across the waters tries to come to America. I am hopeful. Oh God am I hopeful that before I die that I will see that America will move toward a period of real enlightenment—not rhetorical enlightenment, real enlightenment—and that when we are finally faced with the choice of exclusion or inclusion we will choose inclusion because that's what America is supposed to be all about.[20]

Congresswoman Barbara Lee summed up the legacy of Chisholm very well in speaking on how the inauguration of Kamala Harris as the first woman and first woman of color was made possible by Chisholm: "Here you have now this remarkable, brilliant, prepared African-American woman, South Asian woman, ready to fulfill the dreams and aspirations of Shirley Chisholm and myself and so many women of color. This is exciting and is finally a breakthrough that so many of us have been waiting for. And it didn't come easy."[21]

It came because Shirley Chisholm paved the way for leaders such as Harris and Lee. Chisholm was looking into the future when she reflected on her own impact and legacy because she knew she endured the hardships of future generations for them:

> *"The next time a woman of whatever color, or a dark-skinned person of whatever sex aspires to be president, the way should be a little smoother because I helped pave it."*[22]

NOTES

___

Introduction

1. Nichola D. Gutgold, *Still Paving the Way for Madam President* (Lexington Books, 2017), 49.

1. Chisholm's Early Life

1. Winston James, "The History of Afro-Caribbean Migration to the United States," Motion: The African American Migration Experience, Schomburg Center for Research in Black Culture New York Public Library, 2005, http://www.inmotionaame.org (site discontinued).

2. Sarah Fenton, ed., *39-Second New York: The 50 Key Visions, Events and Architects That Shaped the City, Each Explained in Half a Minute* (Ivy Press, 2017), 61.

3. Jane Perlez, "Rep. Chisholm's Angry Farewell," *New York Times*, October 12, 1982, https://www.nytimes.com/1982/10/12/us/rep-chisholm-s-angry-farewell.html.

4. Tammy L. Brown, "'A New Era in American Politics': Shirley Chisholm and the Discourse of Identity," *Callaloo* 31, no. 4 (2008): 1016.

5. Barbara Winslow, *Shirley Chisholm: Catalyst for Change* (Routledge, 2018), 12.

6. Perlez, "Rep. Chisholm's Angry Farewell."

7. Ruth Larsen and Ian Whitehead, *Popular Experience and Cultural Representation of the Great War, 1914–1918* (Cambridge Scholars, 2017), 78.

8. Craig S. Wilder, *A Covenant with Color: Race and Social Power in Brooklyn 1636–1990* (Columbia University Press, 2000), 177.
9. "A Model High School" *New York Times*, April 7, 1895, https://www .nytimes.com/1895/04/07/archives/a-model-high-school-fame-of-the -one-for-brooklyn-girls-widespread.html.
10. Shirley Chisholm, *Unbought and Unbossed* (Houghton Mifflin, 1970), 39.
11. Nichola D. Gutgold, *Paving the Way for Madam President* (Lexington Books, 2006), 54.
12. "'Bright Light'—HH to Chisholm," *Boston Globe*, November 8, 1968.
13. Jason A. Merchey, *Building a Life of Value: Timeless Wisdom to Inspire and Empower Us* (Little Moose Press, 2005), 26.
14. Shirley Chisholm, interview at National Visionary Leadership Project, May 7, 2002, excerpted in Archives of Women's Political Communication, Iowa State University, https://awpc.cattcenter.iastate.edu/2017/03/09 /excerpts-from-the-national-visionary-leadership-project-may-7-2002/.
15. Sheila Rule, "Dean of Black Brooklyn Politics a Power at 85," *New York Times*, October 10, 1982, https://www.nytimes.com/1982/10/10/nyregion /dean-of-black-brooklyn-politics-a-power-at-85.html.
16. Rule, "Dean of Black Brooklyn."
17. Chisholm, *Unbought and Unbossed*, 45.
18. James Haskins, *Fighting Shirley Chisholm* (Dial Press, 1975), 64.
19. Brock Adams, remarks before the US House of Representatives, May 1, 1969, 115 Cong. Rec. 11,162, https://repositories.lib.utexas.edu /bitstream/handle/2152/12421/Chisholm_CR05011969.pdf.
20. Jack Newfield, "Robert Kennedy's Bedford-Stuyvesant Legacy," *New York Magazine*, December 16, 1968, 26.

2. Getting Into and Out of Politics

1. Ron Howell, *Boss of Brooklyn: The Life and Times of Bertram L. Baker* (Fordham University Press, 2019), 68.
2. Stephan Lesher, "The Short, Unhappy Life of Black Presidential Politics," *New York Times*, June 25, 1972, https://www.nytimes.com/1972/06/25 /archives/the-short-unhappy-life-of-black-presidential-politics-1972 -black.html.
3. Frederick Cornish, "Movement for Representation Is at High Point in Municipal Contests," *Freedom* 3, no. 8 (September 1953): http://mc.dlib .nyu.edu/files/books/tamwag_fdm000031/tamwag_fdm000031_lo.pdf, 2.
4. Cornish, 2.

5. Leonard N. Moore, *The Defeat of Black Power: Civil Rights and the National Black Political Convention of 1972* (Louisiana State University Press, 2018), 43.
6. Lesher, "Short, Unhappy Life," https://www.nytimes.com/1972/06/25/archives/the-short-unhappy-life-of-black-presidential-politics-1972-black.html.
7. Gutgold, *Paving the Way*, 57.

3. Getting Back into Politics and the New York State Legislature

1. Wil Mara, *Perspectives on Civil Unrest in the 1960s: Riots and Their Aftermath* (Marshall Cavendish Benchmark, 2010), 50.
2. Julie A. Gallagher, *Black Women and Politics in New York City* (University of Illinois Press, 2012), 97.
3. "Woman Named Aide to Brooklyn Borough Chief; Mrs. Goring Was Insurgent in Ouster of Berman," *New York Times*, November 10, 1964, https://www.nytimes.com/1964/11/10/archives/woman-named-aide-to-brooklyn-borough-chief-mrs-goring-was-insargent.html.
4. Shirley Chisholm to Thomas Jones, October 14, 1963, Schomburg Center for Research in Black Culture, New York Public Library.
5. Adams, remarks, 115 Cong. Rec. 11,160, https://repositories.lib.utexas.edu/bitstream/handle/2152/12421/Chisholm_CR05011969.pdf.
6. Lesher, "Short, Unhappy Life," https://www.nytimes.com/1972/06/25/archives/the-short-unhappy-life-of-black-presidential-politics-1972-black.html.
7. Winslow, *Shirley Chisholm*, 43.
8. Adams, remarks, 115 Cong. Rec. 11,160, https://repositories.lib.utexas.edu/bitstream/handle/2152/12421/Chisholm_CR05011969.pdf.
9. Evelyn M. Simien, *Historic Firsts: How Symbolic Empowerment Changes U.S. Politics* (Oxford University Press, 2016), 24.
10. Robin D. Kelley, *Into the Fire: African Americans Since 1970* (Oxford University Press, 1996), 37.
11. "'Bright Light,'" *Boston Globe*.
12. Winslow, *Shirley Chisholm*, 49.
13. "'Bright Light,'" *Boston Globe*.
14. Adams, remarks, 115 Cong. Rec. 11,162, https://repositories.lib.utexas.edu/bitstream/handle/2152/12421/Chisholm_CR05011969.pdf.
15. United Press International, "Literacy Vote Test Is Made," *Daily Messenger*, May 19, 1965.

16. Adams, remarks, 115 Cong. Rec. 11,160, https://repositories.lib.utexas.edu/bitstream/handle/2152/12421/Chisholm_CR05011969.pdf.

17. Office of Policy Planning and Research, *The Negro Family: The Case for National Action* (US Department of Labor, 1965), 1, https://www.dol.gov/general/aboutdol/history/webid-moynihan.

18. Peter I. Rose, *Americans from Africa: Slavery and Its Aftermath* (Routledge, 2017), 391.

19. Winslow, *Shirley Chisholm*, 54.

20. Jeanne Stevenson, *Women with 2020 Vision: American Theologians on the Voice, Vote, and Vision of Women* (Fortress Press, 2020), 68.

4. Running for Congress

1. Mari Castaneda and Kirsten Isgro, eds., *Mothers in Academia* (Columbia University Press, 2013), 122.

2. Jason Sokol, *All Eyes Are Upon Us: Race and Politics from Boston to Brooklyn* (Basic Books, 2014), 145.

3. Sokol, *All Eyes Are Upon Us*, 146.

4. Edna F. Kelly to Richard Grayson, July 19, 1968, via *Dumbo Books of Brooklyn* (blog), http://who-will-kiss-the-pig.blogspot.com/2011/03/letters-to-richard-grayson-from.html.

5. Sokol, *All Eyes Are Upon Us*, 150.

6. Sokol, *All Eyes Are Upon Us*, 151.

7. Ellen Fitzpatrick, *The Highest Glass Ceiling: Women's Quest for the American Presidency* (Harvard University Press, 2016), 187.

8. Adams, remarks, 115 Cong. Rec. 11,160, https://repositories.lib.utexas.edu/bitstream/handle/2152/12421/Chisholm_CR05011969.pdf.

9. Adams, remarks, 115 Cong. Rec. 11,161, https://repositories.lib.utexas.edu/bitstream/handle/2152/12421/Chisholm_CR05011969.pdf.

10. Adams, remarks.

11. Steven K. Schneider, *Robert F. Kennedy* (Writer's Club Press, 2001), 66.

12. George R. Metcalf, *Up from Within: Today's New Black Leaders* (McGraw-Hill, 1971), 125.

13. Sokol, *All Eyes Are Upon Us*, 152.

14. Howell, *Boss of Brooklyn*, 42.

15. Sokol, *All Eyes Are Upon Us*, 152.

16. "'Bright Light,'" *Boston Globe*.

17. Adams, remarks, 115 Cong. Rec. 11,161, https://repositories.lib.utexas.edu/bitstream/handle/2152/12421/Chisholm_CR05011969.pdf.

18. Sokol, *All Eyes Are Upon Us*, 153.

19. "Assemblyman Tom Fortune Visits," *Workers Voice* 5, no. 1 (August 29, 1975): 7.

20. Sokol, *All Eyes Are Upon Us*, 154.

21. "CHISHOLM, Shirley Anita," US House History, Art & Archives, accessed June 22, 2023, https://history.house.gov/People/Listing/C /CHISHOLM,-Shirley-Anita-(C000371)/.

22. Chisholm, *Unbought and Unbossed*, 89.

23. Chisholm, 89.

24. Office of History and Preservation, *Women in Congress*, 442.

25. US House Office of History and Preservation, *Black Americans in Congress, 1870–2007* (US Government Printing Office, 2008), https://www .govinfo.gov/content/pkg/GPO-CDOC-108hdoc224/pdf/GPO-CDOC -108hdoc224.pdf, 340.

26. Office of History and Preservation, 340.

27. Christine A. Kray, Tamar W. Carroll, and Hinda Mandell, eds., *Nasty Women and Bad Hombres: Gender and Race in the 2016 U.S. Presidential Election* (University of Rochester Press, 2018), 114.

28. Gallagher, *Black Women and Politics*, 170.

29. Stacie Taranto and Leandra Zarnow, eds., *Suffrage at 100: Women in American Politics since 1920* (John Hopkins University Press, 2020), 247.

30. Walter Ray Watson, "A Look Back on Shirley Chisholm's Historic 1968 House Victory," *Morning Edition*, NPR, November 6, 2018, https:// www.npr.org/2018/11/06/664617076/a-look-back-on-shirley-chisholm -s-historic-1968-house-victory.

31. Lucia Raatma, *Leading Women: Shirley Chisholm* (Marshall Cavendish Benchmark, 2011), 5.

32. Christopher C. DeMuth, interview by Timothy Naftali, January 14, 2008, courtesy of the Richard Nixon Presidential Library, https:// www.nixonlibrary.gov/sites/default/files/forresearchers/find/histories /demuth-2008-01-14.pdf.

33. James Farmer, *Lay Bare the Heart: An Autobiography of the Civil Rights Movement* (Texas Christian University Press, 1985), 311.

34. Vernon L. Farmer and Evelyn Shepherd-Wynn, eds., *Voices of Historical and Contemporary Black American Pioneers* (ABC-CLIO, 2012), 33.

5. Congresswoman Shirley Chisholm

1. Brian Reed, "Chisholm Forged a Place for Black Congresswomen," NPR, November 4, 2008, https://www.npr.org/templates/story/story.php? storyId=96516491.

2. Office of History and Preservation, *Women in Congress*, 326.
3. Adams, remarks, 115 Cong. Rec. 11,162, https://repositories.lib.utexas.edu/bitstream/handle/2152/12421/Chisholm_CR05011969.pdf.
4. Ronald E. Kisner, "Shirley Chisholm Kicks Off Campaign for U.S. President," *Jet*, February 10, 1972, 16.
5. "New Faces in Congress," *Ebony*, February 1969, 58.
6. Muriel Morisey, oral history interview, US House Office of the Historian, April 19, 2017.
7. Catherine Ellis and Stephen Drury Smith, eds. *Say It Loud! Great Speeches on Civil Rights and African American Identity* (New Press, 2010), 103.
8. "Congresswoman Chisholm Hit by Thieves in D.C.," *Jet*, January 30, 1969, 12.
9. Kisner, "Shirley Chisholm Kicks Off Campaign," 12.
10. Words of the Week, *Jet*, April 8, 1971, 32
11. Fitzpatrick, *Highest Glass Ceiling*, 193.
12. Chisholm, *Unbought and Unbossed*, 102.
13. Gallagher, *Black Women and Politics*, 157.
14. Richard L. Madden, "Mrs. Chisholm Gets Off House Farm Committee," *New York Times*, January 29, 1969, https://www.nytimes.com/1969/01/30/archives/mrs-chisholm-gets-off-house-farm-committee.html.
15. Office of History and Preservation, *Women in Congress*, 442.
16. Metcalf, *Up from Within*, 132.
17. William H. Hatcher, *U.S. House Journal of William H. Hatcher*, vol. 25 (US House of Representatives, 1969), https://digitalcommons.wku.edu/cgi/viewcontent.cgi?article=1024&context=whnatcher_journals, 46–49.
18. Susan Powell, "Fighting Shirley Chisholm: Husband Conrad Acts as Her 'Shepherd,'" *Jamaica Gleaner*, May 25, 1969, https://gleaner.newspaperarchive.com/kingston-gleaner/1969-05-25/page-36/.
19. Adams, remarks, 115 Cong. Rec. 11,160, https://repositories.lib.utexas.edu/bitstream/handle/2152/12421/Chisholm_CR05011969.pdf.
20. Danny Lewis, "44 Years Ago, Shirley Chisholm Became the First Black Woman to Run for President, *Smithsonian Magazine*, January 29, 2016, https://www.smithsonianmag.com/smart-news/44-years-ago-shirley-chisholm-became-the-first-black-woman-to-run-for-president-180957975/.
21. Susan Brownmiller, "This Is Fighting Shirley Chisholm, *New York Times*, April 13, 1969, https://www.nytimes.com/1969/04/13/archives/this-is-fighting-shirley-chisholm-fighting-shirley-chisholm.html.
22. Chisholm, interview at National Visionary Leadership Project, https://awpc.cattcenter.iastate.edu/2017/03/09/excerpts-from-the-national-visionary-leadership-project-may-7-2002/.

23. Jessyka Finley, "Black Women's Satire as (Black) Postmodern Performance," *Studies in American Humor* 2, no. 2 (2016): 240.
24. Shirley Chisholm, "The White Press: Racist and Sexist," *Black Scholar* 5, no. 1 (1973): 22.
25. Office of History and Preservation, *Black Americans in Congress*, 273.
26. Gutgold, *Paving the Way*, 69.
27. Shirley Chisholm, remarks before the US House of Representatives, March 26, 1969, 115 Cong. Rec. 7,765. https://repositories.lib.utexas.edu/bitstream/handle/2152/12530/_Chisholm_VietnamPolicy.pdf.
28. "Rep. Chisholm to Vote 'No' on Defense Money," *Jet*, April 10, 1969, 3.
29. Marjorie Hunter, "White House Pickets, House Speakers Score War," *New York Times*, March 26, 1969, https://www.nytimes.com/1969/03/27/archives/white-house-pickets-house-speakers-score-war.html.
30. Hunter, "White House Pickets."
31. Paul Findley, remarks before the US House of Representatives, March 25, 1969, 115 Cong. Rec. 7,404, https://www.govinfo.gov/content/pkg/GPO-CRECB-1969-pt6/pdf/GPO-CRECB-1969-pt6-3-1.pdf.
32. Richard W. Leeman and Bernard K. Duffy, eds., *The Will of a People: A Critical Anthology of Great African American Speeches* (Southern Illinois University Press, 2012), 350.
33. Susan Brownmiller, *Shirley Chisholm: A Biography* (Doubleday, 1971), 134.
34. *The Dick Cavett Show*, August 8. 1969, via "The Dick Cavett Show: Black History Month—Shirley Chisholm," Shout! Factory, https://www.shoutfactorytv.com/the-dick-cavett-show/the-dick-cavett-show-black-history-month-shirley-chisholm-august-8-1969/56a2cc4c69702d07f9de7b00.
35. Peter Fonseca, "Chisholm Sees Nation Facing Social Change," *Communicator* 23, no. 3 (October 16, 1970): https://academicworks.cuny.edu/cgi/viewcontent.cgi?article=1087&context=bx_arch_communicator, 1.
36. William E. Farrell, "2 Unknowns Facing Vocal Incumbent in Brooklyn," *New York Times*, October 19, 1970, https://www.nytimes.com/1970/10/19/archives/2-unknowns-facing-vocal-incumbent-in-brooklyn.html.

6. Shirley Chisholm's Legislative Focus

1. Arthur B. Levy and Susan Stoudinger, "The Black Caucus in the 92nd Congress: Gauging Its Success," *Phylon* 39, no. 4 (1978): 322.
2. Louis Stokes, speech to Women's National Democratic Club, October 2, 1972, 118 Cong. Rec. 36,531, https://www.govinfo.gov/content/pkg/GPO-CRECB-1972-pt27/pdf/GPO-CRECB-1972-pt27-3-3.pdf.

3. Stokes, 36, 531.

4. "History," Congressional Black Caucus, accessed June 16, 2023, https://cbc.house.gov/history/.

5. Office of History and Preservation, *Black Americans in Congress*, 391.

6. *Black Caucus of the US House of Representatives against American Broadcasting Co. Inc., Columbia Broadcasting System Inc., and National Broadcasting Co. Inc.*, 40 F.C.C.2d 249 (1973), via "Nicholas Johnson's Federal Communications Commission Opinions," Nicholas Johnson personal website, https://www.nicholasjohnson.org/FCCOps/1972/40F2_249.htm.

7. *Black Caucus against American Broadcasting Co. et al.*

8. Barbara Gold, "New Protest: General Motors Undemocratic?," *Sun*, May 17, 1970.

9. Congressional Black Caucus, *We Have a Lot to Lose: Solutions to Advance Black Families in the 21st Century* (Congressional Black Caucus, 2020), https://cbc.house.gov/uploadedfiles/2017.03.22_cbc_we_have_a_lot_to_lose_v5.pdf, 15.

10. Office of History and Preservation, *Black Americans in Congress*, 387–388.

11. Jennifer E. Manning and Colleen J. Shogan, *African American Members of the United States Congress: 1870–2011* (Congressional Research Service. 2012), 9.

12. US House Committee on Foreign Affairs, *Africa: Observations on the Impact of American Foreign Policy and Development Programs in Six African Countries; Report of a Congressional Study Mission to Zimbabwe, South Africa, Kenya, Somalia, Angola, and Nigeria, August 4–22, 1981* (US Government Printing Office, 1982), 1–2.

13. Milt Freudenheim and Barbara Slavin, "Burned Out but Not Moved Out," The World in Summary, *New York Times*, August 16, 1981, https://www.nytimes.com/1981/08/16/weekinreview/the-world-in-summary-burned-out-but-not-moved-out.html.

14. Shirley Chisholm, "Equal Rights for Women," remarks before the US House of Representatives, May 21, 1969, EdChange Multicultural Pavilion, http://www.edchange.org/multicultural/speeches/shirley_chisholm_women.html.

15. Shirley Chisholm, remarks before US House subcommittee, July 1, 1970, in *Discrimination Against Women: Hearings Before the Special Subcommittee on Education of the Committee on Education and Labor* (US Government Printing Office, 1971), https://www.google.com/books/edition/Hearings/iFQLAAAAIAAJ, 617–619.

16. Shirley Chisholm, "For the Equal Rights Amendment," remarks before the US House of Representatives, August 10, 1970, Archives of Women's Political Communication, Iowa State University, https://awpc.cattcenter .iastate.edu/2017/03/21/for-the-equal-rights-amendment-aug-10-1970/.

17. Lois Mark Stalvey, *The Education of a WASP*, 1st ed. (University of Wisconsin Press, 1970), xi.

18. Stalvey, xii.

19. Lois Mark Stalvey, *The Education of a WASP*, rev. ed. (University of Wisconsin Press, 1989), vii.

20. Shirley Chisholm to House Judiciary Committee chairman Don Edwards, April 14, 1971, Legislative Bill Files of the Committee on the Judiciary for the 92nd Congress, Committee Papers 1813–2011, Records of the US House of Representatives, Record Group 233, National Archives Building, Washington, DC, via DocsTeach, https://www.docsteach.org /documents/document/chisholm-edwards.

21. Remarks before US House subcommittee, April 1, 1971, in *Equal Rights for Men and Women 1971: Hearings Before Subcommittee No. 4 of the Committee on the Judiciary* (US Government Printing Office, 1971), 487.

22. Chana Kai Lee, *For Freedom's Sake: The Life of Fannie Lou Hamer* (University of Illinois Press, 1999), 170.

23. Lee, 170.

24. Jonathan Sposato, *Better Together: 8 Ways Working with Women Leads to Extraordinary Products and Profits* (John Wiley and Sons, 2018), 125.

25. Beverly Guy-Sheftall, *Words of Fire: An Anthology of African-American Feminist Thought* (New Press, 1995), 393.

26. Pat Patterson, "Rep. Chisholm Blasts Black 'Elitists,'" *Manhattan Tribune*, October 25, 1969, via Harvard Library, https://iiif.lib.harvard.edu /manifests/view/drs:483269693$1i.

27. National Advisory Commission on Civil Disorders, report summary, 1968, Homeland Security Digital Library, https://www.hsdl.org/?view &did=35837, 1.

28. National Advisory Commission, 1.

29. Gutgold, *Paving the Way*, 59.

30. Chisholm, "For the Equal Rights Amendment," https://awpc.cattcenter .iastate.edu/2017/03/21/for-the-equal-rights-amendment-aug-10-1970/.

31. "The Irrepressible Shirley Chisholm," *New York Illustrated*, WNBC-TV, September 20, 1969.

32. Shirley Chisholm, remarks before US House subcommittee, March 17, 1970, in *Hearings Relating to Various Bills to Repeal the Emergency*

Detention Act of 1950: Hearings Before the Committee on Internal Security (US Government Printing Office, 1970), 3,034.

33. Louis Fisher, "Detention of U.S. Citizens," Congressional Research Service, April 28, 2005, https://fas.org/sgp/crs/natsec/RS22130.pdf, 3.

34. Shirley Chisholm, speech at Howard University, Washington, DC, April 21, 1969, Archives of Women's Political Communication, Iowa State University, https://awpc.cattcenter.iastate.edu/2018/10/09/speech-at-howard-university-april-21-1969/.

35. Rudy Johnson, "Mrs. Chisholm Joins Campaign to Collect Bail for Joan Bird," *New York Times*, June 9, 1970.

36. Ula Y. Taylor, "Making Waves," *Black Scholar* 44, no. 3 (2014): 33.

37. Heather Ann Thompson, *Blood in the Water: The Attica Prison Uprising of 1971 and Its Legacy* (Pantheon Books, 2016), 6.

38. Clare Crawford, "Mrs. Chisholm 'Took Charge,'" *Evening Star*, October 12, 1972.

39. Shirley Chisholm, remarks at a memorial in Honor of May McLeod Bethune, June 17, 1971, 117 Cong. Rec. 20,707, https://www.govinfo.gov/content/pkg/GPO-CRECB-1971-pt16/pdf/GPO-CRECB-1971-pt16-1-3.pdf.

40. "Mrs. Chisholm, Mrs. Abzug Introduce Child Care Bill," *New York Times*, May 18, 1971, https://www.nytimes.com/1971/05/18/archives/mrs-chisholm-mrs-abzug-introduce-child-care-bill.html.

41. Thomas A. Johnson, "10 in Black Caucus Visit Bases in Study of Charges of Bias," *New York Times*, November 16, 1971, https://www.nytimes.com/1971/11/16/archives/10-in-black-caucus-visit-bases-in-study-of-charges-of-bias.html.

42. Johnson, "10 in Black Caucus."

43. Shirley Chisholm, remarks before the US House of Representatives, October 14, 1972, 118 Cong. Rec. 36,593, https://www.govinfo.gov/content/pkg/GPO-CRECB-1972-pt27/pdf/GPO-CRECB-1972-pt27-3-3.pdf.

44. Charlayne Hunter, "Shirley Chisholm: Willing to Speak Out," *New York Times*, May 22, 1970, https://www.nytimes.com/1970/05/22/archives/shirley-chisholm-willing-to-speak-out-mrs-shirley-chisholm-willing.html.

45. Shirley Chisholm, "Race, Revolution and Women," *Black Scholar* 3, no. 4 (1971): 17–21.

7. Opposition for the White House

1. US Census Bureau, *Money Income in 1972 of Families and Persons in the United States* (U.S. Department of Commerce, 1973).

2. Frederick C. Harris, *The Price of the Ticket: Barack Obama and Rise and Decline of Black Politics* (Oxford University Press, 2012), 9.

3. "Blacks Eye U.S. Presidency, Audacious," *Jet*, May 27, 1971, 7.

4. Gutgold, *Paving the Way*, 62.

5. "Presenting the Real Politicians in the Family," *McCall's*, October 1971, 6.

6. Margaret Chase Smith, "Excerpts from Speech by Senator Margaret Chase Smith," *New York Times*, January 28, 1964, https://www.nytimes .com/1964/01/28/archives/excerpts-from-speech-by-senator-margaret -chase-smith.html.

7. Tom Buckley, "Mrs. Chisholm Finds District Leaders in Opposing Camp," *New York Times*, May 24, 1972, https://www.nytimes.com/1972/05/24 /archives/mrs-chisholm-finds-district-leaders-in-opposing-camp-mrs -chisholm.html.

8. Buckley, "Mrs. Chisholm Finds District Leaders."

9. Mary Breasted, "Shirley Chisholm: 'They Will Remember a 100-Pound Woman,'" *Village Voice*, December 27, 1971, https://www.villagevoice .com/2020/11/09/shirley-chisolm-they-will-remember-a-100-pound -woman/.

10. Jane Howard, "A Shaker-Upper Wants to be Madame President Chisholm," *Life*, November 5, 1971, 81.

11. Harris, *Price of the Ticket*, 16.

12. "Rep. Chisholm Asks Black Men to Get Off Her Back," *Jet*, October 28, 1971, 5.

13. Moore, *Defeat of Black Power*, 59.

14. Simien, *Historic Firsts*, 32.

15. Carl Griffin, "'Black Males Same as White; I'm Different,' Chisholm Says," *Guardian* (Wright State University), November 17, 1971, https:// corescholar.libraries.wright.edu/cgi/viewcontent.cgi?article=1220& context=guardian, 3–4.

16. "Archive: Shirley Chisholm on Why She Should Be President," BBC, January 26, 2016, https://www.bbc.com/news/av/magazine-35376524.

17. Breasted, "Shirley Chisholm," https://www.villagevoice.com/2020/11/09 /shirley-chisolm-they-will-remember-a-100-pound-woman/.

18. Moore, *Defeat of Black Power*, 58.

19. Thomas A. Johnson, "Mrs. Chisholm Chides Black Caucus," *New York Times*, November 20, 1971, https://www.nytimes.com/1971/11/20 /archives/mrs-chisholm-chides-black-caucus.html.

20. Breasted, "Shirley Chisholm," https://www.villagevoice.com/2020/11/09 /shirley-chisolm-they-will-remember-a-100-pound-woman/.

21. Sheila Moran, "Shirley Chisholm's Running No Matter What It Costs Her," *Free Lance Star*, April 8, 1972.

22. Lesher, "Short, Unhappy Life," https://www.nytimes.com/1972/06/25 /archives/the-short-unhappy-life-of-black-presidential-politics-1972 -black.html.

23. Lesher, "Short, Unhappy Life."

24. Shirley Chisholm, presidential candidacy announcement, January 25, 1972, Archives of Women's Political Communication, Iowa State University, https://awpc.cattcenter.iastate.edu/2017/03/09/declaring -presidential-bid-jan-25-1972/.

25. Richard M. Nixon, radio address, February 9, 1972, American Presidency Project, https://www.presidency.ucsb.edu/documents/radio -address-about-the-third-annual-foreign-policy-report-the-congress.

26. Robert C. Smith, "National Black Political Convention," in *Encyclopedia of African American Politics* (Facts on File, 2003), 242.

27. Reginald Wilson, "Mixed Legacy," *New Politics* 15, no. 3 (July 1, 2015): 119.

28. Gary Declaration, 1972, BlackPast.org, https://www.Blackpast.org /african-american-history/gary-declaration-national-Black-political -convention-1972/.

29. Wilson, "Mixed Legacy," 119.

30. Michael Puente, "Richard Hatcher, First Black Mayor of Gary, Dies at 86," NPR, December 16, 2019, https://www.npr.org/local/309/2019 /12/16/788368369/richard-hatcher-first-black-mayor-of-gary-dies-at-86.

31. Justin Driver, "The Report on Race That Shook America," *Atlantic*, May 2018, https://www.theatlantic.com/magazine/archive/2018/05 /the-report-on-race-that-shook-america/556850/.

32. Harris, *Price of the Ticket*, 149.

33. Leah Wright Rigueur, *The Loneliness of the Black Republican: Pragmatic Politics and the Pursuit of Power* (Princeton University Press, 2015), 134.

34. Frank Lynn, "What Makes Shirley Run," *New York Times*, January 30, 1972, https://www.nytimes.com/1972/01/30/archives/what-makes-shirley -run-candidates.html.

35. Richard Iton, *In Search of the Black Fantastic: Politics and Popular Culture in the Post–Civil Rights Era* (Oxford University Press, 2008), 332.

36. Paul Delaney, "Blacks Are Divided on the Convention," *New York Times*, July 16, 1972, https://www.nytimes.com/1972/07/16/archives/blacks -are-divided-on-the-convention.html.

8. On the Campaign Trail

1. Harris, *Price of the Ticket*, 10.
2. Kareem Crayton, "The Changing Face of the Congressional Black Caucus," *Southern California Interdisciplinary Law Journal* 19 (2010): 483–484.
3. James M. Naughton, "Muskie Rules Out a Black Running Mate," *New York Times*, September 9, 1971, https://www.nytimes.com/1971/09/09 /archives/muskie-rules-out-a-black-running-mate.html.
4. Dan T. Carter, *The Politics of Rage: George Wallace, the Origins of the New Conservatism, and the Transformation of American Politics*, 2nd ed. (Louisiana State University Press, 2000), 109.
5. George Lardner Jr. and Walter Pincus, "Kennedy, Muskie, Jackson Eyed for Nixon Dirty Tricks in '71," *Washington Post*, October 30, 1997, https://www.washingtonpost.com/wp-srv/politics/special/nixon /stories/103097trick.htm.
6. Robert M. Teeter, Wallace strategy memorandum to the Honorable John N. Mitchell, April 11, 1972, courtesy of the Richard Nixon Presidential Library, https://www.nixonlibrary.gov/sites/default/files/virtuallibrary /documents/contested/contested_box_13/Contested-13-14.pdf, 71.
7. Shirley Chisholm, letter and statement to Messrs. Nader and Green, February 18, 1972, in *Role of Giant Corporations: Hearings before the Subcommittee on Monopoly of the Select Committee on Small Business, United States Senate* (US Government Printing Office, 1973), 3, 139.
8. Dolores Barclay, "Conrad Chisholm Willingly Standing in Shadow While Wife Runs for Presidency," *Bee* (Danville, VA), February 29, 1972, WikiTree, https://www.wikitree.com/photo.php/8/8d/Hill-31352-1.jpg.
9. Barclay, "Conrad Chisholm Willingly Standing."
10. Gutgold, *Paving the Way*, 64.
11. "School Busing Halted by Vote in U.S. House," *Jet*, November 25, 1971, 28.
12. David S. Broder, "Candidates Differ on Busing, Again," *Washington Post*, February 15, 1972, courtesy of the Richard Nixon Presidential Library, https://www.nixonlibrary.gov/sites/default/files/virtuallibrary /documents/contested/contested_box_13/Contested-13-02.pdf, 50.
13. Russell M. Lawson and Benjamin A. Lawson, eds., *Race and Ethnicity in America: From Pre-contact to the Present* (ABC-CLIO, 2019), 55.
14. Saswat Pattanayak, "Shirley Chisholm: The Original Boss Lady of American Politics," *Medium*, February 10, 2020, https://saswatblog .medium.com/shirley-chisholm-the-original-boss-lady-of-american -politics-d29af66774ab.

15. Stuart Emmrich, "'Unbought and Unbossed': How Shirley Chisholm Helped Paved the Path for Kamala Harris Nearly Five Decades Ago," *Vogue*, August 20,2020, https://www.vogue.com/article/how-shirley -chisholm-made-history-at-the-1972-democratic-national-convention.

16. Shola Lynch, "Shirley Chisholm Fought the Good Fight," *Crisis* 12, no. 1 (January–February 2005): 58.

17. "The First Black Woman to Run for President," *Radio Diaries*, NPR, October 17, 2008, https://www.npr.org/transcripts/95828537.

18. Karen Foerstel and Herbert N. Foerstel, *Climbing the Hill: Gender Conflict in Congress* (Praeger, 1996), 30.

19. John J. O'Connor, "TV: Woman Alive!," *New York Times*, October 22, 1975, https://www.nytimes.com/1975/10/22/archives/tv-woman-alive -new-magazine-series-is-on-channel-13-babe-drama.html.

20. Kisner, "Shirley Chisholm Kicks Off Campaign," 14.

21. Fitzpatrick, *Highest Glass Ceiling*, 215.

22. Fitzpatrick, *Highest Glass Ceiling*, 216.

23. Winifred D. Wandersee, *On the Move: American Women in the 1970s* (Twayne Publishers, 1988), 27.

24. Gloria M. Steinem, *Outrageous Acts and Everyday Rebellions* (Open Road Integrated Media, 2012), 100.

25. Laurie Johnston, "Dream for Women: President Chisholm," *New York Times*, February 14, 1972, https://www.nytimes.com/1972/02/14 /archives/dream-for-women-president-chisholm.html.

26. Johnston, "Dream for Women."

27. Michele A. Paludi, ed., *The Psychology of Women at Work: Challenges and Solutions for Our Female Workforce* (ABC-CLIO, 2008), xii.

28. Brown, "'A New Era,'" 1014.

29. Jackson Landers, "'Unbought And Unbossed': When a Black Woman Ran for the White House," *Smithsonian Magazine*, April 25, 2016, https:// www.smithsonianmag.com/smithsonian-institution/unbought-and -unbossed-when-black-woman-ran-for-the-White-house-180958699/.

30. Eric Blakemore, "Here's What People Once Said About How a Woman Would Never Be the Democratic Nominee," *Time*, June 7, 2016, https:// time.com/4359610/shirley-chisholm-nominee/.

31. Elaine Woo, "Estelle Ramey, 89; Doctor, Sharp-Tongued Feminist," *Los Angeles Times*, September 17, 2006.

32. Blakemore, "Here's What People Once Said," https://time.com/4359610 /shirley-chisholm-nominee/.

33. Blakemore, "Here's What People Once Said," https://time.com/4359610/shirley-chisholm-nominee/.

34. Warren Weaver Jr. "'72 Election Set Spending Record," *New York Times*, April 25, 1976, https://www.nytimes.com/1976/04/25/archives/72-election-set-spending-record-137-million-went-for-major-parties.html.

35. Landers, "'Unbought and Unbossed,'" https://www.smithsonianmag.com/smithsonian-institution/unbought-and-unbossed-when-black-woman-ran-for-the-White-house-180958699/.

36. Emmrich, "'Unbought and Unbossed,'" https://www.vogue.com/article/how-shirley-chisholm-made-history-at-the-1972-democratic-national-convention.

37. Jessica Lawson, "'Unbossed and Unbought': Shirley Chisholm and the Voice of the People," Iowa Women's Archives, November 25, 2014 https://blog.lib.uiowa.edu/iwa/2014/11/25/unbossed-and-unbought-shirley-chisholm-and-the-voice-of-the-people/.

38. Fitzpatrick, *Highest Glass Ceiling*, 219.

39. "She Had Her Own Ideas on Ways, Means of Politics," *Sydney Morning Herald*, January 7, 2005, https://www.smh.com.au/national/she-had-her-own-ideas-on-ways-means-of-politics-20050107-gdkg10.html.

40. Landers, "'Unbought And Unbossed,'" https://www.smithsonianmag.com/smithsonian-institution/unbought-and-unbossed-when-black-woman-ran-for-the-White-house-180958699/.

41. Jonathan Capehart, "How Segregationist George Wallace Became a Model for Racial Reconciliation," episode 6 of *Voices of the Movement* (podcast), *Washington Post*, May 16, 2019, https://www.washingtonpost.com/opinions/2019/05/16/changed-minds-reconciliation-voices-movement-episode/.

42. Landers, "'Unbought And Unbossed,'" https://www.smithsonianmag.com/smithsonian-institution/unbought-and-unbossed-when-black-woman-ran-for-the-White-house-180958699/.

43. Shirley Chisholm, *The Good Fight* (Harper & Row, 1973), 79.

44. Nora Sayre, "Film: Women in Protest," *New York Times*, January 26, 1974, https://www.nytimes.com/1974/01/26/archives/film-women-in-protest.html.

45. Rebecca Traister, *Good and Mad: The Revolutionary Power of Women's Anger* (Simon & Schuster, 2018), 110.

46. Gloria M. Steinem, *My Life on the Road* (Random House, 2015), 134.

47. *Issues and Answers*, ABC, June 4, 1972, transcript via Minnesota Historical Society, http://www2.mnhs.org/library/findaids/00442/pdfa/00442-03513 .pdf.

48. *Issues and Answers*, ABC.

49. Walt Wurfel, "Bogus News Releases Issued on Humphrey Letterhead, Denounced by Top Humphrey Aide," Humphrey '72 News, June 5, 1972, courtesy of the Richard Nixon Presidential Library, https://www .nixonlibrary.gov/sites/default/files/virtuallibrary/documents/contested /contested_box_34/Contested-34-09.pdf, 142.

50. Lynch, "Shirley Chisholm Fought," 58.

51. *Meet the Press*, NBC News, January 9, 2005, https://www.nbcnews.com /id/wbna6805000.

52. Will Kohler, "Gay History—July 12, 1972: First Gay Delegates Speak at the Democratic National Convention. Sort Of . . . ," Back2Stonewall, July 12, 2019, http://www.back2stonewall.com/2019/07/gay-history-july -12-1972-gay-delegates-speak-Democratic-national-convention.html.

53. Robert D. Novak, *The Prince of Darkness: 50 Years Reporting in Washington* (Three Rivers Press, 2007), 225.

54. Rhonda Y. Williams, *Concrete Demands: The Search for Black Power in the 20th Century* (Routledge, 2015), 257.

55. Michele A. Paludi, ed., *Why Congress Needs Women: Bringing Sanity to the House and Senate* (ABC-CLIO, 2016), 37.

56. "Dellums Endorses McGovern After Caucus Speech," *Palm Beach Post*, July 10, 1972.

57. Clara Bingham, *Women of the Hill: Challenging the Culture of Congress* (Time Books, 1997), 22.

58. Percy Sutton, "In Nomination for the Presidency the Name of Congresswoman Shirley Chisholm," *Massachusetts Review* 13, no. 4 (1972), 703–707.

59. Anastasia Curwood, "Black Feminism on Capitol Hill: Shirley Chisholm and Movement Politics, 1968–1984," *Meridians: Feminism, Race, Transnationalism* 13, no. 1(2015), 204.

60. Shirley Chisholm, "Sexism and Racism: One Battle to Fight," *Personnel & Guidance Journal* 51 (1972), 123.

61. Chisholm, 125.

62. Simien, *Historic Firsts*, 32.

63. Lawson and Lawson, *Race and Ethnicity in America*, 55.

64. Suzanne O'Dea Schenken, *From Suffrage to the Senate: An Encyclopedia of American Women in Politics* (ABC-CLIO, 1999), 140.

65. Schenken, 758.

66. Sherie M. Randolph, *Florynce "Flo" Kennedy: The Life of a Black Feminist Radical* (University of North Carolina Press, 2015), 202.

67. Hanes Walton Jr., *Invisible Politics: Black Political Behavior* (State University of New York Press, 1985), 94.

68. Molly A. Mayhead and Brenda D. Marshall, *Women's Political Discourse: A 21st-Century Perspective* (Rowman & Littlefield, 2005), 37.

9. Back in Congress

1. "Women of the Year," *Ladies' Home Journal*, 1973, clipping in "4/8/76—New York City—'Women of the Year,'" box 23, Sheila Weidenfeld Files, Gerald R. Ford Presidential Library, https://www.fordlibrarymuseum.gov/library/document/0126/1489645.pdf, 34.

2. Reed Ueda, *America's Changing Neighborhoods: An Exploration of Diversity Through Places* (ABC-CLIO, 2017), 281.

3. Gregg Simms, "Leaders Ask Ford to Pardon Blacks," *Jet*, September 26, 1974, 8.

4. Shirley Chisholm to President Gerald Ford, August 12, 1974, collected in "Vice President—House Suggestions, A-Mh (3)," box 19, Robert T. Hartmann Files, Gerald R. Ford Presidential Library, https://www.fordlibrarymuseum.gov/library/document/0011/18540897.pdf, 12.

5. Linda Charlton, "Rep. Chisholm in Drive for Rockefeller," *New York Times*, December 17, 1974, https://www.nytimes.com/1974/12/17/archives/rep-chisholmin-drive-for-rockefeller-albert-sees-vote-thursday-ford.html.

6. Shirley Chisholm, prepared statement, November 27, 1974, in *Nomination of Nelson A. Rockefeller to be Vice President of the United States: Hearings Before the Committee on the Judiciary, House of Representatives* (US Government Printing Office, 1974), 678–679.

7. Paul Delaney, "Big Rise Noted in Total of Black Elected Officials," *New York Times*, April 23, 1974, https://www.nytimes.com/1974/04/23/archives/big-rise-noted-in-total-of-black-elected-officials-special-to-the.html.

8. Joshua D. Farrington, *Black Republicans and the Transformation of the GOP* (University of Pennsylvania Press, 2016), 157.

9. Suraya Khan, "Transnational Alliances: The AAUG's Advocacy for Palestine and the Third World," *Arab Studies Quarterly* 40, no. 1(2018): 61.

10. Michael R. Fischbach, *Black Power and Palestine: Transnational Countries of Color* (Stanford University Press, 2019), 165.

11. Fischbach, *Black Power and Palestine*, 170.
12. Khan, "Transnational Alliances," 60.
13. Khan, 60.
14. Fischbach, *Black Power and Palestine*, 166.
15. "JTA Exclusive Interview: Mrs. Chisholm Now Favors Direct Mideast Talks; Says Going to Israel 'To See,'" Jewish Telegraphic Agency, August 2, 1972, https://www.jta.org/1972/08/02/archive/jta-exclusive -interview-mrs-chisholm-now-favors-direct-mideast-talks-says-going -to-israel-to-see.
16. "Black Representatives Back Israel in UN," *Southern Africa* 8, no. 9 (October 1975): 39, MSU Libraries, http://kora.matrix.msu.edu /files/50/304/32-130-A37-84-al.sff.document.nusa197510.pdf.
17. "Black Representatives Back Israel," 39.
18. Betty Holcomb, "The Political Scene," *Working Mother*, April 1988, 71.
19. Shirley Chisholm, "Welfare Reform, a Beginning," remarks before the US House of Representatives, May 26, 1969, 115 Cong. Rec. 13,806, https://www.govinfo.gov/content/pkg/GPO-CRECB-1969-pt10/pdf /GPO-CRECB-1969-pt10-8-3.pdf.
20. Shirley Chisholm, "Welfare Reform," remarks before the US House of Representatives, February 22, 1973, 119 Cong. Rec. 5,070–5,071.
21. Shirley Chisholm, "Chisholm Works for Senior Citizens," constituent outreach mailer, Fall 1973, 2, AVOICE Online, Congressional Black Caucus Foundation, https://avoice.cbcfinc.org/wp-content /uploads/2022/05/njr-chisholm-5-5-1973fall.pdf.
22. Donald M. Fraser, remarks before US House subcommittees, October 5, 1973, in *The Repeal of the Rhodesian Chrome Amendment: Hearings Before the Subcommittee on Africa and the Subcommittee on International Organizations and Movements of the Committee of Foreign Affairs* (US Government Printing Office, 1973), 2–3, No Easy Victories, http://www .noeasyvictories.org/congress/uscg009.pdf.
23. Shirley Chisholm, "Setting the Record Straight on School Desegregation," remarks before the US House of Representatives, May 16, 1974, 120 Cong. Rec. 15,252–15,253.
24. Milliken v. Bradley, 418 U.S. 717 (1974).
25. Glenn L. Starks, *African Americans by the Numbers: Understanding and Interpreting Statistics on African American Life* (ABC-CLIO, 2017), 8.
26. Starks, *African Americans by the Numbers*, 11.
27. Shirley Chisholm, remarks before US House subcommittee, May 8, 1974, in *Juvenile Justice and Delinquency Prevention and Runaway Youth:*

Hearings Before the Subcommittee on Equal Opportunities of the Committee on Education and Labor (US Government Printing Office, 1974), 434.

28. Shirley Chisholm, remarks before US House subcommittee, March 31, 1982, in *Oversight Hearing on the Office of Juvenile Justice and Delinquency Prevention: Hearing Before the Subcommittee on Human Resources of the Committee on Education and Labor* (US Government Printing Office, 1982), 17–18, https://files.eric.ed.gov/fulltext/ED230851.pdf.

29. David M. Alpern and Thomas DeFrank, "The Black Backlash," *Newsweek*, August 27, 1979, 20.

30. Jimmy Carter to Andrew Young, July 17, 1975, Heritage Auctions, https://historical.ha.com/itm/political/small-paper-1896-present-/very -historic-handwritten-political-letter-from-jimmy-carter-to-andrew -young-longhand-letters-by-recent-presidents-are-few/a/625-26472.s.

31. G. Thomas Kingsley and Karina Fortuny, "Urban Policy in the Carter Administration," Urban Institute, May 2010, https://www.urban.org /sites/default/files/publication/28631/412091-Urban-Policy-in-the-Carter -Administration.PDF.

32. Shirley Chisholm et al., statement on Haitian refugees, April 2, 1980, in *Caribbean Refugee Crisis, Cubans and Haitians: Hearing Before the Committee on the Judiciary, United States Senate* (US Government Printing Office, 1980), 216–217.

33. Brenda Pillors, "Political Repression Continues in Haiti" (press release), Office of Congresswoman Shirley Chisholm, 1980, via University of Florida Digital Collections, http://ufdcimages.uflib.ufl.edu /AA/00/06/21/20/00001/LEH40520433003.pdf.

34. "Rep. Chisholm Blasts U.S., Reagan, on Refugee Policy," *Jet*, August 27, 1981, 7.

35. "Rep. Chisholm Blasts U.S.," 7.

36. Carl Lindskoog, *Detain and Punish: Haitian Refugees and the Rise of the World's Largest Immigration Detention System* (University of Florida Press, 2018), 83.

37. Shirley Chisholm, "Should Congress Establish a Separate Cabinet-Level U.S. Department of Education?," *Congressional Digest* 57, no. 11 (1978): 277.

38. Chisholm, 277.

10. Chisholm's Final Years in Congress

1. Frank Lynn, "In Tristate Area, Key Contests Will Be Affected by National Strategy, *New York Times*, September 5, 1976, https://www.nytimes

.com/1976/09/05/archives/in-tristate-area-key-contests-will-be-affected
-by-national-strategy.html.

2. Shirley Chisholm, remarks before US House subcommittee, May 16, 1979, in *Fair Housing Amendments Act of 1979: Hearings Before the Subcommittee on Civil and Constitutional Rights of the Committee on the Judiciary* (US Government Printing Office, 1979), 469–470.

3. Regents of the University of California v. Bakke, 438 U.S. 265 (1978).

4. Congressional Black Caucus to President Jimmy Carter, September 9, 1977, courtesy of the Jimmy Carter Presidential Library and Museum, https://www.jimmycarterlibrary.gov/digital_library/sso/148878/40/SSO_148878_040_05.pdf, 12.

5. "Mrs. Chisholm Named First Black Woman on House Rules Unit," *New York Times*, January 19, 1977.

6. "Guts, Stamina, Audacity: Shirley Chisholm's House Career," Whereas: Stories from the People's House, US House of Representatives, January 3, 2019, https://history.house.gov/Blog/2019/January/1-3-Chisholm/.

7. Food Stamp Act of 1977, Pub. L. No. 88-525, US Department of Agriculture, Food and Nutrition Service, https://www.fns.usda.gov/snap/leghistory/food-stamp-act-1977-amended-dec-2000.

8. Janet Tara, "World Almanac Chose America's 25 Most Influential Women" (press release), World Almanac & Book of Facts, 1977, box 37, Sheila Weidenfeld File, Gerald R. Ford Presidential Library, https://www.fordlibrarymuseum.gov/library/document/0126/1489780.pdf, 23.

9. "Shirley Chisholm Denies She's Leaving Husband," *Jet*, February 1976, 45.

10. "Rep. Chisholm Picks Escort for Gala White House Party," *Jet*, January 1975, 21.

11. New York State Black, Puerto Rican, Hispanic and Asian Legislative Caucus, *1917–2014: A Look at the History of Legislators of Color* (New York State Assembly, 2014), 14, https://nyassembly.gov/comm/BlackPR/20140213/index.pdf.

12. Wayne Dawkins, *City Son: Andrew W. Cooper's Impact on Modern-Day Brooklyn* (University Press of Mississippi, 2012), 98–99.

13. Perlez, "Rep. Chisholm's Angry Farewell."

14. Morisey, oral history interview.

15. Shirley Chisholm, "Vote for the Individual, Not the Political Party," *Vital Speeches of the Day* 44, no. 21 (1978): 670.

16. Chisholm, 670.

17. Shirley Chisholm, commencement address, Mount Holyoke College, South Hadley, MA, May 24, 1981, Archives of Women's Political

Communication, Iowa State University, https://awpc.cattcenter.iastate
.edu/2018/10/10/commencment-address-at-mt-holyoke-college-may-24
-1981/.

18. Steve Kornacki, "1980: Carter vs. Kennedy Left African Americans
Feeling Ignored," NBC News, July 29, 2019, https://www.nbcnews.com
/politics/elections/1980-carter-vs-kennedy-left-african-americans-feeling
-ignored-n1029591.

19. Laila Kazmi and Stephen Hegg, "What Former Presidential Candidate Shirley Chisholm Said About Facing Gender Discrimination,"
PBS.org, September 13, 2016, https://www.pbs.org/newshour/politics
/what-former-presidential-candidate-shirley-chisholm-said-about
-facing-gender-discrimination.

20. "'Salute to Black Business': 1982 Twelfth Annual Legislative Weekend," Congressional Black Caucus, 1982, 11, AVOICE Online, Congressional Black Caucus Foundation, https://avoice.cbcfinc.org/exhibits
/origins-of-the-congressional-black-caucus/attachment/salute-to-black
-business/.

21. Tom Wicker, "Subsidizing Racism," In the Nation, *New York Times*,
January 12, 1982, https://www.nytimes.com/1982/01/12/opinion
/in-the-nation-subsidizing-racism.html.

22. William Foster, *On Our Backs . . . Came the Chosen* (Xlibris, 2011), 74.

23. Michelle O'Donnell and James Barron, "Shirley Chisholm: 'Unbossed'
Pioneer in Congress, Dies January 3, 2005," *Black Scholar* 35, no. 1
(2005): 38-39.

24. Bob Frishman, "Chisholm to Leave Congress" (press release), Office
of Congresswoman Shirley Chisholm, 1982, AVOICE Online, Congressional Black Caucus Foundation, https://avoice.cbcfinc.org/exhibits
/women-of-the-cbc/attachment/chisholm-to-leave-congress/.

25. Jane Perlez, "Mrs. Chisholm Plans to Retire from Congress," *New York
Times*, February 11, 1982, https://www.nytimes.com/1982/02/11/ny
region/mrs-chisholm-plans-to-retire-from-congress.html.

26. Perlez, "Mrs. Chisholm Plans to Retire."

27. "'Salute to Black Business,'" Congressional Black Caucus, 62, https://
avoice.cbcfinc.org/exhibits/origins-of-the-congressional-black-caucus
/attachment/salute-to-black-business/.

28. Jacqueline Trescott, "Shirley Chisholm in Her Season of Transition,"
Washington Post, June 6, 1982, https://www.washingtonpost.com/archive
/lifestyle/1982/06/06/shirley-chisholm-in-her-season-of-transition
/058aaa51-36d4-412b-a8e4-def321b61366/.

29. Yvonne Shinhoster Lamb, "Pioneering Politician, Advocate Shirley Chisholm Dies," *Washington Post*, January 4, 2005, https://www.washingtonpost.com/archive/local/2005/01/04/pioneering-politician-advocate-shirley-chisholm-dies/c2801230-6ae1-449d-b5a2-ec458c3cdfaf/.

30. Glenn L. Starks and F. Erik Brooks, *Thurgood Marshall: A Biography* (ABC-CLIO, 2012), 79.

31. Tim Naftali, "Ronald Reagan's Long-Hidden Racist Conversation with Richard Nixon," *Atlantic*, July 30, 2019, https://www.theatlantic.com/ideas/archive/2019/07/ronald-reagans-racist-conversation-richard-nixon/595102/.

32. Michael Mueller, "Shirley Chisholm 1924– ," Contemporary Black Biography, Encyclopedia.com, May 23, 2018, https://www.encyclopedia.com/people/social-sciences-and-law/social-reformers/shirley-chisholm.

11. Life After Congress

1. Jeroline D. McCarthy, "Palm Coaster Witnesses History at White House Ceremony," *Daytona Times*, December 3, 2015, https://daytonatimes.com/2015/12/03/palm-coaster-witnesses-history-at-white-house-ceremony/.

2. Mount Holyoke College Alumnae Association, "Catalyst for Change: Shirley Chisholm's Time in Congress, on Campus and Beyond," *Mount Holyoke College Alumnae Quarterly*, Fall 2019, https://alumnae.mtholyoke.edu/blog/catalyst-for-change-shirley-chisholms-time-in-congress-on-campus-and-beyond/.

3. Diane Casselberry Manuel, "For Shirley Chisholm, Life in Academia Is Hardly Sedentary," *Christian Science Monitor*, December 13, 1983, https://www.csmonitor.com/1983/1213/121310.html.

4. Manuel, "For Shirley Chisholm, Life in Academia."

5. Shirley Chisholm, "A Coalition of Conscience," speech at Greenfield High School, Greenfield, MA, October 3, 1983, Archives of Women's Political Communication, Iowa State University, https://awpc.cattcenter.iastate.edu/2017/03/09/a-coalition-of-conscience-oct-3-1983/.

6. Will Bunch, *Tear Down This Myth: The Right-Wing Distortion of the Reagan Legacy* (Free Press, 2009), 110.

7. Shirley Chisholm, commencement address, Massachusetts Institute of Technology, Cambridge, MA, June 4, 1984, Archives of Women's Political Communication, Iowa State University, https://awpc.cattcenter.iastate.edu/2018/10/12/mit-commencement-address-june-4-1984/.

8. Betsy Sandberg, "Shirley Chisholm Sees Pat Robertson as Threat," *Schenectady Gazette*, February 18, 1988, Google News, https://news.google

.com/newspapers?nid=1917&dat=19880218&id=XREhAAAAIBAJ
&sjid=nXIFAAAAIBAJ&pg=793,4324248.

9. Sandberg, "Shirley Chisholm Sees Pat Robertson."

10. National Women's Political Caucus gala, July 11, 1991, CSPAN, https://
www.c-span.org/video/?19097-1/national-womens-political-caucus
-gala-party.

11. NWPC gala, CSPAN.

12. "President Names Chisholm Ambassador to Jamaica" (press release),
White House Office of the Press Secretary, July 29, 1993, https://
clintonwhitehouse6.archives.gov/1993/07/1993-07-29-president-names
-shirley-chisholm-ambassador-to-jamaica.html.

13. Press release, White House Office of the Press Secretary, October 13, 1993, https://clintonwhitehouse6.archives.gov/1993/10/1993
-10-13s-chisholm-release.html.

14. "Shirley Chisholm," National Women's Hall of Fame, accessed June 21,
2023, https://www.womenofthehall.org/inductee/shirley-chisholm/.

15. "A Look Back On Shirley Chisholm's Historic 1968 House Victory,"
1968: How We Got Here, NPR, November 6, 2018, https://www.npr
.org/transcripts/664617076.

16. "POV: Chisholm '72—Unbought & Unbossed," Peabody Awards, 2005,
http://www.peabodyawards.com/award-profile/p.o.v.-chisholm-72
-unbought-unbossed.

17. Gutgold, Still Paving the Way, 49.

18. "Shirley Chisholm," Biography.com, May 4, 2021, https://www.biography
.com/political-figure/shirley-chisholm.

19. Clem Richardson, "Preserving Shirley Chisholm's Legacy Is a Labor of
Love for William Howard and Barbara Bullard," New York Daily News,
March 2, 2012, https://www.nydailynews.com/new-york/preserving
-shirley-chisholm-legacy-labor-love-william-howard-barbara-bullard
-article-1.1031344.

20. James Barron, "Shirley Chisholm, 'Unbossed' Pioneer in Congress, Is
Dead at 80," New York Times, January 3, 2005, https://www.nytimes
.com/2005/01/03/obituaries/shirley-chisholm-unbossedpioneer-in
-congress-is-dead-at-80.html.

21. Lamb, "Pioneering Politician, Advocate," https://www.washingtonpost
.com/archive/local/2005/01/04/pioneering-politician-advocate-shirley
-chisholm-dies/c2801230-6ae1-449d-b5a2-ec458c3cdfaf/.

22. Lamb, "Pioneering Politician, Advocate."

23. "Film Update: *Chisholm '72*—Shirley Chisholm," POV.org, 2005, http://archive.pov.org/chisholm/film-update/.

24. "Shirley Chisholm, Nation's First Black Woman to Serve in Congress, Dies," *Jet*, January 24, 2005, 14.

25. "Shirley Chisholm, Nation's First," 15.

26. A Resolution Honoring Shirley Chisholm for Her Service to the Nation and Expressing Condolences to Her Family, Friends, and Supporters on Her Death, S. Res.52 (2005), https://www.congress.gov/bill/109th-congress/senate-resolution/52/text.

27. Pub. L. No. 109-50 (2005).

12. The Legacy of Shirley Chisholm

1. *Discrimination Against Women*, 914.

2. Aimee Molloy, "Shirley Chisholm's Legacy," *Brooklyn Rail*, February 2005, https://brooklynrail.org/2005/02/express/shirley-chisholms-legacy.

3. Landers, "'Unbought And Unbossed,'" https://www.smithsonianmag.com/smithsonian-institution/unbought-and-unbossed-when-black-woman-ran-for-the-White-house-180958699/.

4. Renee Montagne, "Shirley Chisholm, First Black Congresswoman, Dies at 80," *Morning Edition*, NPR, January 3, 2005, https://www.npr.org/templates/story/story.php?storyId=4256177.

5. Alexis Pauline Gumbs, "Peta for Prez: A Black Feminist Socialist Presidential Candidate Speaks!," *Feminist Wire*, May 22, 2012, https://thefeministwire.com/2012/05/peta-for-prez-a-black-feminist-socialist-presidential-candidate-speaks/.

6. Hechinger Report, "College System Pushes Many Graduates into Middle Class," *U.S. News*, February 5, 2018, https://www.usnews.com/news/best-states/articles/2018-02-05/new-york-college-system-pushes-many-graduates-into-middle-class-and-beyond.

7. Stephon Johnson, "Brooklyn State Office Building Named After Chisholm," *New York Amsterdam News*, April 4, 2011, http://amsterdamnews.com/news/2011/apr/12/brooklyn-state-office-building-named-after/.

8. "Governor Paterson, Assemblyman Jeffries, Dignitaries Rename State Building in Honor of Congresswoman Chisholm," New York State Office of the Governor (press release), October 4, 2010, readMedia, http://readme.readmedia.com/Governor-Paterson-Assemblyman-Jeffries-Dignitaries-Rename-State-Building-in-Honor-of-Congresswoman-Chisholm/1735839/.

9. "U.S. Postal Service Honors Shirley Chisholm: First African-American Woman Elected to Congress Joins Popular Black Heritage Stamp Series" (press release), US Postal Service January 31, 2014, https://about .usps.com/news/national-releases/2014/pr14_005.htm.

10. Barack H. Obama, remarks at Medal of Freedom ceremony, November 24, 2015, White House Office of the Press Secretary, https://obamawhite house.archives.gov/the-press-office/2015/11/24/remarks-president-medal -freedom-ceremony.

11. Nancy D. O'Reilly, *In This Together: How Successful Women Support Each Other in Work and Life* (Adams Media, 2019), 65.

12. Vanessa Williams, "Analysis: 'Unbought and Unbossed'—Shirley Chisholm's Feminist Mantra Is Still Relevant 50 Years Later," *Washington Post*, January 26, 2018, https://www.washingtonpost.com/news /post-nation/wp/2018/01/26/unbought-and-unbossed-shirley-chisholms -feminist-mantra-is-as-relevant-today-as-it-was-50-years-ago/.

13. Barbara J. Lee, "Congresswoman Lee's Statement on the 50th Anniversary of Shirley Chisholm's Historic Election to Congress," Office of Congresswoman Barbara Lee, November 5, 2018, https://lee.house.gov /news/press-releases/congresswoman-lees-statement-on-the-50th -anniversary-of-Chisholm-chisholms-historic-election-to-congress.

14. "She Built NYC: De Blasio Administration Announces Shirley Chisholm, First Black Woman to Serve in Congress, Selected for New City-Funded Monument" (press release), City of New York, November 30, 2018, https://www.nyc.gov/office-of-the-mayor/news/579-18/she-built-nyc -de-blasio-administration-shirley-chisholm-first-black-woman-serve-in.

15. "An Inspiration to Women Candidates in 2018: Remembering Shirley Chisholm," National Organization for Women, November 5, 2018, https://now.org/media-center/press-release/an-inspiration-to-women -candidates-in-2018-remembering-shirley-chisholm/.

16. Kamala Harris, "Harris, Clarke Reintroduce Legislation to Commission Statue Honoring U.S. Representative Shirley Chisholm" (press release), Office of Senator Kamala Harris, March 7, 2019, https://www .harris.senate.gov/news/press-releases/harris-clarke-reintroduce-legislation -to-commission-statue-honoring-us-representative-shirley-chisholm (page discontinued).

17. "Governor Cuomo Announces Opening of $20 Million First Phase of Shirley Chisholm State Park in Brooklyn" (press release), Office of the Governor of New York, July 2, 2019, https://www.governor.ny.gov

/news/governor-cuomo-announces-opening-20-million-first-phase -shirley-chisholm-state-park-brooklyn (page discontinued).

18. "New York State Announces Opening of $20 Million First Phase of Shirley Chisholm State Park in Brooklyn" (press release), New York State Parks, Recreation and Historic Preservation, July 2, 2019, https://parks .ny.gov/newsroom/press-releases/release.aspx?r=1523.

19. Marianne Schnall, "How History Can Bring Us Hope Right Now," CNN, March 28, 2020, https://www.cnn.com/2020/03/27/opinions /womens-history-month-trailblazers-amid-coronavirus-schnall/index .html.

20. "Shirley Chisholm," Voice of America, February 19, 2005, https://learning english.voanews.com/a/a-23-a-2005-02-19-1-1-83124567/124271.html.

21. Lisa Lerer and Sydney Ember, "Kamala Harris Makes History as First Woman and Woman of Color as Vice President," *New York Times*, August 26, 2020, https://www.nytimes.com/2020/11/07/us/politics/kamala -harris.html.

22. Joan Potter, *African American Firsts: Famous, Little-Known and Unsung Triumphs of Blacks in America* (Kensington, 2014), 172.

INDEX

Page numbers in *italics* refer to illustrations. SC = Shirley Chisholm.